D1739325

The Plight of the Palestinians

Also by William A. Cook

*A Time to Know*
*Psalms for the 21st Century*
*Tracking Deception: Bush Mid-East Policy*
*The Unreasoning Mask* (co-authored with Darcy Jones Cook)
*The Agony of Colin Powell*
*Hope Destroyed, Justice Denied: The Rape of Palestine*
*The Chronicles of Nefaria*

# The Plight of the Palestinians

## A Long History of Destruction

*Edited by*
William A. Cook

palgrave
macmillan

THE PLIGHT OF THE PALESTINIANS

First published in 2010 by
PALGRAVE MACMILLAN®
in the United States—a division of St. Martin's Press LLC,
175 Fifth Avenue, New York, NY 10010.

Where this book is distributed in the UK, Europe and the rest of the world,
this is by Palgrave Macmillan, a division of Macmillan Publishers Limited,
registered in England, company number 785998, of Houndmills,
Basingstoke, Hampshire RG21 6XS.

Palgrave Macmillan is the global academic imprint of the above companies
and has companies and representatives throughout the world.

Palgrave® and Macmillan® are registered trademarks in the United States,
the United Kingdom, Europe and other countries.

ISBN: 978-0-230-10037-4

Library of Congress Cataloging-in-Publication Data

The plight of the Palestinians : a long history of destruction / edited by
William A. Cook.
    p. cm.
    ISBN 978-0-230-10037-4 (hardback)
    1. Palestinian Arabs—Crimes against. 2. Palestinian Arabs—
Government policy—Israel. 3. Palestinian Arabs—History—20th century.
4. Arab-Israeli conflict. I. Cook, William A.

DS113.7.P57 2010
323.1192'74—dc22                                        2009044766

A catalogue record of the book is available from the British Library.

Design by Newgen Imaging Systems (P) Ltd., Chennai, India.

First edition: June 2010

10 9 8 7 6 5 4 3 2 1

Printed in the United States of America.

*To the memory of the innocent victims of the
Nakba and its aftermath.*

# CONTENTS

x                  *Contents*

# GRAPHS AND TABLES

## Graphs

## Tables

# ACKNOWLEDGMENTS

This book represents at least two years of cooperative effort by writers from many countries. To them I acknowledge my deepest gratitude. In some instances, publishers granted access to their writers; that, too, must be recognized, with special acknowledgment going to Truthdig editor Zuade Kaufman of www.truthdig.com, the Internet site that carries an ongoing column by Chris Hedges; similarly, Alexander Cockburn of the political newsletter *Counterpunch*, www.counterpunch.com, provided articles by Robert Fisk and Patrick Cockburn, both contributors to that Internet publication; in addition, Chris Gunness, the director of the United Nations Relief and Works Agency (UNRWA), aided my efforts to acquire copyright permission from Karen Koning Abu Zayd, a kind service on his part; my gratitude also goes to Ms. Jan Olberg, who gave permission to use Dr. Richard Falk's article published by the Transnational Foundation for Peace and Future Research; and, finally, I'd like to thank Matt Bargannier, editor at Antiwar.com, for his ongoing assistance in acquiring copyright permission from Jon Utley.

I must also acknowledge the invaluable assistance of my wife, Darcy Jones Cook, who undertook the arduous task of converting the scanned documents for each chapter from their original source into Microsoft Word format, always conscious of the intrusion of the Chicago stylebook on all the articles. Her devotion to this project provided ongoing inspiration to the very end. I also owe my gratitude to Ms. Betty Wailing Tsang, who spent untold hours scanning the articles that make up the individual chapters in this book and compiling them into a single document, a thankless task for which I am very grateful. Brian Tresner, the University of La Verne's guru of information technology, gave valuable assistance regarding the transitioning from published text to book format. In addition, Ms. Krystal Carrillo compiled the first drafts of the author's biographies and, with the aid of Ms. Erin Gratz of the University of La Verne's Wilson Library, developed a working index.

Finally, I'd like to acknowledge the help provided by our Humanities secretary, Ms. Melanie Brown, as she aided in converting many of the compiled works into corrected Word format.

Lastly, I must acknowledge a group of writers who had granted me preliminary copyright permission to use their work only to find that the publisher controls the end product, at least as far as the number of words and pages is concerned. As a result, I could not use all who offered their work and I apologize to them for that. However, I have provided a bibliography at the end of the book that includes the names of the pieces that I had hoped to use, along with the names of others that address the principal issue of this text—genocide.

# AUTHORS' BIOGRAPHIES

**Dr. Elias Akleh** is an Arab writer of Palestinian descent, born in the town of Beit-Jala. His family was first evicted from Haifa after the *Nakba* of 1948 (the catastrophe), then from Beit Jala after the *Nakseh* of 1967 (the war of 1967, the setback). He lives now in the United States and contributes to numerous online publications in both English and Arabic, including *Global Research, Media with a Conscience, Dissident Voice, Information Clearing House, Palestine Think Tank*, and *The Palestine Chronicle*. "Gaza's Holocaust" appeared in *MWC News*.

**Uri Avnery** is an Israeli writer and founder of the Gush Shalom peace movement, and served as a member of the Knesset from 1965–74 and 1979–81. The owner of *HaOlam HaZeh*, an Israeli newsmagazine from 1950 until it closed in 1993, Avnery is famous for crossing the lines during the Battle of Beirut to meet Yasser Arafat on July 3, 1982—the first time the Palestinian leader ever met with an Israeli. Avnery has written several books about the Israeli-Palestinian conflict, including *1948: A Soldier's Tale, the Bloody Road to Jerusalem* (2008); *Israel's Vicious Circle* (2008); and *My Friend, the Enemy* (1986). "Slow-Motion Ethnic Cleansing" appeared in *Counterpunch*.

**Omar Barghouti**, who was born in Qatar and later moved to Ramallah, holds a bachelor's and master's degree in electrical engineering from Columbia University. He contributed to the philosophical volume *Controversies and Subjectivity* (2005) as well as *The New Intifada: Resisting Israel's Apartheid* (2001). Barghouti is a founding member of the Palestinian Campaign for the Academic and Cultural Boycott of Israel (PACBI) and a leader of the boycott, divestment, and sanctions (BDS) campaign against Israel. As an independent Palestinian political and cultural analyst, Barghouti's works have appeared in numerous publications, and his article "9.11 Putting the Moment on Human Terms" was chosen among the "Best of 2002" by the *Guardian*. "Relative Humanity" appeared in *Counterpunch*.

**Ramzy Baroud:** A Palestinian-American journalist, author, and former Al-Jazeera producer, Ramzy Baroud taught mass communication at Australia's Curtin University of Technology and is the editor-in-chief of the *Palestine Chronicle*. Baroud's work has been published in hundreds of newspapers and journals worldwide, including the *Washington Post*, the *International Herald Tribune*, the *Christian Science Monitor*, the *Philadelphia Inquirer*, the *Seattle Times*, the *Miami Herald*, the *Japan Times*, *Al-Ahram Weekly*, *Asia Times,* and nearly every English-language publication throughout the Middle East. He has been a guest on numerous television programs, including CNN International, the BBC, ABC Australia, National Public Radio, Al-Jazeera, and many others. He has contributed to many anthologies, and his works *Searching Jenin: Eyewitness Accounts of the Israeli Invasion* (2002) and *The Second Palestinian Intifada: A Chronicle of a People's Struggle* (2006) have received international recognition. His *My Father Was a Freedom Fighter: Gaza's Untold Story*, was published by Pluto Press in March 2010. "Big Bang or Chaos: What's Israel Up To?" appeared in *California Chronicle*.

**Francis A. Boyle** is a leading American expert in international law. He was responsible for drafting the Biological Weapons Anti-Terrorism Act of 1989, the American implementing legislation for the 1972 Biological Weapons Convention. He served on the board of directors of Amnesty International (1988–1992) and represented Bosnia-Herzegovina at the World Court. He served as a legal adviser to the Palestine Liberation Organization (PLO) on the Palestinian Delegation to the Middle East peace negotiations from 1991 to 1993. In 2007, he delivered the Bertrand Russell Peace Lectures. Professor Boyle teaches international law at the University of Illinois, Urbana-Champaign, and has written extensively on the relationship between international law and politics, including *Breaking All the Rules: Palestine, Iraq, Iran and the Case for Impeachment* (2008); *Protesting Power: War, Resistance and Law* (2007); *Biowarfare and Terrorism* (2005); and *Foundations of World Order: The Legalist Approach to International Relations* (1898–1922) (1999). His latest work, *Tackling America's Toughest Questions: Alternative Media Interviews*, was published in 2009 by Clarity Press. "Palestine Should Sue Israel for Genocide" appeared in *Media Monitors*.

**Kathleen and Bill Christison** write on Palestinian issues and on U.S. foreign policy, and they travel regularly to Palestine. They are former CIA (Central Intelligence Agency) political analysts; Bill Christison was a senior official of the CIA, and Kathleen Christison was a political analyst working on Arab-Israeli issues. They co-authored *Palestine in Pieces: Graphic Perspectives on the Israeli Occupation*(2009). Kathleen Christison is the author of *Perceptions of Palestine: Their Influence on U.S. Middle East Policy* (2001) and *The Wound of Dispossession: Telling the Palestinian Story* (2002). They live in Santa Fe, New Mexico. "Genocide or Erasure" appeared in *Counterpunch*.

**Patrick Cockburn**, Middle East correspondent of the *Independent* and author of *The Occupation: War, Resistance and Daily Life in Iraq* (2006), has been visiting Iraq since the late 1970s. After several years at the *Financial Times*, he worked for the *Independent* as a Jerusalem correspondent between 1995 and 1999. He was awarded the 2004 Martha Gellhorn Prize for war reporting, the 2006 James Cameron Memorial Award, and the 2009 Orwell Prize in Journalism, in recognition of his writing on Iraq. He is the author of a memoir, *The Broken Boy* (2005), and has co-written, with Andrew Cockburn, *Saddam Hussein: An American Obsession* (2000). His latest book, *Muqtada: Muqtada al-Sadr, the Shia Revival, and the Struggle for Iraq*, was published by Faber & Faber in April 2008, and he is a writer for *Counterpunch* and the *London Review of Books*. "Gaza Is a Jail; Gaza Is Dying" appeared in *Counterpunch*.

**Jonathan Cook** is a British writer based in Nazareth, Israel. He was a staff journalist on the the *Guardian* and the *Observer* newsletters, and has also written about the Israeli-Palestinian conflict for *The Times*, *Le Monde Diplomatique*, the *International Herald Tribune*, *Al-Ahram Weekly*, *Counterpunch*, *Al Jazeera English*, *ZNet*, and the *Electronic Intifada*. He is the author of three books: *Blood and Religion: The Unmasking of the Jewish and Democratic State* (2006); *Israel and the Clash of Civilisations: Iraq, Iran and the Plan to Remake the Middle East* (2008); and *Disappearing Palestine: Israel's Experiments in Human Despair* (2008). "Israel Plots Another Palestine Exodus" appeared in *AntiWar*.com.

**William A. Cook** is a professor of English at the University of La Verne in southern California. He serves as a senior editor at *MWC News*, *Prout World Assembly*, and the *Palestine Chronicle*. He also writes for *Counterpunch*, *Pacific Free Press*, *Atlantic Free Press*, *Dissident Voice*, and many other Internet publications. His works include *Tracking Deception: Bush Mid-East Policy*, (2006), *The Rape of Palestine*, (2008). *The Chronicles of Nefaria (a Novella)* (2008) *and Psalms for the 21st Century* (2003), among others. Additional information is available at www.drwilliamcook.com. "Hope Destroyed, Justice Denied: The Rape of Palestine" appeared in *Counterpunch*.

**Paul de Rooij** is a Dutch mathematician, economist, and writer living in London. De Rooij has been a committed activist on Palestine since the first intifada. He has written for *Z Magazine*, *Agenda*, *Counterpunch*, *Arab Media Internet Network*, *Miftah*, and numerous media research journals. "Palestine Misery in Perspective" appeared in *Dissident Voice*.

**Curtis F. J. Doebbler** is an international human rights lawyer who has represented individuals before international human rights bodies in Africa, Europe, and the Americas, as well as the United Nations. Doebbler has advised the Palestinian National Authority and the Hamas government and has published numerous articles in academic journals and newspapers. His latest works include *The Principle of Non-Discrimination under International Law* (2007); *International Human Rights Law: Cases and Materials* (2004); *Getting to Know International Human Rights Law* (2004); *An Introduction to International Humanitarian Law* (2006); *An Introduction to International Human Rights Law* (2006); and *International Criminal Law* (2007). Doebbler has also been a regular contributor to the Egyptian newspaper *Al-Ahram* and to the online legal forum *JURIST*. "Genocide among Us" appeared in *uruk.net.info*.

**Jon Elmer** is a Canadian freelance writer and photojournalist specializing in the Middle East. He has researched and reported from the West Bank and Gaza Strip—based in Jenin and Gaza—during the al-Aqsa intifada (2003), following Israel's "disengagement" from the Gaza Strip (2005), and during the sanctions regime and factional strife (2007). Jon has photographed in over a dozen countries, including Nepal (1998), the Basque region (2000), Morocco (2000), Israel (2003), Palestine (2003, 2005, 2007), Jordan (2005) and Lebanon (2006). He has also covered globalization summits and accompanying protests throughout North America, including Washington, D.C.; New York; and Quebec City. Jon completed an honors degree in political science at Dalhousie University in Halifax, Nova Scotia; his thesis, "Pulling from the Roots," was a study of Israel's policy of assassination during the al-Aqsa intifada. He also served as an editor and columnist at the *Dalhousie Gazette* during that time, from 1999 to 2003. "A Slow, Steady Genocide" appeared in *Zmag.net*.

**Richard Falk** is the Albert G. Milbank Professor Emeritus of International Law at Princeton University and Visiting Distinguished Professor in Global and International Studies at the University of California, Santa Barbara. His most recent book, *The Great Terror War* (2003), considers the American response to September 11, including its relationship to the patriotic duties of American citizens. In 2001, he served on a three-person Human Rights Inquiry Commission for the Palestine Territories that was appointed by the United Nations and, previously, on the Independent International Commission on Kosovo. He is the author or coauthor of over 37 books; his most recent works include *The Costs of War: International Law, the UN, and World Order after Iraq* (2007); *Israel-Palestine on Record: How the New York Times Misreports Conflict in the Middle East* (2007); *Achieving Human Rights* (2008); and *International Law and the Third World: Reshaping Justice* (Routledge-Cavendish Research in International Law, 2008). He serves as the chair of the Nuclear Age Peace Foundation's board of directors and as honorary vice president of the American Society of International Law. Falk also acted as counsel to Ethiopia and Liberia in the Southwest Africa Case before the International Court of Justice. He received his B.S. from the Wharton School, University of Pennsylvania; L.L.B. from Yale Law School; and J.S.D. from Harvard University. "Slouching toward a Palestine Holocaust" appeared in *Transnational Foundation for Peace and Future Research.*

**Robert Fisk** is an award-winning journalist and Middle East correspondent of the *Independent.* Fisk is one of few Westerners to interview Osama bin Laden, interviewing him three times between 1993 and 1997. Fisk holds more British and international journalism awards than any other foreign correspondent, including a Jacob's Award, two Amnesty International UK Press Awards, seven British Press Awards' International Journalist of the Year, the David Watt Prize, the Martha Gellhorn Prize for Journalism, and the Lannan Cultural Freedom Prize. Fisk is the author of several books, including *The Point of No Return: The Strike Which Broke the British in Ulster* (1975), *In Time of War: Ireland, Ulster and the Price of Neutrality, 1939–1945* (2001); *Pity the Nation: Lebanon at War* (2001); *The Great War for Civilisation: The Conquest of the Middle East* (2005); and *The Age of the Warrior: Selected Writings* (2008). "A Conveniently Forgotten Holocaust" appeared in *Counterpunch.*

**Dr. Jeff Halper** is a professor of anthropology, author, lecturer, political activist, and co-founder and coordinator of the Israeli Committee against House Demolitions (ICAHD). He was nominated for the Nobel Peace Prize by the American Friends Service Committee for his work "to liberate both the Palestinian and the Israeli people from the yoke of structural violence" and "to build equality between their people by recognizing and celebrating their common humanity." Halper has also served on the steering committee of the United Nations Conference on the Exercise of the Inalienable Rights of the Palestinian People. His book *Obstacles to Peace* (2005) is a resource manual of articles and maps on the Israeli-Palestinian conflict and is published by ICAHD. Additional works include *Between Redemption and Revival: The Jewish Yishuv in Jerusalem in the Nineteenth Century* (1991) and *An Israeli in Palestine: Resisting Dispossession, Redeeming Israel* (2008). "The Problem with Israel" appeared in the ICAHD publication.

**Chris Hedges:** Pulitzer Prize–winning American journalist, author, and veteran war correspondent, Chris Hedges is currently a senior fellow at The Nation Institute. Specializing in American and Middle Eastern politics and societies, Hedges was a foreign correspondent for nearly two decades for the *New York Times*, the *Dallas Morning News*, the *Christian Science Monitor* and National Public Radio. He was a member of the team that won the 2002 Pulitzer Prize for Explanatory Reporting for the *New York Times'* coverage of global terrorism, and he received the 2002 Amnesty International Global Award for Human Rights Journalism. He has taught at Columbia University,

New York University, and Princeton University. Hedges is the author of the bestseller *American Fascists* and is a National Book Critics Circle finalist for *War Is a Force That Gives Us Meaning.* His most recent works are *Collateral Damage: America's War Against Iraqi Civilians* (2008) and *Empire of Illusion: The End of Literacy and the Triumph of Spectacle*(2009). "The Lessons of Violence" appeared in Hedges' regular column in *Truthdig.com.*

**Andrea Howard** is a psychiatric case manager in the central United States. She has organized for local and national organizations focusing on social justice issues. "Israeli Immunity for Genocide" appeared in *Axis of Logic.*

**Sonja Karkar** is the founder and president of Women for Palestine, a Melbourne-based human rights group that seeks to raise awareness about the plight of the Palestinians through various media. She is also the co-founder of Australians for Palestine (AFP), which advocates for Palestine at all levels of Australian society. Her articles have been published in numerous online journals such as *Counterpunch, ZNet,* and *Electronic Intifada,* among others. She works voluntarily full-time for Palestine and is the editor of the AFP news website, australiansforpalestine.com, and the special website for the Nakba, 1948.com.au. "The Olive Trees of Palestine Weep" appeared in *Counter Currents.*

**Karen Koning AbuZayd** has been a commissioner-general for the United Nations Relief and Works Agency for Palestine Refugees in the Near East (UNWRA) since 2005. From her base in Gaza, she helps to oversee the education, health, social services, and micro-enterprise programs for 4.6 million Palestine refugees. Before joining UNRWA, Karen worked for the Office of the United Nations High Commissioner for Refugees for nineteen years. She began her humanitarian career in Sudan in 1981, dealing with Ugandan, Chadian, and Ethiopian refugees fleeing from war and famine in their own countries. Before joining UNHCR, Karen lectured in political science and Islamic Studies at Makerere University in Kampala, Uganda, and at Juba University in southern Sudan. She earned her B.Sc. at DePauw University in Indiana and her M.A. in Islamic Studies at McGill University in Canada. "The Brutal Siege of Gaza" appeared in the *Guardian.*

**Steve Lendman** is an independent, progressive economist who, with his colleague Professor Michel Chossudovsky, coordinates the Center for Global Research in Canada. He received a B.A. from Harvard University and an M.B.A from the Wharton School at the University of Pennsylvania. He worked as a marketing research analyst for several large U.S. corporations before focusing his attention on small business enterprises, progressive nonprofit organizations, economic and political research on finance, war and peace issues, social equity, and the humanitarian crises among Palestinians and Haitians. A regular contributor to numerous publications including the *Atlantic Free Press*, *Counterpunch*, and *OpedNews*, Lendman is also a co-host of *The Global Research News Hour* broadcast on the Republic Broadcast Network. "Israel's Slow-Motion Genocide" appeared in *Global Research* and "The Russell Tribunal in Palestine" in *Op-Ed News*.com.

**Adi Ophir:** The Israeli philosopher Adi Ophir is an associate professor at the Cohn Institute for the History and Philosophy of Science and Ideas at Tel Aviv University. He is also a fellow at the Van Leer Jerusalem Institute, where he directs an interdisciplinary research project titled "Humanitarian Action in Catastrophes: The Shaping of Contemporary Political Imagination and Moral Sensibilities." Recent works include *Order of Evils* (2007); *Terrible Days: Between Disaster and Utopia* (2002), a collection of critical essays on the current political situation in Israel; *Working for the Present* (2001), a collection of deconstructive readings of some major texts and events in contemporary Israeli culture; and "The Identity of the Victims and the Victims of Identity: A Critique of Zionist Ideology for a Post-Zionist Age," published in *Mapping Jewish Identities* (2000). Ophir also founded and edited *Theory and Criticism*, Israel's leading journal for critical theory. "A Response to Benny Morris" appeared in *Counterpunch*.

**Ilan Pappe:** The Israeli historian Ilan Pappe is currently the chair of the Department of History at the University of Exeter and a codirector of the Exeter Center for Ethno-Political Studies. Pappe served as the academic head and founder of the Institute for Peace Studies in Givat Haviva, Israel (1992–2000) and the chair of the Emil Touma Institute for Palestinian Studies in Haifa (2000–2008). Pappe's publications include *The Ethnic Cleansing of Palestine* (2006); *A History of Modern Palestine: One Land, Two Peoples* (2006); *The Modern Middle East* (2005); *Britain and the Arab-Israeli Conflict* (1988); *Jordan in the Middle East: The Making of a Pivotal State 1948–1988* (1994); *The Making of the Arab-Israeli Conflict 1947–51* (1994); *The Israel/Palestine Question* (Rewriting Histories) (1999); and *Middle Eastern Politics and Ideas: A History from Within* (1998). "The Necessity of Cultural Boycott" and "Genocide in Gaza" appeared in *Electronic Intifada*.

**James Petras** is a Bartle Professor (emeritus) of Sociology at Binghamton University, New York, and adjunct professor at Saint Mary's University, Halifax, Nova Scotia. He is the author of sixty-six books published in thirty-one languages and over 600 articles in professional journals, including the *American Sociological Review*, *British Journal of Sociology*, *Social Research*, and

*Journal of Peasant Studies.* He has published over 2,000 articles in nonprofessional publications such as the *New York Times,* the *Guardian,* the *Nation, Christian Science Monitor, Foreign Policy, New Left Review, Partisan Review, TempsModerne,* and *Le Monde Diplomatique,* and his commentary is widely carried on the Internet. He is a winner of the Career of Distinguished Service Award from the American Sociological Association's Marxist Sociology Section; of the Robert Kenny Award for Best Book, 2002; and of the Best Dissertation, Western Political Science Association, in 1968. His most recent titles include *Unmasking Globalization: Imperialism of the Twenty-First Century* (2001), *System in Crisis* (2003), *What's Left in Latin America* (2009), and *World Depression Regional Wars* (2009). "The Final Solution and Jose Saramago" appeared in *Canadian Dimension,* and "The Israeli Agenda and the Scorecard of the Zionist Power" appeared in *itszone.co.uk.*

**John Pilger:** A renowned investigative journalist and documentary filmmaker, John Pilger is one of only two people to have twice won British journalism's top award, and his documentaries have won academy awards in both the UK and the United States. Pilger began his career as a Vietnam War correspondent for the *Daily Mirror.* He has written close to a dozen books and made over fifty documentaries, and his latest works include the books *Reporting the World: John Pilger's Great Eyewitness Photographers* (2001); *The New Rulers of the World* (2002); *Tell Me No Lies: Investigative Journalism and Its Triumphs* (2004); and *Freedom Next Time* (2006); and the films *Palestine Is Still the Issue* (2002); *The War on Democracy* (2007); *Behind the Facades* (2008); and *Reporting the World* (2008). "From Belsen to Gaza" appeared in *Global Research.*ca.

**Dr. Gideon Polya** recently retired from a senior post at La Trobe University, Melbourne, Australia, after four decades of teaching and research in biochemistry. He continues to teach part-time at La Trobe University and at the University of the Third Age (U3A), Melbourne. Author and coauthor of over 100 scientific papers, he recently published a huge pharmacological text, *The Biochemical Targets of Plant Bioactive Compounds* (2003); two further works, *Body Count: Global Avoidable Mortality since 1950* (2008); and an updated edition of his 1998 book *Jane Austen and the Black Hole of British History* (2008). Dr. Polya is an active antiracism, antiwar, pro-environment, pro-peace, pro-humanity researcher, scientist, writer, lecturer, advocate, and artist. "Ongoing Palestinian Genocide" appeared in *MWC News.*

**Tanya Reinhart:** Israeli linguist, author, and peace activist, Dr. Tanya Reinhart (1943–2007) wrote frequently on the Israeli-Palestinian conflict, contributing columns to the Israeli newspaper *Yediot Aharonot* and longer articles to the *Counterpunch, Znet,* and *Israeli Indymedia* websites. Reinhart studied philosophy and Hebrew literature at the Hebrew University, Jerusalem, as an undergraduate, where she later received an M.A. in comparative literature and philosophy. In 1976 she obtained a Ph.D. from the Massachusetts Institute of Technology. Her thesis supervisor was Noam Chomsky. Reinhart was a former professor of linguistics and literary theory at Tel Aviv University. She was also a guest lecturer at Duke University and at Utrecht University in the Netherlands, and ended her international career as Global Distinguished Professor at New York University (NYU). "A Slow, Steady Genocide" appeared in *Zmag.net.*

**Paul Craig Roberts** is an economist and a nationally syndicated columnist for Creators Syndicate. He served as an assistant secretary of the Treasury in the Reagan administration, earning fame as the "Father of Reaganomics." He is a former editor and columnist for the *Wall Street Journal, Business Week,* and *Scripps Howard News Service.* He is a graduate of the Georgia Institute of Technology and holds a Ph.D. from the University of Virginia. Roberts was a post-graduate at the University of California, Berkeley, and Oxford University, where he was a member of Merton College. In 1992, he received the Warren Brookes Award for Excellence in Journalism. In 1993, the Forbes Media Guide ranked him as one of the top seven journalists in the United States. His writings frequently appear on OpEdNews.com, Antiwar.com, VDARE.com, *Counterpunch,* and the *American Free Press.* "The Shame of Being American" appeared in *AntiWar.*com.

**Jon Basil Utley** is associate publisher of *The American Conservative,* a Robert A. Taft Fellow for International and Constitutional Studies at the Ludwig von Mises Institute, and a Fellow with the Atlas Economic Research Foundation. He has written widely on third-world development economics and foreign policy. He is a graduate of Georgetown University's School of Foreign Service. He has written for the *Harvard Business Review,* the *Washington Post,* the *Washington Times, National Review, Human Events,* and the *Miami Herald* and is listed in *Who's Who in the World* and *Who's Who in America.* In 1990, Utley cofounded the Committee to Avert a Mid-East Holocaust, which opposed the American attack on Iraq. He is now the chairman of Americans Against World Empire. He has served on the board of directors or advisory councils of many leading conservative and libertarian organizations, including Accuracy in Media, Conservative Caucus, Council for Inter-American Security, the Ethics and Public Policy Center, Reason Foundation, and Solidarity America. "America's Armageddonites" appeared in *AntiWar.*com.

# Introduction

## WILLIAM A. COOK

## The Untold Story of the Zionist Intent to Turn Palestine into a Jewish State

(Based on classified documents seized by the British Mandate Police from the Jewish Agency and its affiliated organizations, materials that confirm that the Zionist-controlled Jewish community intended to remove the Arab inhabitants of Palestine from their land and make the whole of Palestine a Jewish State, an intent that continues to the present day, as the chapters in this book attest.)

> Jewish villages were built in the place of Arab villages. You do not even know the names of these Arab villages, and I do not blame you because geography books no longer exist, not only do the books not exist, the Arab villages are not there either... There is not one single place built in this country that did not have a former Arab population
>
> (Moshe Dayan, address to the Technion, Haifa, as quoted in *Ha'aretz*, April 4, 1969, as cited in Walid Khalidi, *All That Remains*. Institute for Palestine Studies: Washington, D.C., xxxi).

Thus began in November 1947 what is euphemistically called the ethnic cleansing of Palestine by the combined forces of the Jewish armies—the Haganah, the Stern, and the Irgun—as they drove more than 700,000 Palestinian Arabs from their homes, leaving them destitute, homeless, and abandoned without a country in what is now the largest refugee Diaspora in the world.

More truthfully, the evacuation of the Palestinians that began so ruthlessly in 1947, and is now called the *Nakba*, was an intentional, calculated campaign to force the Palestinian Arabs out of Palestine, a systematic genocide of a people as defined by the United Nations in its adoption of Raphael Lemkin's term in 1948.[1]

This book yokes together two charged words. Both require clarification because both are, paradoxically, ancient and new, and both are fraught with entwined intellectual and emotional responses. "Palestine" can be traced back to prepatriarchal times and the peoples from Asia Minor and Greece, a migratory group called "Plesheth" (eventually, "Philistines"), who were not Semites and did not speak Arabic but occupied what is now Palestine and areas of Jordan. Eventually, the Roman emperor Hadrian changed the name *Roman Provincia Judaea* to *Provincia Syria Palaestina,* which, in short-ened form, became Palestine. The term, referencing both a place and a people, has become a controversial one since the declaration of the Jewish state.

"Genocide," a word now coupled with Palestine as a result of Israeli policy against the Palestinians, is a neologism coined in 1944 by Raphael Lemkin that links the Greek *genos,* referring to tribe or race, with the suffix "cide," from the Latin *caedere,* meaning "to kill." Genocide thus resides next to frat-ricide and patricide as descriptive of the worst of evils inherent in humans, an evil that can be traced back to Cain and Abel. Lemkin designed the term in response to the atrocities rampant during World War II.

Today, Palestine is a geographical area in the Mid-East created after World War I that borders Lebanon on the north, Jordan on the east, the Sinai on the south, and the Mediterranean on the west. The United Kingdom had mandatory authority from the League of Nations to gov-ern the area with the establishment of the Palestine Mandate in 1922, an action that imposed a Western colonial and national mind-set on an area familiar with tribal and imperial authority. Prior to the official implemen-tation of the mandate in 1922, the British government had enunciated a "declaration" concerning the desirability of His Majesty's government in the "establishment of a national home for the Jewish people," called the Balfour Declaration.

His Majesty's government view with favor the establishment in Palestine of a national home for the Jewish people, and will use their best endeav-ors to facilitate the achievement of this object, it being clearly understood that nothing shall be done which may prejudice the civil and religious rights of existing non-Jewish communities in Palestine, or the rights and political status enjoyed by Jews in any other country.[2]

Discussions that resulted in the final text of the Balfour Declaration clarify the intention of its wording. The term "national home" was used intentionally instead of "state." Additionally, the first draft of the declaration referred to the principle *"that Palestine should be* reconstituted *as the National Home of the Jewish people"* (italics in original). In the final text, the word *that* (in this first draft) was replaced with *in* to avoid committing all of Palestine to the Jews only.[3]

At the time of the mandate's implementation, the Muslim population exceeded 757,182, or 78 percent of the total population of Palestine, the Jewish 11 percent, and the Christian 9.6 percent, as determined by the British census of 1922. By 1931 there were 761,922 Muslims, representing 74 percent of the total population, with 16 percent now Jewish and 8.6 percent Christian. In 1945 the Muslim population had reached 1,061,270, or 60 percent, with the Jewish at 31 percent and the Christian at 2.8 percent. In 1947, at the time of the partitioning of Palestine by the United Nations, the successor to the League of Nations, Jews owned 6 percent of the land in Palestine.[4] These figures played a significant role when the mandate came into effect, as the British government in Palestine attempted to not "prejudice the civil and religious rights of existing non-Jewish communities in Palestine." The increase in the numbers of legally admitted Jews and those entering illegally account for the disproportionate rise in the Jewish population from 11 percent to 31 percent in just 23 years. Aware of the dramatic increase occurring in the 1930s, the Mandate Government issued a white paper in 1939 placing limits on the numbers of Jews allowed to enter Palestine in an attempt to maintain a balance between the new immigrants and the existing population. Various factions in the Jewish community revolted against this imposed limitation.

It is this confrontation between the Mandate Government and the Jewish community's organizations that is the subject of this Introduction, as it provides a historical link to the ten years covered by the essays in this book. Between 1939 and 1947, the Mandate Government found it more and more difficult to maintain its position as the responsible governing force servicing the Arab population and the growing Jewish population, determining by 1947 that these two populations could not coexist. As a result, the British government placed the resolution of the problem in the hands of the United Nations. That in turn resulted in a plan to partition the land of Palestine, proposed in November 1947 to the General Assembly, to be implemented in May 1948.

At the root of this conflict between the Jewish organizations and the Arab population, and subsequently the British Mandate government, was the intent of the Zionist-led group that dominated the organizations that worked on behalf of the Jewish community in Palestine. Zionism arose in the late 1880s in Europe as a national revival movement, according to Ilan Pappe in his book *The Ethnic Cleansing of Palestine,* and by the time of the mandate had evolved into a secularized and nationalized Judaism.[5] Both Pappe and the Israeli historian Benny Morris have shown that the Jewish Agency, which served as the principal power in Palestine serving the Jewish community, had intentions of acquiring complete control over all the land of Palestine and to expel by any means necessary the indigenous population. This brings us to the second word of crucial significance in this book—genocide.

In 1944 the term "genocide" appeared in Raphael Lemkin's *Axis Rule in Occupied Europe.* This passage by Frank Chalk and Kurt Jonassohn summarizes Lemkin's understanding:

> Under Lemkin's definition, genocide was the coordinated and planned annihilation of a national, religious, or racial group by a variety of actions aimed at undermining the foundations essential to the survival of the group as a group. Lemkin conceived of genocide as "a composite of different acts of persecution or destruction." His definition included attacks on political and social institutions, culture, language, national feelings, religion, and the economic existence of the group. Even nonlethal acts that undermined the liberty, dignity, and personal security of members of a group constituted genocide if they contributed to weakening the viability of the group. Under Lemkin's definition, acts of ethnocide—a term coined by the French after the war to cover the destruction of a culture without the killing of its bearers—also qualified for genocide.[6]

According to Lemkin, "Genocide has two phases: one, destruction of the national pattern of the oppressed group; the other, the imposition of the national pattern of the oppressor."[7]

It was Lemkin's work that paved the way for the Convention passed by the United Nations in 1948, a document signed by the nascent Jewish State at a later date. Lemkin's "composite of different acts of persecution or destruction" includes attacks on a people's political institutions, its culture, its national feelings, its religion, and its economic existence. It also includes non-lethal acts that undermine the liberty, dignity, and personal security of members of the group as they result in weakening the viability of the group.

These are the criteria that determine genocide under the UN Convention.

Article II:
In the present Convention, genocide means any of the following acts committed with intent to destroy, in whole or in part, a national,

ethnical, racial, or religious group, as such:
a. Killing members of the group;
b. Causing serious bodily or mental harm to members of the group;
c. Deliberately inflicting on the group conditions of life calculated to bring about its physical destruction in whole or in part;
d. Imposing measures intended to prevent births within the group;
e. Forcibly transferring children of the group to another group.

Article III:
The following acts shall be punishable:
a. Genocide;
b. Conspiracy to commit genocide;
c. Direct and public incitement to commit genocide;
d. Attempt to commit genocide;
e. Complicity in genocide.[8]

The Convention assumes that all signers will abide by its terms. Therefore, once the State of Israel was created by the Jewish leaders of the area by declaration on May 14, 1948, and subsequently was recognized for membership in the UN in 1949, it was expected to abide by the UN Convention.[9]

## The View from Inside the Mandate

One of the curious ambiguities that surrounds the decade that preceded the declaration by the Jewish leaders in Palestine of the State of Israel is the dearth of information and perspective from the British Mandate forces governing Palestine between 1940 and May 15, 1948, the date of implementation of the partition resolution. Fortunately, Sir Richard C. Catling has left us a file that provides insight into conditions that prevailed in Jerusalem while he was the deputy head of the Special Branch of the Criminal Investigation Division in Jerusalem in 1944 and, a year later, assistant inspector general. Catling's "Top Secret" file lay untouched in the Rhodes House archives of the Bodleian Libraries of Oxford University until two years ago, when I received permission to cite its contents by the Chief Archivist for Rhodes Library.

Two documents dominate the file, with sixty-two appendices of evidence totaling close to 500 pages of materials. The first is a dispatch sent to the secretary of state, dated October 16, 1941, by the high commissioner of Palestine, Harold MacMichael, labeled "Most Secret"; the second, a top-secret "Memorandum on the Participation of the Jewish National Institutions in Palestine in Acts of Lawlessness and Violence," prepared by the Criminal Investigation Department headquarters, the Palestine Police, Jerusalem, dated July 31, 1947.[10]

Together, these documents provide a British Mandate government perspective on the forces that controlled the evolving Jewish presence in Palestine; on the intent of those forces to take full control of the land of Palestine after the mandate period; and on the ruthlessness of their operations against the British Palestine government and the Palestinian people, including their removal, transfer, expulsion, and death, and their awareness of the awesome power the Zionists brought, both politically and militarily, to the achievement of that goal. In short, the accumulated evidence of an ethnic cleansing of Palestine, as documented by Dr. Ilan Pappe, based on the Israeli (Jewish Agency) archives, finds corroboration here as recorded and documented by seized materials from the Jewish Agency, Haganah, Irgun, and related sources.

What should be obvious now, after the carefully researched and scholarly work of Dr. Pappe and the equally well-researched work of Dr. Morris, both based on recently released evidence from the Israeli archives and those of the Israel Defense Forces Archives, complemented now with the materials preserved by Sir Richard C. Catling, is the truth about the creation of the State of Israel: the acceptance of UN Resolution 181 by the Jewish Agency Provisional Government as the designated Jewish State was not done with intent to abide by the goal of the UN General Assembly—to provide a state for two peoples in the land of Palestine—but rather to use it as a means to gain eventual control of all the land and cleanse that land of its indigenous people to whatever extent possible. Put bluntly, as the essays in this volume attest, the current government in Israel continues the practices of past Israeli governments: to cleanse the land of its rightful inhabitants to make that land part of the Jewish state. This is what is termed in numerous articles in this volume "slow-motion genocide."

## Jump-Starting the State

Consider the events of April 9–11, 1948, the extermination of the citizens of the town of Deir Yassin, a month before the agency declared the existence of the Israeli state and the implementation of the UN Resolution to Partition. This massacre became then, and remains, the signature example of the intent of the Zionist Consultancy and its agents to ethnically cleanse Palestine of its non-Jewish inhabitants. A plethora of documents abound that claim insight into the events that transpired during those three days, yet all attest to the extermination of the town's citizens, differing only as to numbers and agents responsible. Since Benny Morris relies on official documents released by the government and the military, I will use his summation as an example.

> Deir Yassin is remembered…for the atrocities committed by the IZL (National Military Organization) and LHI (Freedom Fighters of Israel) troops during and immediately after the drawn-out battle: Whole families were riddled with bullets…men, women, and children were mowed down as they emerged from houses; individuals were taken aside and shot. Haganah intelligence reported "there were piles of dead. Some of the prisoners moved to places of incarceration, including women and children, were murdered viciously by their captors…LHI members…relate that the IZL men raped a number of Arab girls and murdered them afterward" (we don't know if this is true). Another intelligence operative (who visited the site hours after the event) reported the "adult males were taken to town Jerusalem in trucks and paraded in the city streets, then taken back to the site and killed…Before they were put on the trucks, the IZL and LHI men searched the women, men, and children [and] took from them all the jewelry and stole their money." Finally, the "Haganah made great efforts to hide its part in the operation."[11]

Despite Morris's account, fifty years after the events at Deir Yassin, Morton Klein, the president of the Zionist Organization of America, attempted to revise history by denying that a massacre took place in his book *Deir Yassin, History of a Lie*. Why? Why go to such lengths to deny what is so thoroughly documented? The answer is simple. Deir Yassin is a symbol of ethnic cleansing, of the determination of the Jews in Israel, controlled by the Zionist Consultancy and its armed forces, to "transfer" or kill the indigenous people of Palestine.

Matthew C. Hogan and Daniel A. McGowen, in an essay titled "Anatomy of a Whitewash," have provided a detailed rebuttal of Klein's work, noting that

> not unlike the historical revisionists who deny the Holocaust, Klein's work 'Deir Yassin: History of a Lie,' has the appearance of scholarship. It is heavily footnoted, and documented and relentlessly plods through every quote and claim made about the events in Deir Yassin.…He uses half quotes, specious arguments and *ad hominem* attacks in an effort to confound an ordinary reader. He admits what cannot be denied, but minimizes its importance.

The real reason for Klein's effort, as Hogan and McGowen note, is "to rewrite history by eliminating from its record one of Zionism's more odious events."

The truth symbolized by Deir Yassin is the calculated Zionist strategy "to terrorize Arabs in order to expel them on the way to depopulating their villages in order to repopulate them with new Jewish immigrants or to erase them from the map."[12] During the six months between the adoption of UN Resolution 181 and in subsequent months, the new state of Israel launched a massive military incursion into territory designated for the Palestinian people by that same resolution, creating in its wake, as Walid Khalidi notes, "three quarters of a million Palestinian refugees," the destruction of "hundreds of entire villages...not only depopulated but obliterated...and houses blown up or bulldozed." Khalidi's massive study focuses on 418 villages, once the homes of Palestinians, 292 completely destroyed, 90 others "largely destroyed," the remainder replaced by Jews called "Israeli settlers."[13]

Perhaps one of the ironic twists resulting from Klein's work occurs when he recounts evidence that attests to accusations of rape at Deir Yassin. Morris notes that the IZL had raped women at Deir Yassin based on LHI statements to that effect. Klein reports:

> The original source of the Deir Yassin rape accusation was a senior British police official. Since the British Mandatory authorities were still in power at the time of the Deir Yassin battle—they were not due to leave Palestine until May 15, more than a month later—the British police carried out their own investigation of the events, led by Richard C. Catling, Assistant Inspector General of the Mandatory regime's Criminal Investigation Division and a specialist in Jewish matters. Catling was not, however, the most objective person to be investigating whether or not the IZL and Lehi had carried out atrocities against Arab civilians. For much of the previous decade, Catling had played a prominent role in the Mandate regime's violent struggles with the Jewish fighting forces and with the IZL and Lehi in particular, who had assassinated numerous leading British police officers and military officials, and had publically humiliated the English forces with retaliatory hangings, public whippings, assaults on supposedly-invulnerable police stations and army bases, and spectacular prison breaks.[14]

Klein's unabashed gloating over the British embarrassment caused by the Jewish terrorists against the United Nations's mandated government in Palestine reflects his attitude that the abominations inflicted on the people of Deir Yassin are of little relevance or consequence in the larger developments that gave Israel control over virtually all of Palestine by the time of his book's appearance. However, it might be instructive for us to see these events through the eyes of Sir Richard C. Catling, the specialist in Jewish affairs, as even Klein asserts, and the man who interviewed the women raped.

While Klein cites Catling's specialization in Jewish affairs and even notes his narrowly escaping assassination at the hands of the IZL and his subsequent miraculous escapes from death at the hands of Jewish terrorists, including his presence in the King David Hotel lobby when it was bombed by the IZL in a "false flag" operation in 1946, he gives no credence to Catling's expertise in understanding how the Zionist Consultancy operated and controlled the Jewish forces and the Jewish people during the years leading up to the assumption of statehood in May 1948. (The Rhodes House documents include a communiqué by J. P. I. Pforde, assistant inspector general, that identifies the connection between Haganah forces and the National Military Organization (NMO) as responsible for the false flag operation, with NMO's own admission of that connection.)[15]

One might think that a man of Catling's experience and knowledge would be the most appropriate person to investigate the occurrences at Deir Yassin. Given the documents that he retained from that period, it would appear that he understood more than most what capabilities the Jewish Agency, the Consultancy, and the military "gangs" (read armies) had at their disposal as they undertook an all-out sabotage of the British Mandate government between 1941 and May 15, 1948. In hindsight, Sir Richard had to live out his retirement in Britain, from 1964 to 2005, conscious of the materials that would explain the perceived failure of the mandate period even as he observed Britain's capitulation to the Zionist influences in the U.K. that dominated discourse about the evolving Jewish state

## Perceiving the Reality

The "dispatch" sent by MacMichael to the secretary of state resulted from an investigation into the funding practices and use of those funds by various Jewish organizations.

> The memorandum illustrates—indeed, brings into full limelight—the fact that the Mandatory is faced potentially with as grave a danger in Palestine from Jewish violence as it has ever faced from Arab violence, a danger infinitely less easy to meet by the methods of repression which have been employed against Arabs. In the first place, the Jews ... have the moral and political support ... of considerable sections of public opinion both in the United Kingdom and the United States of America. ... all the influence and political ability of the Zionists would be brought to

bear to show that the Jews in Palestine were the victims of aggression, and that a substantial body of opinion abroad would be persuaded of the truth of the contention.[16]

This last observation is exceedingly prescient, as it shows that MacMichael recognizes the power of deception that will be used by the Zionist machine to stamp the Jewish community as victims of overwhelming forces—both Arab and British—while the reality of Jewish military power remains hidden.

Quite obviously, MacMichael understood that the Mandatory had little power at home over the zealous actions of the Zionists as they manipulated public and political opinion, even as they expanded their terrorism against the British Mandate government in Palestine. This was an untenable position to be in: responsible for government control and security of those under its authority—that is, Palestinians as well as Jews—and knowing that the Jews were set on driving the British out of Palestine, and knowing that the home government could offer little help.

To bolster his points, MacMichael offers the following data:

> The Jews in Palestine are by no means untrained in the use of arms...large numbers have received training in the Palestine Police...or in His Majesty's Forces. At the present time, in addition to approximately 10,000 Jews in His Majesty's Forces, there are 5,800 in various units of the police force and 15,400 special policemen (31,000)...When to those men...are added the illicit "defence" organizations of the Jews [Haganah alone had an estimated 60–70,000 men by 1945, see Mss, Med. S20 Appendix XXI], it will be evident that the Jewish people in arms would numerically and in calibre be a very formidable adversary.[17]

This was in 1941, before the full deployment of Jewish terrorism against the legitimate Palestine government was under way. How different the truth from the deception: propaganda, perception, and reality.

MacMichael and Catling found themselves missing one of Catling's primary supports for the waging of "irregular warfare," drawn from his image of the three-legged stool that required the support of the people, the commander and his army, and the government, an image, no doubt, from his childhood in Suffolk, where his family were butchers and farmers. Needless to say, both had to confront the "facts on the ground": the Zionist Executive movement's resistance to Britain's limitation of immigrants into Palestine, as enunciated in the white paper of 1939, and the outright terrorism of the Stern "gang" that "deemed Britain to be the bitter enemy of Zionism." LEHI (Lohamei 'Herut Yisrael), the official name for the Stern "gang," from the Hebrew for Fighters for the Freedom of Israel, emphasized anti-British rebellion, including robbing of banks, indiscriminate killing of British police, and the assassination of the British minister-resident Lord Moyne in 1944 even as "the Nazi death machinery continued to swallow European Jewry." But the situation only got worse as the end of World War II loomed. "The Haganah carried out anti-British military operations—liberation of interned immigrants from the Atlit camp; the bombing of the country's railroad network; sabotage raids on radar installations and bases of the British police mobile force; sabotage of British vessels...and the destruction of all road and railroad bridges on the borders." All of this terrorism was conducted against the Mandate Government while the home government remained silent under the pall of Israeli Zionist propaganda.[18]

But recording the acts of terrorism does not do justice to the conditions the Mandate Government faced. MacMichael describes the reality of the forces aligned against the police in Palestine.

> A second matter which deeply impressed me is the almost Nazi control exercised by the official Jewish organizations over the Jewish community, willy nilly, through the administration of funds from abroad, the issue of labor certificates in connection with the immigration quota, the forced contributions to funds and the power of the Histadruth. The Royal Commission were, in my view, fundamentally at error in describing the Jewish community in Palestine as "intensely democratic"... The Zionist organization, the whole social structure which it has created in Palestine, has the trappings but none of the essentials of democracy. The community is under the closed oligarchy of the Jewish official organizations which control Zionist policy and circumscribe the lives of the Jewish community in all directions—the Mapai, the Histadruth, the Vaad Leumi and the Jewish Agency. The reality of power is in the Agency, with the Haganah, the illegal military organization, always in the background.[19]

These conditions prevailed in 1941. The mandate may be "in force," as MacMichael's notes, but the Jewish Agency is in control of the Jews in Palestine. Their forced loyalty is to the agency. "The Zionist discipline so firmly welds the majority of Jews in Palestine into one body that measures against the Haganah would inevitably become measures against the Jewish community as a whole." And so the authorities in Palestine, the legal authorities, had no power to enforce measures that would curtail terrorism against their own police. "The use of force cannot be contemplated at present as any such action would have to be on a very large scale." MacMichael understands that he can get no help from the Jewish community, even from those who

find themselves at odds with the agency's methods or morality. The consequences to the individual Jew for disobedience was horrendous, as the second
document seized from the Zionists in 1947 attests.

Perhaps one of the most frightening observations MacMichael's makes
comes at the very end of his dispatch: "As matters now stand it seems to
me inevitable that the Zionist Juggernaut which has been created with such
intensity of zeal for a Jewish national state will be the cause of very serious
trouble in the Near East." Prophetic words indeed.

## Between Two Worlds

Nothing makes more obvious the meaning of the "Zionist Juggernaut"
than Catling's Top Secret "Memorandum of the Criminal Investigation
Department" of July 31, 1947, a three-inch-thick file filled with seized Jewish
organization documents collated to provide evidence on each of the sections
detailed in the cover report of forty-three pages.

> The purpose of this memorandum is to furnish documentary evidence of
> the extent to which the supreme Jewish national institutions in Palestine
> and their principal officials have been parties to acts of sedition, vio-
> lence, incitement and other offences against the laws of Palestine.... The
> bulk of the memorandum concerns the war and post war years.... The
> trends which thenceforth led up to serious outbreaks of active resistance
> towards the end of 1945 and early 1946 are well known and the memo-
> randum will therefore concern itself solely with an attempt to establish
> the links between the supreme Jewish bodies and illegal activity.[20]

Catling's memorandum begins with an understanding of the "intri-
cate Jewish political, social and economic structure in Palestine." A series
of appendices chart these structures, marking in passing that "the Palestine
Royal Commission Report of 1937 understood 'The Agency is obviously not
a 'governing body'; it can only advise and cooperate in a certain wide field.'
But allied as it is with the Vaad Leumi, and commanding the allegiance of
the great majority of the Jews in Palestine, it unquestionably exercises, *both in
Jerusalem and in London,* a considerable influence on the conduct of government." Catling's frustration with the actual control of the Jews over British
policy in Palestine glares through this document. *"This powerful and efficient
organization amounts, in fact, to a government existing side by side with the Mandatory
Government"* [emphasis mine].[21]

What Catling doesn't state in that sentence, but what he demonstrates in the memorandum, is that the Jewish Agency and its affiliated organizations are at war with the UN authority in Palestine, the British Mandate government. The appendices include detailed information on the personnel in interlocking Jewish organizations and the function of each, noting specifically the presence of leading Jewish personalities. Special emphasis is given to the power of the Mapai (Palestine Labor Party) as it controls key executive positions so that it in effect controls the Yishuv—the Zionist-controlled Jewish Agency—and directs its policies. "Ben Gurion stated, 'In a Jewish Community of some 600,000 there are more than 170,000 organized workers, men and women....' *Evidence will show how these organized workers are penalized if they dare to oppose the arbitrary commands of the national institutions"* [emphasis mine]. The British Mandate government had long suspected that the subversive activities against the Palestine government were not the sole responsibility of the "gangs," like the resistance groups, the NMO, and the Stern gang. With the evidence provided in this memorandum, it became obvious that the "Jewish national institutions, or groups of their officials have placed the legally constituted framework and organs of these bodies at the discreet disposal of the para-military organization, 'Irgun Hagana.'"

The memorandum goes further. It notes that the activities of the Jewish Agency through its controlled organizations send emissaries and instructors abroad "to stir up Zionist sentiments among the Jewish communities and displaced persons, to bring pressure to bear upon the Palestine problem, to organize illegal immigration and engage in espionage." As a result of its investigations, the department itemizes six areas of subversive activities undertaken by the Jewish Agency against the British Mandate government:

a. Maintenance of a secret army and espionage system;
b. Smuggling, theft and manufacture of arms;
c. Illegal immigration;
d. Violence and civil disobedience;
e. Seditious and hostile propaganda;
f. Encroachment upon the civil rights of Jewish citizens.[22]

In short, the Yishuv actively undermined the Mandate Government's legal authority in Palestine even as it operated to undermine support for that government in Britain, placing UK forces in harm's way as they attempted to fulfill their authorized responsibilities in Palestine. It also demonstrates the determination of the agency's leadership in undermining the very nation that gave it a means of establishing a "homeland" in Palestine through the Balfour Declaration. Needless to say, Catling and his CID forces recognized the impossible position this defiance placed them in and understood the deception and violent means used by the Zionists to ensure that their will and theirs alone would be fulfilled at any cost. On page seventy-four of the appendices, this assertion by the unnamed head of command, the Jewish Resistance Movement, March 25, 1946, establishes the reality of this point:

> But if the solution (i.e., that Britain would not repeal the White Paper) is anti-Zionist, our resistance will continue, spread and increase in vigor.... There are precepts in Jewish ethics which oblige a man to be killed rather than trespass. The precept of defense of our national existence is at the head of these. We shall not trespass.... Our resistance is liable to result in the creation of a new problem in this country—the British problem, the problem of British security in Palestine, and this problem will be resolved only by the Zionist solution. It would be better if the Zionist solution were proclaimed in recognition of the world Jewish problem and the justice of our work in Palestine. We do not threaten. We only wish you to know our intentions clearly.

The chutzpah represented by this statement, that in effect declares open war against the Mandate Government, receives confirmation in the following words:

> We shall not accept the status of a minority in our own land, whether the minority is 33% or 49%.... We shall not accept a symbolic independence in a dwarflike token state which will not give us the chance of developing all the resources of the country and creating here a safe asylum for all Jews who are compelled or wish to come... In all the crises of the past and until today, the Arabs have always acquiesced in the facts we have created here and have expressed their opposition only to the creation of a new state of affairs. If they were to be faced now with the fait accompli of the Jewish State, they will at length acquiesce in that too.[23]

Recognize the absoluteness of these comments: "resistance will continue," "result in the creation of a new problem—the British problem," "the problem of British security in Palestine," "this problem will only be resolved by the Zionist solution," "our land," "developing all the resources of the country, "Arabs have always acquiesced in the facts we have created," and "they will...acquiesce in that too." For the Zionists, there is no alternative but the total takeover of the land of Palestine, regardless of the existence of an indigenous people or an existing government.

It is not the purpose of this chapter to provide all the particulars of the CID memorandum, but it is important to provide an understanding of what these papers reveal about the conditions that existed from 1941 to 1948 as the Mandate Government had to contend with the terrorism of the Jews in Palestine. What they reveal is a Zionist mind-set that had a predetermined intent of full acquisition of the land of Palestine regardless of the Balfour Declaration intent, regardless of the British Mandate government's responsibilities as the authorized government until May of 1948, regardless of Resolution 181 as it set borders by partitioning Palestine for two peoples, and regardless of the rights of the indigenous population to their homes and villages. These papers also provide insight into the processes used by the Zionists to gain their ends, including violence, civil disobedience, seditious acts, deception, and encroachment on civil and human rights of Jews and Palestinians.

The evidence presented in this chapter demonstrates that the original intent of the Zionists was the complete takeover of Palestine by extermination, expulsion, or submission of the Palestinians. Consider how the Jewish Agency waged its war against the Mandate Government through violence, civil disobedience, and seditious acts. Section D, page thirty-six of the memorandum, provides evidence that yokes the actions of the illegal resistance movement to the agency, including its complicity in the bombing of the British headquarters at the King David Hotel (July 22, 1946). Indeed, the documents include an admission of culpability by Haganah in Appendix LVa. But as is always the case, deception plays its role. "There is no doubt that the Haganah is maintaining the designation 'Jewish Resistance Movement' to cover the continuation of its sabotage activities against those instruments of Government which are directly preventing illegal immigration." Yet even as the Haganah pleads innocence to that crime when it occurred, Ben-Gurion mouths these words as he runs for reelection: "If need be, we shall take the country by force. If Palestine proves too small—her frontiers will have to be extended." No recognition of borders here, no acceptance of the UN or Britain as authorities of international law.

Yet the agency continues its ostensible role as the accepted government organization cooperating with the Mandate Government, issuing statements of innocence while deploring acts of terror, even as it sabotages members of the British forces and authorizes bombings that kill hundreds. While deception is the norm with the agency as it feigns cooperation, it speaks its intent to the Jewish community through "the clandestine publications of the 'Haganah', such as 'Eshnav,' 'Hahoma,' and the 'Kol Israel' broadcasts which preach anything short of open revolt against the British authorities."

What form does this indoctrination take that is pumped into the Jewish community?

> The public is reminded incessantly that the Government's policy has no legal basis and therefore all the evils of terrorism, illegal immigration, the death of hundreds of thousands of Jews in Europe, the plight of the Jewish D.P.s are the making of the Government whose sinister aim is to destroy the Zionist movement and, limit the Yishuv to an everlasting ghetto.

> Another form of subversive activity was the insidious propaganda directed at British troops and police with the object of undermining their sense of loyalty. Such activity might be deemed to amount to incitement to mutiny.[24]

## Inside the Zionist Mind

Perhaps the most insidious of the strategies employed by the Zionist Consultancy and its agents comes via encroachment on the civil rights of Palestinian and Jewish citizens. That encroachment comes stealthily out of the dark recesses of a spider's hole, the Red House, where, as recorded by Ilan Pappe in *The Ethnic Cleansing of Palestine,* the Zionist eleven of the Consultancy held its clandestine meetings, where the strategies that were to guide the affairs of the nascent Jewish "state" were hatched. Parallel this image then, between the years 1930 and 1948, with the situation in the United States since World War II, as Jewish forces asserted their control from lobbies in Washington D. C. that began to encase America's governing organizations in a web of interlocking deceptions that effectively took control of America's policies in the Mid-East.

The eggs hatched behind the closed doors of the Red House emerged as executives of the various organizations established to provide for the welfare of the ever-increasing Jewish community in Palestine. Initially, Chaim Weizman and David Ben-Gurion, worked with the Mandate forces by forming the Jewish Agency, the former serving as president and the latter as chairman, to serve the needs of this new community as it entered Palestine, legally providing personnel that could speak the languages of the various Jews arriving, arranging jobs for them, and orienting them to their new homeland. Clandestinely, the agency served the purposes of Zionist ideology through the Consultancy, where Ben-Gurion also served as chief executive.

The Consultancy established a network of allied organizations, ostensibly to aid the agency, the Yishuv community, on behalf of the Mandate Government, but in each case headed by a small group of Consultancy Zionists. Thus, the political department of the agency, headed by Arie Liebman and

Shlomo Dostroski, interacted with the Mandate Police Forces to ensure that the Consultancy had access to the inner workings of the CID and police in Jerusalem and Haifa. Clandestinely, the Consultancy organized Hagana as a military operation distinct from Mandate Forces to ensure that the Jewish community carried out the will of the Zionist enterprise, an operation that built in numbers by 1945, according to Weizman, from 80,000 to 200,000 (XXB 209–212). The immigration department, with Eliyhu Dobkin and Mosha Shapiro serving as joint directors, provided knowledge of the mandate's policies regarding immigration, especially policies that countermanded the intentions of the Zionists regarding limitations on Jewish immigration. The Labour Department, with Dr. Schmovak serving as the head, had its parallel operation serving the Consultancy, the Histadruth, that provided the means to control job placement for immigrants and thus a means to control the immigrants. Finally, for the limited purposes of this paper, the Department of Youth established to work with the Mandate Forces to provide education for the new arrivals became the work of Director Dr. Georg Landauer. Education for the Consultancy became the responsibility of the Vaad Leumi, about which Catling's memorandum has this to say: "Perhaps it is true to say that it is in the Jewish educational system which allows political forces to contaminate its charges that Jewish civil rights are fundamentally challenged. With the politically controlled Vaad Leumi it is not surprising that such a state of affairs should exist" (42). The memorandum refers then to a "Report of the Commission of Enquiry into the System of Education of the Jewish Community in Palestine, 1945" in appendix LVII. So out of the darkness of the Zionist dictatorship comes the indoctrination of the Jewish youth.

> The peremptory order of the national institutions that all girls and boys aged 17–18 are obliged to give a complete year's national service (see Appendices XL e-g) is an instance where their control of the school system usually leaves the pupil no alternative but to obey for information indicates that the dissenter's school leaving or examination certificates are withheld until such time as he has satisfied the national demands. (42)

This network of intertwined webs enabled the Zionists to create the illusion of a democratic Jewish community that permitted Jews to run for elected office in the agency but that in fact was dictated by a few through an insidious network of moral compulsion, coercion, extortion, and threats of physical harm and death. "Many are the evils of a regime founded on such a highly organized national dictatorship as exists in the Yishuv today."[25]

But what natural forces inherent in the web govern the creation of its means of survival in a world indifferent to its needs? What compels the multitude of mafias around the world—in China, America, Columbia, Israel, and elsewhere—to create such a web of deceit to achieve their ends? The answer to that question is not the purpose of this chapter, but the awareness of the existence of such power is. It's necessary then to understand how this interlocking of the web structure thrusts out from that central dark hole to force its will on all entwined in its mesh. That in itself is complicated but comprehensible.

The Zionists who took control of the Jewish immigrants entering Palestine had predetermined goals: the establishment of a Jewish State and the expulsion of the existing population in the land of Palestine by whatever means necessary. The reality of these goals is undeniable following the research disclosures of Benny Morris and Ilan Pappe, corroborated now by Catling's file that adds the understanding of the British Mandate Forces to the conditions they faced during the decade that ended with the establishment of the Jewish State. To effectively force their goals on their constituents, the Zionist Consultancy enlisted the beliefs of the Jewish people by injecting into their political intentions the sacred biblical iterations of the "Promised Land," the Zion of the Psalms, for example, "By the streams of Babylon we sat down and wept when we remembered Zion" (137:1). Although the Zionists were, for the most part, secular in thinking, they used the Jewish yearning for the Promised Land as a goad for acceptance of their leadership.

However, the real power behind their efforts, what effectively held together the multiple strands of the web, was the use of extortion on all the Jewish people in Palestine, "the extortion of money for unauthorized funds and self imposed taxes to further the illicit political ends of the national institutions" (42). Catling's memorandum provides evidence of how effective this consolidation of the web's network operated in appendices XXXVIe through XXXVIIt, including the systematic compilation of all wage earners, measures to be adopted in event of refusal to pay, publishing of names of those who failed to contribute, deductions from salary, sanctions on businesses, compulsory assessment, withholding of immigrants' certificates, and Jewish Agency officials' assessments. Out of the eggs hatched in that dark hole poured those held responsible for enacting the policies and procedures of the various organizations that the agency clandestinely controlled. In a translated document seized from the Jewish Agency's Recruiting Office in Tel Aviv on April 29, 1943, the details of the rules and regulations for the imposition of discipline in connection with services and obligations demonstrate the magnitude of this control:

1. When the recruit has been designated to a specific service...and undertaken his task, he receives a badge and certificate of fulfillment of his duty. The badge...must be worn constantly in a prominent and visible position on the jacket or suit.

2. Every man in the Yishuv aged 17–35 must take care that he gets his
badge and certificate not later than 31.8.42. Every one who on and after
31.8.42 is seen in the streets or in any other public place without the
above mentioned badge will be considered a shirker.[26]

There follows the measures to be taken against shirkers, including actions to
be taken against anyone aiding a shirker. There is no need to go into the details
of these imposed actions; the consequences amount to total ostracism of an
individual from his or her community to kidnapping and disappearance.
For those entering the military forces of the Jewish Agency, the Hagana,
the badge is replaced with the Hagana Oath (XVI A 157).

I hereby declare that of my own free will and in free recognition I enter
the Jewish defence organization of the Land of Israel (Irgun Haganana
Haivri Be'Eretz Israel).

I hereby swear to remain loyal all the days of my life to the defense
organization, its laws and its tasks as defined in its basic regulations by
the High Command.

I hereby swear to remain at the disposal of the defense organization
all my life, to accept its discipline unconditionally and without limit,
and at its call to enlist for active service at any time and in any place, to
obey all its orders and to fulfill all its instructions.

I hereby swear to devote all my strength, and even to sacrifice my life,
to defense and battle for my people and my Homeland, for the freedom
of Israel and for the redemption of Zion.[27]

In one sense, these two methodologies of control, one imposed by fear, the
second by moral obligation, make comprehensible the complete control the
Zionists were able to achieve over a protracted period of time toward their
distant goals. The fear imposed by extortion rests on its use in providing
access to jobs made possible by the Histadruth certificates, the protection
offered by the "gangs" and Haganah forces, and the enforcement of the rules
and regulations as itemized above.

The Haganah Oath goes deeper than fear. In effect, it declares that an individual has surrendered his or her conscience over to the High Command, thus
accepting what is right and what is wrong as determined by that authority
regardless of local, state, or international law, indeed, regardless of the morals, values, and traditions of Judaism. This commitment is forever, to death.
It is bolstered by a document issued to the Commander and Troops of the
Haganah labeled "Security Instructions" that notes at the outset, "Remember,
you are a member of an illegal military organization according to the Laws of

the government, its existence, activity and membership of it is forbidden." The remainder of the document obligates the recruit to unconditional obedience, absolute silence, and the pragmatic and utilitarian virtues of deceit and lying.[28]

## Selling the Soul

From the moment an individual takes the Haganah Oath, they are committed to a life of secrecy and hence of disloyalty and betrayal to those they are most intimate with in their day-to-day life. Neither their actions nor their true identity is discernible to those with whom they interact regularly. This is a life that encapsulates the necessity of lies, deceit, coercion, extortion, and obedience to a group that dictates the actions one must pursue; freedom no longer exists, self-direction no longer exists, loyalty to others no longer exists, indeed, friendship with others is compromised or impossible, one becomes the subject of that group, a veritable slave to their desires and wills. The mind-set that promotes such control allows for spying, for deception of friends, for ostracism in one's own community for thinking differently, for imprisonment without due process, for torture, even for extrajudicial executions. It is a total commitment to a cause that supersedes all others, determined and dictated by an oligarchy in silence, and subject to no legitimate institution and to no one.

The darkness of the Zionists' deceit was and is camouflaged by the appearance of civil structures existing within the framework of a legal authority, the Mandatory Government's accepted agency for the Jewish community in Palestine and, today the presence of lobbies, think tanks, controlled media of communication, and legalization of policies that allow for dual citizenship among others. Fear still operates, fear of the nonfriendly, enemy states that surround the friendly, democratic state of Israel, promoted as existentially threatening to America's security; fear for representatives in Congress who dare not confront the desires of the American Israel Public Affairs Committee (AIPAC) and its affiliates lest they find themselves bereft of political support and consequently bereft of their position, and fear induced by corporate media that fears offending the power base represented by the lobby.

Until Israel's fall 2006 blitzkrieg of Lebanon, when the world had an opportunity to witness the ruthlessness of Israeli Zionist violence unimpeded by concern for helpless civilians fleeing for their lives, orphans unable to take shelter from missiles, or children returning home after fearful flight from invading forces only to find toy-like cluster bombs left intentionally to maim or slaughter, the world's communities felt a sympathy for the offspring of those victimized by the Nazis. Prior to that destruction wrought by a military of enormous power, the people of the world knew little of what went on in Palestine and knew only that the Jews of Palestine in 1948 and 1967 had to fight against overwhelming odds against Arabs of many nations intent on pushing them into the sea, making them victims of human violence once again. Then came December 27, 2008, Israel's Christmas bombing of Gaza: holiday giving with a vengeance. Once again, the might of Israel's state-of-the-art military—its air force, navy, army—invaded the defenseless, imprisoned, physically destitute residents of Gaza. Once again, the world witnessed the ruthlessness of Israel's Zionist intent to subjugate, humiliate, and obliterate the indigenous people of Palestine. Now the world knows the truth: the Zionist Consultancy that ruled the Jewish people in Palestine in the 1930s and 1940s, like their counterparts in the Israeli government of Ehud Olmert in December 2008 and January 2009, and the continuing siege of Gaza under Netanyahu in 2010 that imprisons the people, destroys their economy, and inflicts intense psychological suffering, is, in the end, a policy designed to expel the people of Palestine from their land by military means, against an anemic enemy incapable of defending itself.

There is an unraveling of the lies of omission that have quilted the truth these many years. As each square rots in the sun now shed on it, the plight of the people of Palestine becomes more and more apparent. Benny Morris revealed in June 2009 that "there were far more acts of massacre than I had previously thought (with the new documents made available)...and many cases of rape...and (between April-May 1948) units of Haganah were given operational orders that stated explicitly that they were to uproot the villagers, expel them and destroy the villages themselves." Morris continued in response to the interviewer's questions: "Because neither the victims nor the rapists liked to report these events, we have to assume that the dozen cases of rape that were reported...are not the whole story. They are just the tip of the iceberg"; "The worst cases (of massacre) were Saliha (70–80) killed, Deir Yassin (100–110), Lod (250), Dawayima (hundreds) and perhaps Abu Shusha (70); Ben Gurion "covered up for the officers who did the massacres"; "Yes...the commander of the Northern Front, Moshe Carmel, issued an order in writing to his units to expedite the removal of the Arab population"; "From April 1948, Ben-Gurion is projecting a message of transfer....The entire leadership understands that this is the idea"; and quoting Morris himself, "Without the uprooting of the Palestinians, a Jewish state would not have arisen here."[29]

In *The Ethnic Cleansing of Palestine*, Ilan Pappe states, "The Zionist project could only be realized through the creation in Palestine of a purely Jewish state, both as a safe haven for Jews from persecution and a cradle for a new Jewish nationalism. And such a state had to be exclusively Jewish not only in its socio-political structure but also in its ethnic composition." Pappe's accounting of the ethnic cleansing is not pleasant reading. It is a detailed presentation of calculated ruthlessness. Considered alongside Walid Khalidi's *All That Remains,* it provides the reader with a visual context that forces consideration of the mothers and fathers and children who once lived and worked and played and prayed in the 418 villages destroyed. It is that human element that can give meaning to "Never Again."[30]

## Slow-Motion Genocide

The reader of this book will notice that the chapters contained in it come almost exclusively from well-known Internet publications with international distribution. Indeed, many of these pieces have been reissued in other Internet publications following the original date of publication. In short, the Internet provides a worldwide audience in the millions and has, as a consequence, altered how and where current news is obtained. Quite obviously, even hard-copy journalists rely now on Internet news. Its value rests in good measure on the scholars, activists, NGO spokespeople, trained journalists and reporters, and sundry "muckrakers" that find voice on the Internet. Nothing is sacred and out of bounds here; all topics can be addressed if they are well written, well researched and substantiated and refereed by experienced, articulate, and morally responsible editors.

Given the source of these chapters, it is imperative that the reader recognize the nonacademic character of the writing. These pieces were not developed for academic journals; the issues at hand cannot wait for next year before they are published. They are rather responses to real and ongoing events and hence dependent on evidence that is current yet subject to change as days go by, information gathered by journalists, NGOs, or local organizations such as B'Tselem in Jerusalem or the Palestine Center for Human Rights (PCHR) in Palestine, and guided by the writer's conscience as he or she confronts the ambiguities, the contradictions, and the hypocrisy of what is claimed to be truth versus the reality. Because the Internet is a fluid medium, finding original sources can be frustrating, especially when unknown forces remove documents or a site closes.

No one can now doubt the impact of Internet publications. They are so pervasive and so impactful that governments attempt to control access to sources they deem objectionable. Even as this is written, the U.S. government is moving to control the Internet in ways that exceed the use of software devices that prevent children from getting to sites that have been determined as potentially harmful to them. The *New York Times* reported on June 13, 2009, that "Privacy May Be a Victim in Cyberdefense Plan," an article by Thom Shanker and David Sanger.

A plan to create a new Pentagon cybercommand is raising significant privacy and diplomatic concerns, as the Obama administration moves ahead on efforts to protect the nation from cyberattack and to prepare for possible offensive operations against adversaries' computer networks.[31]

While the intent here is not to close or control content in Internet publications, the consequence of the means to control coupled with the rationale that uses national security as the need to control, could become the means to silence those who criticize the government.

This volume provides perceptions by a multitude of writers on the subject of genocide in Palestine. These are recent pieces that delve into current events. They cover material rarely heard or read in the mainstream media, especially in the United States. That makes access to these ideas and arguments a necessity if the primary issue they address is to be aired at all. That issue is, in essence, one word—justice.

★   ★   ★

The narrative that runs as an undercurrent in this Introduction finds corroboration in chapter 20, Robert Fisk's "The British in Palestine, 1945–48: A Foreign Holocaust," a recounting of the "lost" years of British rule in Mandate Palestine. This piece complements the perceptions brought by the contributors of this volume devoted to genocide in Palestine. Dr. Francis Boyle's early piece, written in 2001, details the reality of the genocide and the legal apparatus that could be used to bring justice to the Palestinians if only the world would stop watching and act. James Petras's "The Final Solution," Omar Barghouti's "Relative Humanity: the Essential Obstacle," and Paul de Rooij's "Palestinian Misery in Perspective," all written before 2005, attest to the anguish, the suffering, the psychological humiliation, and frustration visited upon the people of Palestine as an indifferent world turns away from their plight. That same concern for the inhumanity being wrought upon a defenseless people finds reiteration in subsequent years through the voices of Andrea Howard's "Israeli Immunity for Genocide," Paul Craig Roberts's "The Shame of Being American," and Patrick Cockburn's "Gaza Is a Jail."

Jeff Halper, Ilan Pappe, Richard Falk, and Gideon Polya give voice to the Jew of conscience, voices able to feel the truth of "Never Again" that rises in the soul where love, compassion, and respect reside for all who suffer the atrocities of their fellow beings. Kathleen and Bill Christison, Ramzy

Barhoud, and Jonathan Cook investigate the actions of the Israeli government as they inflict policies that defy international law and cry for justice. Some of these chapters reflect careful research, some detail statistical evidence many find boring, neglecting to confront the suffering such statistics reflect, and some are polemical, giving voice to the emotional trauma that the reality portrays.

The purpose of this volume is to provide the full depth of concern that those who know the truth can offer. Chris Hedges's "The Lessons of Violence" gives pause to reflect on the inner consequences to every human that lives in indifference to the crimes being perpetrated in their name. Perhaps Hedges's closing paragraph can act as a warning to all of us as we reflect on the men and women from many continents and many countries who have voiced their perceptions in this volume that scrutinizes the agonies of unending violence that characterizes the conflict between Palestinians and Israelis.

> The cycle of violence that began decades ago, that turned a young Palestinian refugee with promise and talent into a militant and finally a martyr, is turning small boys today into new versions of what went before them. Olmert, Bush's vaunted partner for peace, has vowed to strike at Palestinian militants "without compromise, without concessions and without mercy," proof that he and the rest of his government have learned nothing. It is also proof that we, as the only country with the power to intervene, have become accessories to murder.[32]

This collection provides the reader with an incredible range of voices—academic scholars, journalists, editors, lawyers, United Nations agency personnel, activist organizers in Israel, Palestine, Australia, and Canada—that speak about the ongoing, slow-motion genocide that is happening in Palestine. It covers the first decade of the twenty-first century, indicating that the awareness of this illegal and inhumane behavior of the state of Israel has been known, at least to those who have devoted their attention to it. The primary focus of these thirty-two chapters forces the reader to confront genocide as it spreads throughout the occupied territories linked to an Introduction that uses heretofore classified files from the Mandate period to identify the intent of the Zionists who sought the eradication of the Arabs living in Palestine. The chapters are arranged not in chronological order from 2001 to 2009, but rather, by areas of focus that hover above the reality on the ground, yet cry to us to be witness to the atrocity being played out on the hapless people of Palestine: The Human Tragedy, Propaganda, Perception and Reality, and Rule by Law or Defiance.

The writers featured here come from many countries, including Israel and Palestine. They reflect cautioned, critical, carefully analyzed, and documented presentations that confront the realities of Israel's policies as they are antithetical to the moral principles that give meaning to the UN's Universal Declaration of Human Rights , the Geneva Conventions, and the UN Charter. They provide documentable evidence that should shake the complacency and indifference that characterizes the governments that accept in silence the ruthlessness of the occupying power that has decided to impose its will on the hapless people of Palestine by destroying their culture and identity even as it imposes on all in Palestine the national pattern of the oppressor. That, in effect, is the definition of genocide.

## Notes

1. Raphael Lemkin. (1944). *Axis Rule in Occupied Europe.* Washington D.C.: Carnegie Endowment for International Peace. 79–95.
2. Me. E. Yapp (1987). *The Making of the Modern Near East 1792–1923.* Harlow, England: Longman. 290.
3. Leonard Stein. (1961). *The Balfour Declaration.* New York: Simon and Schuster. 470.
4. The figures provided here are drawn from the first and second British Census of 1922 and 1931 respectively as noted in Wikipedia under the heading British Mandate of Palestine at www.en.wikipedia.org/wiki/British_Mandate_of_Palestine#Population. It should be noted here as well that the White Paper of 1939, issued by the British Mandate government placed immigration restrictions on the Jews, and stated that the Jewish population "has risen to some 450,000...(and was) approaching a third of the entire population of the country." Additional statistics of varying estimates question the British census figures. However, it must be stated that the actions of the British Mandate were based on the known figures at the time. See for recent arguments on these statistics Fred M. Gotthell . "The Smoking Gun: Arab Immigration into Palestine, 1922–1931." *Middle East Quarterly* (Winter 2003). 4–5.
5. Ilan Pappe. (2006). *The Ethnic Cleansing of Palestine.* Oneworld: Oxford. 11.
6. Frank Chalk, and Kurt Jonassohn. (1990). *The History and Sociology of Genocide.* New Haven, CT: Yale University Press. 8–9.
7. Lemkin, *Axis Rule,* 80.
8. United Nations Convention on Genocide. (1948). December 9, 1948. New York. www.un.org/millenium/law/iv-1/htm. April 11, 2009. Note: Entered into force January 12, 1951.
9. Jim Harb. "The UN Did Not Create Israel." June 11, 2009. www.philipweiss.org/mondoweiss/2009/04/what-the-un-did-not-create-israel.html. The United Nations does not appropriate to itself the authority to create states. The United Nations only authorizes itself to recognize states for membership, states that are formed or proclaimed by the people of said state.
10. Sir Richard C. Catling. Personal File, Classified "Top Secret." Rhodes House Archives #145, Mss.Med.S20. Bodleian Library, Oxford.
11. Benny Morris. (1999). *Righteous Victims: A History of the Zionists-Arab Conflict, 1881–2001.* New York: Knopf.

12. Matthew C. Hogan, and Daniel A. McGowen. "Anatomy of a Whitewash," in *Remembering Deir Yassin*. 1. www.deiryassin.org/op0005.html.
13. Walid Khalidi. (1992). *All That Remains*. Institute for Palestine Studies: Washington, D.C. xv.
14. Morton Klein. (1998). *Deir Yassin: History of a Lie*. Zionist Organization of America.
15. Catering files, Appendix L Va, 431–434. Communique by J.P.I. Pforde, Assistant Inspector General.
16. Harold MacMichael. (1947). "Memorandum on the Participation of the Jewish National Institutions in Palestine in Acts of Lawlessness and Violence." The Palestine Police, Jerusalem, July 31, 1947 in Catling file.
17. MacMichael, "Despatch." 1.
18. Ibid. 2.
19. Ibid. 2.
20. Sir Richard C. Catling (1947). "Memorandum." 1–2.
21. Ibid. 2–3.
22. Ibid. 5.
23. Ibid. 75, 76.
24. Ibid., 40.
25. Ibid. 42.
26. Ibid. Appendix XLb, 301.
27. Catling, Appendix XVIA. 157.
28. Catling, Appendix XDVIII. 219.
29. Ari Shavit. (2004). "Survival of the Fittest." *Ha'aretz* January 9, 2004. 15. Quoting Benny Morris.
30. Pappe, *Ethnic Cleansing*. 15.
31. Thom Shanker and David Sanger. "Privacy May Be a Victim in Cyberdefense Plan." *New York Times*, June 13, 2009.A1.
32. Chris Hedges. "The Lessons of Violence." Truthdig.com. January 21, 2008. www.truthdig.com/report/item/20080121_the_lessons_of_violence.

# PART 1

## The Human Tragedy

Seventy years ago, following the slaughters of World War II that left 100 million people killed, wounded, or disabled, including both soldiers and civilians, the United Nations was formed to "prevent a World War Three in the future." Today, 192 nation-states are members of the United Nations.

Sixty-one years ago, the Jewish people residing in the British Mandate area of Palestine, through their Yishuv, the Jewish Agency, declared the existence of the state of Israel based on the area provided for it through Resolution 181 of the United Nations and so declared in a letter to the president of the United States, Harry S. Truman, on May 14, 1948.

Tradition holds that 6 million of that 100 million were victims of the Nazi war machine that determined a "Final Solution" that became known as the Holocaust. Throughout the world, the Jews who died in the concentration camps are remembered in ceremonies held in synagogues, town squares, auditoriums, and Holocaust museums. Two words have become the clarion call of that remembrance, a cry to all to never forget: "Never Again."

Ironically, this volume responds to that very call, that desperate cry to never forget, to not replicate what the world witnessed seventy years ago; pathetically, the cry is pointed to the descendents of those Jewish victims of Nazi terror who now inflict on the indigenous people of Palestine a crime equally horrendous, a prolonged, merciless attempt to erase a people from their land by whatever force is needed.

The chapters in this section will make that call ring to the heavens; it's a knell that rings for justice at last by placing the horrors of the crimes perpetrated on the Palestinians before our eyes that we may hear our inner voice plead to the Jews of Israel and to all the world that mercy, compassion, and love will purge vengeance, hatred, and racism from our souls.

# CHAPTER ONE

# Israel's Slow-Motion Genocide in Occupied Palestine

## STEVE LENDMAN

## (11-26-2008)

Israel is a serial human rights international law abuser. The UN Human Rights Commission affirms that it violates nearly all 149 articles of the Fourth Geneva Convention, which governs the treatment of civilians in war and under occupation, and is guilty of grievous war crimes.[1] Imagine life under these conditions: Living in limbo under a foreign occupier; having no self-determination, no right of return, and no power over your daily life; being in constant fear, economically strangled, and collectively punished; having your free movement denied by enclosed population centers, closed borders, regular curfews, roadblocks, checkpoints, electric fences, and separation walls; having your homes regularly demolished and land systematically stolen to build settlements for encroachers in violation of international law prohibiting an occupier from settling its population on conquered land; having your right to essential services denied—emergency health care, education, employment, and enough food and clean water; being forced into extreme poverty, having your crops destroyed, and being victimized by punitive taxes; having no right for redress in the occupier's courts under laws only protecting the occupier; being regularly targeted by incursions and attacks on the ground and from the air; being wilfully harassed, ethnically cleansed, arrested, incarcerated, tortured, and slaughtered on any pretext, including for your right of self-defence;

having no rights on your own land in your own country for over six decades and counting; vilified for being Muslims and called terrorists, Jihadists, crazed Arabs, and fundamentalist extremists. Victimized by slow-motion genocide to destroy you.

According to the Israeli historian Ilan Pappe, Israel has conducted state-sponsored genocide against the Palestinians for decades and intensively in Gaza. In a September 2006 *Electronic Intifada* article titled "Genocide in Gaza," he wrote:

> A genocide is taking place in Gaza.... An average of eight Palestinians die daily in the Israeli attacks on the Strip. Most of them are children. Hundreds are maimed, wounded and paralyzed. [It's become] a daily business, now reported [only] in the internal pages of the local press, quite often in microscopic fonts. The chief culprits are the Israeli pilots who have a field day, like shooting fish in a barrel. Why not, they're only Muslims, so who'll notice or care.[2]

The international law expert Francis Boyle does care, and in March 1998 he proposed that "the Provisional Government of [Palestine] and its President institute legal proceedings against Israel before the International Court of Justice (ICJ) in the Hague for violating the Genocide Convention." He stated that "Israel has indeed perpetrated the international crime of genocide against the Palestinian people (and the) lawsuit would... demonstrate that undeniable fact to the entire world."[3]

Geneva, Nuremberg, and other international human rights laws guarantee what Article 3 of the Universal Declaration of Human Rights states: that everyone has the right to life, liberty and security of person." Article 6 (1) of the International Covenant on Civil and Political Rights also affirms it by saying that every "human being has the inherent right to life." Official Israeli policy is to deny this right to Palestinians under occupation, especially Gazans under siege. On November 5, the siege was egregiously tightened after Israel closed all commercial crossings and banned virtually all permissible items—previously severely restricted and in limited amounts.

On November 21, 2008, *Ha'aretz* reported that Karen AbuZayd, the United Nations Relief and Works Agency (UNRWA) commissioner-general, said that Gaza faces a humanitarian "catastrophe" if Israel maintains its blockade. She called the current closure the gravest since the early days of the Second Intifada eight years ago: "It's been closed for so much longer than ever before... and we have nothing in our warehouses... It will be a catastrophe if this persists, a disaster."[4]

UNRWA provides vitally needed rations for 820,000 of Gaza's 1.5 million refugees, and the UN World Food Program aids another 200,000 people. They supply about 60 percent of daily needs, now effectively shut off and nearly exhausted—including food, medicines, fuel, and other basic essentials. On November 17, 2008, thirty-one containers of foods and medicines were allowed in through Karm Abu Salem (Kerem Shalom) crossing, southeast of Rafah. It had been closed, along with other border crossings, for the previous two weeks. These amounts are hugely deficient and amount to less than 10 percent of what entered Gaza before Israel's June 2007 imposed siege. Also allowed in was 427,000 liters of fuel, or barely enough to operate Gaza's power plant for a day. It's effectively shut down, and at least 30 percent of the population is without electricity and around 70 percent experience lengthy power outages for days or weeks. On November 20, AP reported that Israeli officials "stood by [their] decision to shut cargo crossings into the Gaza Strip, brushing off pleas to ease the blockade from United Nations chief Ban Ki-moon." Of course, the Strip has been mostly isolated since Israel's imposed siege eighteen months ago that created a humanitarian crisis now intensified.

Why so was stated to the *Jerusalem Post* by the senior IDF general Amos Gilad: Because "Hamas is committed to the destruction of the state . . . it [also] wants to take over the PLO." Unmentioned are the facts that refute this assertion. After Ismail Haniyeh became the Hamas prime minister in 2006, he offered the Bush administration peace and a long-term truce in return for an end to Israel's (illegal) occupation. He was rebuffed the way he was by Israel for the same offer.

Again why so? Israel and Washington are allied in a joint enterprise and need enemies, a.k.a "terrorists." While maintaining the illusion of a "peace process," in reality, none whatsoever exists, nor is any effort made to address equity for the Palestinians. What matters is joint control of the region: Israel as the local *hegemon* and America as part of its world empire and all vital resources in it, especially oil, of course.

In the 1980s, the former prime minister Yitzhak Shamir admitted that Israel waged war against Lebanon in 1982 because there was "a terrible danger . . . not so much a military one as a political one." So a pretext was arranged the way it always is to invent threats and avoid resolution.

In January 2006, Israel employed a political maneuver to control the PLO after Hamas won a resounding democratic majority in the Palestinian Legislative Council (PLC). As a result, they and the Palestinians paid dearly. Israel, America, and the West ended all outside aid, imposed a crippling economic embargo and sanctions, and politically isolated the ruling Hamas government. An intensive crackdown followed that continues to this day—regular interventions, attacks, ruthless repression, and the imposition of a medieval siege on Gaza, now intensified.

On November 19, 2008, the territory's largest flour mill shut down for a lack of wheat, and the UN suspended cash grants to 98,000 poor Gazans because of a shortage of Israeli currency.

The world community has been silent. Conditions continue to deteriorate, and Christian Aid is speaking out. It accused Israel of collective punishment in violation of international law. Under the Fourth Geneva Convention, Article 33,

No protected person (under occupation) may be punished for an offense he or she has not personally committed. Collective penalties and likewise all measure of intimidation or of terrorism are prohibited (as well as) reprisals against protected persons and their property.[5]

Costa Dabbagh from the Near East Council of Churches (a Christian Aid partner) says, "Simply letting food into Gaza is not enough," and precious little is arriving. Its people "are fed and kept alive without dignity and the international community should be blamed for it." It's "not acceptable to be waiting for food to come. (Gazans) want to live freely with Israel and other countries in peace. (They're) not against any individual or government (but) are against imprisonment."[6]

They're also against starving, extreme deprivation, no effective outside aid, and no support from world or other Arab leaders on their behalf. At the moment, three of five mills have stopped operating, and the two others are about to close for lack of wheat. Several bakeries are closed for lack of flour, fuel, cooking gas, and electricity.

Of Gaza's seventy-two bakeries, forty-seven produce Syrian bread (the most popular kind); twenty-nine of them stopped operating; eight others are at partial capacity; ten bake Iraqi bread, and fifteen others different varieties and pastries. None are in full operation, and all may have to close for lack of supplies and power. Gazans are being strangled and starved.

Health facilities are also in crisis, and their patients are endangered because of their limited ability to provide services. In addition, forty-five vital medicines are embargoed and unavailable. Another unconscionable act.

Shifa Hospital is Gaza's largest and most seriously hampered. Besides a lack of power, medicines, and other supplies, its equipment needs repair and has no readily available spare parts. Its main generator is in disrepair. Its MRI machine can't operate without electricity. It is short on gas for disinfection and to prepare food for patients. Concern is growing that other essential equipment may also stop working or have to shut down for lack of power.

Shifa's director, Hassan Khalaf, and the Red Cross describe the situation as critical. Lives are at risk. The intensive care unit can't operate. Electronic equipment in the newborn-baby unit doesn't function, and the staff has to manually pump oxygen to all infants. In addition, stocks of about 160 essential medicines have run out, and another 120 are running low. Shifa can't run very long under these conditions. Nor can Gaza's other hospitals and all other operations in the Occupied Territories—an intolerable situation barely reported on by the mainstream U.S. media. Inverting the truth, they portray Israel heroically as a democratic island in a hostile Arab sea.

They won't explain that Israel is obligated to provide essentials under the Fourth provision of Geneva's Article 55. It states:

> To the fullest extent of the means available to it, the Occupying Power has the duty of ensuring the food and medical supplies of the population; it should, in particular, bring in the necessary foodstuffs, medical stores and other (essential) articles if the resources of the occupied territory are inadequate.[7]

Israel continues to violate this law and all others. As Andrea Becker of the UK-based Medical Aid for Palestinians states, for Israelis, "international law was tossed aside long ago." The result for Gazans is "exhaustion gripping hold of (them) all. Survival leaves (them) little if no room for political engagement—and beyond, exhaustion, anger, and frustration are all that is left."

## A Partial Border Reopening

On November 24, 2008, *Ha'aretz* reported that "Israel partially (opened) its border crossings with the Gaza Strip (today) to allow the transfer of humanitarian aid (after) all but completely (keeping them) shut for (the past) nineteen days." Defense officials let in "44 trucks with basic goods...through Kerem Shalom crossings" in the south.

According to the *Ma'an News Agency*, another 200 truckloads of UN humanitarian aid and 25 more containing food will also be allowed through Kerem Shalom. This is helpful but woefully short of what the Strip needs regularly to care for its 1.5 million people, most of whom rely solely or mainly on outside aid.

Whether this additional aid will even arrive is now open to question, according to *Ha'aretz* (on November 25, 2008). It reported that Israel "closed its crossings with Gaza again," supposedly after two Qassam rockets were fired on Sunday, one on Monday, and another on Tuesday. Unmentioned are the regular and devastating IDF attacks against Palestinian civilians who have little more than crude weapons for self-defense and are no match against Israel's overpowering force.

According to *Ha'aretz* on November 26, 2008, some aid may be forthcoming, surprisingly from Libya. It "sent a ship carrying 3000 tons of humanitarian aid to Gaza" to break Israel's blockade. The International Middle East Media Center called on other Arab states to do the same—flout the blockade and send aid even with no assurance Israel will allow it in. It's been very effective preventing most everything so far and shows no signs of relenting.

## A Shocking Red Cross Report

On November 15, 2008, the London *Independent* headlined an article titled "Chronic Malnutrition in Gaza Blamed on Israel." The writer Donald Macintyre referred to a leaked Red Cross report he called "explosive."

It chronicled "the devastating effect of the siege that Israel imposed after Hamas (took control of Gaza) in June 2007 and notes that the dramatic fall in living standards triggered a shift in diet that will damage the long-term health of (Gaza's population). Alarming deficiencies (showed up) in iron, vitamin A and vitamin D."

The report goes on to say that

> heavy restrictions on all major sectors of Gaza's economy, compounded by a cost of living increase of at least 40 percent, is causing progressive deterioration in food security for up to 70 per cent of (the) population. That in turn is forcing people to cut household expenditures down to survival levels.[8]

Chronic malnutrition is rising steadily, and "micronutrient deficiencies are of great concern." Since 2007, the report cited a switch to "low cost/high energy" cereals, sugar, and oil and away from higher-cost animal products, fresh fruits, and vegetables. This type of diet assures long-term, harmful consequences.

The Red Cross said that "the (18 month) embargo has had a devastating effect for a large proportion of households who have had to make major changes on the composition of their food basket." They now rely 80 percent on cereals, sugar, and oil. In addition, people are selling assets, cutting back on clothing and children's education, scavenging for discarded items, and doing virtually anything to survive. The report refers to economic disintegration and that prolonging the current situation risks permanently damaging households and their capacity to recover. The study was conducted from May to July 2008.

Mark Regev, spokesman for the Israeli prime minister Ehud Olmert, had little response except to say that the people of Gaza were being "held hostage" to Hamas' "extremist and nihilist" ideology. In fact, Hamas wants peace and has repeatedly been conciliatory, and its founder, Sheikh Ahmed Yassin, said earlier that armed struggle would cease "if the Zionists ended (their) occupation of Palestinian territories and stopped killing Palestinian women, children and innocent civilians."

That offer is repeatedly rejected. More recently, Hamas offered to maintain peace and recognize Israel in return for a Palestinian state inside pre-1967 borders, its Occupied Territories. That, as well, is a nonstarter for Israel. It conflicts with its West Bank plan to colonize the Territory and ethnically cleanse its rightful inhabitants in violation of international law.

## Israeli Clampdown on Human Rights
## Organizations and the Media

Over twenty human rights organizations sought entry to Gaza but were denied to prevent them from seeing and reporting on conditions on the ground. A delegation representing the Coordination Forum of the Association of International Development Agencies (AIDA), arrived at Erez Crossing with the required permit and were still prevented from entering. International journalists are also banned. The AP head and Israeli Foreign Press Association chairman, Steven Gutkin, said journalists called and complained. In response, the association appealed to the government without success. "We consider it a serious problem for freedom of the press. We think that journalists have to be placed in a special category. A blanket ban on people going into Gaza should not apply to journalists," Gutkin explained. "We are hoping that this is not the start of a policy of banning journalists from Gaza. We would like to point out that when times are tough, and when things heat up, it is important for journalists to be able to enter" and report on it.

A BBC media crew was also refused entry, along with Conny Mus from the Dutch television station RTL after being told he and his crew had permission. Even *Ha'aretz* objected in an editorial titled "Open Gaza to media coverage." It stated:

To serve their function sufficiently, representatives of the Israeli and international press must be in Gaza, just like in any other conflict region around the world. There is no way to cover (events there) without free access.[9]

*Ha'aretz* called on the Israel Press Council, journalist associations, editors, writers, and the public to "raise their voices in protest." It also asked the defense establishment "to immediately lift the media closure." The Israeli press has been banned from entering Gaza for the past two years. Only the *Ha'aretz* correspondent Amira Hass has been there. She then left and could only get back in by sea, and not easily or safely. Orwell would appreciate how the coordinator of government activities in the Territories, Peter Lerner, responded: "There is no decision not to allow journalists in." The Israeli foreign ministry said that no restrictive order had been issued in spite of clear evidence that one was being enforced.

## Hostilities in Gazan Waters

The Israeli navy is also in action. It arrested three human rights activists—Darlene Wallach from America, Andrew Muncie from Britain, and Vittorio Arrigoni from Italy—as they accompanied Gaza fishermen in waters nowhere near ones under Israeli control. The three were imprisoned, are on hunger strike in protest, and may face deportation or worse, as Israeli justice is harsh and not forthcoming against opponents of its policies.

Under the Oslo Accords, Palestinians can fish as far out as thirty kilometers. Forty thousand fishermen and their dependents rely on their catch for their livelihoods and sustenance. Israel egregiously impedes them, and after Hamas took control of Gaza, it restricted fishing to within six kilometers of the shore (in less productive shallow waters) and rigorously enforces it. Those exceeding the limit risk being shot or arrested and their boats confiscated or destroyed—another serious international law violation. Saber Al-Hissie is one of them. He's been fishing in Gazan waters for fifteen years, his father and grandfather before him. He has spent half his life at sea, "but every day we face problems from Israeli gunboats," he explained. "They follow us, and then they start shooting at us because they want to force us to stop working."

Thousands of fishermen live in Gaza, mostly in and around Gaza City, where the main harbor is located. Al-Hissie describes the restrictions Israel imposes on him and others trying to earn a living from the sea. "If we sail six miles out to sea, then maybe we will be safe. But if we go any further, the Israelis always harass us. They circle the boats, they shoot towards us, and recently they started using water cannon to attack us." He won't exceed the limit to protect his boat, but it's scarred with bullet holes anyway.

He and others aren't safe wherever they fish. They're harassed and attacked daily. "Unless you see it for yourself, you cannot believe the situation we are facing," he explains. It has decimated local fishing. Ten years ago, Gazan fishermen caught about three thousand tons a year. 'This figure has now come down to less than five hundred; consequently, Israel's control of the sea becomes another part of the Gaza siege, Israel's war on its people, and its ongoing slow-motion genocide. "We just want to fish and support our families," says Saber. "We are not committing any crimes, but they are."

### End the Israeli Blockade and Stop the Genocide

On November 24, 2008, the UN General Assembly president Miguel D'Escoto Brockmann said that Israel's treatment of the Palestinians was like "the apartheid of an earlier era." His remarks were at an annual debate marking the International Day of Solidarity with the Palestinian people. He added: "We must not be afraid to call something what it is" since the UN passed the International Convention against the crime of apartheid. Israel's response was familiar. Its UN ambassador, Gabriela Shalev, called Brockmann an "Israel hater." He's a seventy-five-year old Catholic priest. If he were Jewish, she'd have accused him of being "self-hating."

On November 20, 2008, the UN High Commissioner for Human Rights, Navanethem Pillay, called for an immediate end to Israel's blockade. In response, the Ministry of Foreign Affairs (MFA) audaciously expressed shock at what it called a one-sided statement. The high commissioner's call came after mounting reports of human rights and humanitarian concerns. For its part, Israel claims its siege is a necessary response to mortar and rocket attacks on Israeli towns and military posts. They're little more than pin pricks and only occur in response to sustained and brutal Israeli attacks against Gazan civilians, including men, women, and children—a long-standing practice for decades with overwhelming force against light arms and homemade weapons as well as children throwing rocks. It hardly justifies a medieval siege against 1.5 million people and the horrific fallout it causes; and for what?

For five months through November 3, Hamas and Israel were at peace as a result of an agreed on Egyptian-brokered *hudna* (or truce). On November 4, it ended when the Israeli Defense Forces (IDF) entered Gaza (without cause) and killed six Hamas officers supposedly because of tunnels close to the Kisufim roadblock. Thereafter, and in spite of both sides calling for peace, IDF hostilities continued.

Israel is a serial aggressor. Hamas responds in self-defense (as do West Bank Palestinians). Reality is turned on its head. Lightly-armed Gazans are called terrorists, and the world's fourth most powerful military its victims. In fact, Gazans are grievously harmed, impoverished, slaughtered, and now starved. Israel claims it as a right. International law is a nonstarter, and a state of war exists against innocent men, women, and children with no world efforts made to stop it. If conditions in Gaza worsen, "Arab rulers should expect an earthquake that would shake their countries and regimes." It's high time something shook them out of their silent complicity with decades of slow-motion genocide.

The Washington-Israeli axis believes that strife, instability, and a "war on terror" can remake the Middle East and place it firmly under their control. No matter that it failed hugely in Iraq, the same in Afghanistan, and for over six decades in occupied Palestine.

Today, starving Gazans won't be silenced. They keep protesting, and according to Hamazah Mansur, the head of the Jordanian-based Islamic Action Front's six-member parliamentary bloc, if conditions in the Territory worsen, "Arab rulers should expect an earthquake that would shake their countries and regimes." It's high time something shook them out of their silent complicity with decades of slow-motion genocide, now worse than ever in Gaza under siege.

## Notes

1. "United Nations Rights Council Report on Israel's Human Rights Violations in Gaza," March 20, 2009. http://www.ohchr.org.
2. Ilan Pappe, "Genocide in Gaza," *Electronic Intifada*, September 2, 2006. http://www.electronicintifada.net/v2/articles5656.shtml.
3. Francis Boyle, "Palestine Should Sue Israel for Genocide," *Media Monitors*, December 13, 1997. http://www.mediamonitors.net/francis.html.
4. Karen Koning AbuZayd, "Brutal Siege of Gaza," *Guardian*, January 28, 2008. http://www.guardian.co.uk/commentisfree/2008/jan/23.
5. International Humanitarian Law, ICRC, Convention IV, Geneva, August 12, 1949. http://www.ICRC.org/IHL.nsf.
6. Agency Reporter, "Israel Using Food and Medicines as Weapons," November 20, 2008. http://www.eklesia.co.uk/noe/8011.
7. International Humanitarian Law, 4 Geneva Convention, Article 55. http://www.ICRC.org/IHL.nsf.
8. Donald McIntyre, "Chronic Malnutrition in Gaza Blamed on Israel," *Independent*, November 15, 2008. http://www.independent.co.uk/news/world/middle-east/chronic.
9. Editorial, "Open Gaza to Media Coverage," *Ha'aretz*, November 23, 2008. http://www.haaretz.com/hasen/spages/1039951.

CHAPTER TWO

# Ongoing Palestinian Genocide

GIDEON POLYA

(3-6-2008)

## Israel-US and Nazi Death Ratios Compared

The world continues to look on with horror as apartheid Israel continues to police its Gaza concentration camp with tanks, shells, bombs, and rockets. According to the United Nations Relief and Works Agency (UNRWA) for 4.2 million United Nations (UN)-registered Palestinian refugees in the Middle East, 254 Palestinians have been killed by the Israeli military so far in 2008 as compared to 301 in 2007. Last week alone, 123 Palestinians, 27 of them children and 28 of them unarmed civilians, died in Israeli attacks. Five Israelis were killed in the same period, four in Palestinian-killing military operations in Gaza, and one by a rocket that landed in Israel[1] (and which, together with hundreds of home-made rocket attacks, precipitated the latest horrendous instance of Israeli violence).

How do civilized, antiracist humanitarians respond linguistically to such utterly disproportionate, misplaced, and deadly violence? It is perhaps most useful and surely most evidently "unbiased" in relation to Zionist Jewish Israelis to see the views of outstanding, antiracist, humanitarian Jewish scholars—noting that the primary messages from the Jewish Holocaust (6 million dead) are "zero tolerance for racism" and "never again to *anyone*."

Thus, the outstanding Jewish Israeli scholar Dr. Ilan Pappe has described what is happening in 2008 as a "Gaza Genocide" and a "West Bank ethnic

cleansing." The outstanding Jewish American linguistics scholar Professor
Noam Chomsky of MIT describes the Occupied Palestinian Territory (OPT)
as a highly abusive "prison"—noting that half of the 4 million inmates are
children.[2] Others use the term "concentration camp," noting that we have
to go back to the Nazi-era, postwar U.S. atrocities in Asia and apartheid
atrocities in South Africa to see routine, violent, deadly, military policing of
indigenous people in concentration camps. Indeed, the Jewish South African
Ronnie Kasrils—leader in the fight against apartheid and now a South African
government minister—has described apartheid Israel rule over the Holy Land
thus: "Israel 2007: Worse Than Apartheid."[3]

## What do Palestinians, Scholars Think?

The situation has been recently described as a Palestinian Holocaust by the
Palestinian scholar Dr. Elias Akleh, who is exiled from his homeland and is
now living in the United States. It has been frequently described by others as
a Palestinian genocide, a term that is amply justified in relation to the definitions [of Article 2} of the UN Genocide Convention as outlined below.

> In the present Convention, genocide means any of the following acts
> committed with intent to destroy, in whole or in part, a national, eth-
> nic, racial or religious group, as such: a) Killing members of the group;
> b) Causing serious bodily or mental harm to members of the group;
> c) Deliberately inflicting on the group conditions of life calculated to
> bring about its physical destruction in whole or in part; d) Imposing
> measures intended to prevent births within the group; e) Forcibly trans-
> ferring children of the group to another group.

Using the latest available UN Agency data we can systematically analyze
these UN Genocide Convention points thus:

> "Intent to destroy in whole or in part"—sustained (and frequently
> asserted) intent over about 150 years of the Zionist colonial project;
> 0.75 million Palestinian refugees in 1948; currently 7 million Palestinian
> refugees, and 4.2 million Palestinian refugees registered with the UN
> in the Middle East; over forty years of illegal Israeli occupation of the
> West Bank and Gaza; post-1967 excess deaths 0.3 million; post-1967
> under-five infant deaths 0.2 million; 2,400 OPT (Occupied Palestinian
> Territory) infants under five years of age die avoidably each year in the
> OPT "prison" owing to apartheid Israeli war crimes.

(a) Killing—about 50,000 Palestinians killed since 1948; post-1967 excess deaths 0.3 million; post-1967 under-five infant deaths 0.2 million; 2,400 OPT infants under five years of age die avoidably each year in the OPT "prison" owing to Israel's ignoring of the Geneva Convention; 254 OPT Palestinians killed by the Israeli military in the last two months of 2008 alone, 301 killed thus in 2009.[4]

(b) Causing serious bodily or mental harm—see (a) and the shocking UNICEF reports of the appalling conditions psychologically scarring OPT children.

(c) Conditions to cause destruction in whole or in part—see (a) and (b); Professor Noam Chomsky describes the OPT as a highly abusive "prison"; others use the valid term "concentration camp" and make parallels with the Warsaw ghetto; one has to turn to US-guarded Vietnamese hamlets and the Nazi-era atrocities to see routine, horrendously violent, and deadly military policing of civilian concentration camps.

(d) Measures intended to prevent births—see (a), (b) and (c) above; dozens of pregnant women dying at road blocks; other killing of pregnant Palestinian women; high rate of infant mortality in the OPT, with the occupier in gross violation of the Geneva Convention.

(e) Forcible transferring of children—irreversible transferring by killing of children—0.2 million postinvasion infant deaths; twenty-seven OPT children violently killed in the last week alone, mass imprisonment of 2 million OPT children; hundreds of Palestinian children in abusive Israeli high-security prisons; forcible separation of families by racist Israeli apartheid, marriage, and immigration laws.

As indicated above, we have to turn to the Nazi crimes of World War II and postwar U.S. war crimes in its post-1950 Asian wars for baseline comparisons for horrendous maltreatment and mass murder of conquered indigenous civilians. It is accordingly instructive to look at quantitative "us and them" "death ratios" in these other conflicts, as for example, the Ardeatine Caves Massacre in Italy in 1944, when such ratios became ten to one after Hitler ordered the execution of ten Italian civilians for every German soldier killed in a prior partisan bombing.

In World War II the Axis civilian deaths totaled 5.1 million as compared to Allied civilian losses in Europe and Asia totaling 54 million; U.S., British, Axis, and Soviet military losses totaled 0.29 million, 0.45 million, 5.9 million, and 13.6 million, respectively. Accordingly, the "enemy civilian"/"military death" "kill ratios" were 0:4 (for the Soviet forces), 9:2 (Axis), 11:3 (the British Empire) and 17:6 (the United States). The following "enemy civilian avoidable mortality"/"US combat death" "kill ratios" have been calculated for the

Korean War (1950–1953) (23.8), the Indo-China War (1957–1975) (276.5), the Gulf War and Sanctions War (1990–2003) (12,259), the Afghanistan War (2001–2005) (15,716), and the Iraq War (2003–2005) (323.9). The "death ratio" in Gaza in the last week (123 Palestinians killed by the Israelis in response to one Israeli killed by a rocket) is over twelve times that advocated by arch-fiend Adolph Hitler but consonant with the war-criminal, civilian-targeting, postwar military technology and strategy used by the United States and its allies—notably, the UK, Australia, Canada, NATO, and Israel—in post-1950 Asian wars against indigenous Asians (excess indigenous Asian deaths in post-1950 US Asian Wars now total 24 million).

The primary messages from the Jewish Holocaust (6 million dead) and of the World War II holocaust as a whole (30 million Slavs, Jews, and Roma dead) are "zero-tolerance for racism" and "never again to anyone"—those responsible for the Palestinian Holocaust and Palestinian Genocide are thus grossly violating the memory of the martyred 6 million and grossly violating the fundamental moral messages of the World War II Holocaust. Indeed, the Palestinian Holocaust (postinvasion excess deaths of 0.3 million out of an average 1967–2008 population of 2.6 million) makes shocking comparison with the Jewish Holocaust in Hungary in 1944–1945 (0.2 million Jewish deaths out of a Hungarian Jewish population of 0.7 million).

What can decent people do? Silence kills and silence is complicity—we cannot walk by on the other side. As I have put it in a recent article in *MWC News*, "We are all Palestinian." We are obliged to (a) inform everyone we can and (b) to act ethically by collective, individual, intranational, and international sanctions and boycotts as citizens, voters, and consumers in all our avoidable dealings with racist Zionists, apartheid Israel, and all those countries, corporations, and individuals complicit in the Palestinian Holocaust.[5]

## Notes

1. "Call for End to Cycle of Attacks as Gaza Death Toll Soars to 234," *Cape Times*, March 5, 2008.
2. http://www.zmag.org/content/showarticle.cfm?itemID=10577.
3. Ronnie Kasrils, "Israel 2007: Worse Than Apartheid," *Mail* and *Guardian* Online. May 21, 2007.
4. Lena C. Endresen and Geir Ovensen, "The Potential of UNRWA-Data for Research on Palestinian Refugees, a Study of UNRWA Administrative Data," 1994. www.fafo.no/pub/176.htm. See also "Epidemicological Bulletin for Gaza Strip," Weekly Reports, 2009. www.ochaopt.org/cluster/admin/output/files.
5. A postscript that complements these gruesome statistics should be mentioned: in December 2008–January 2009, in what is known as "the Gaza massacre," Israelis killed 1,350 (60% children) and severely wounded 5,450 (40% children) in response to zero Israeli deaths from Gaza rockets in the preceding year (2008).

# CHAPTER THREE

## The Lessons of Violence

### CHRIS HEDGES

### (1-28-2008)

The Gaza Strip is rapidly becoming one of the worst humanitarian disasters in the world. Israel has cordoned off the entire area, home to some 1.4 million Palestinians, blocking commercial goods, food, fuel, and even humanitarian aid. At least thirty-six people have been killed in Israeli strikes since Tuesday and many more wounded. Hamas, which took control of Gaza in June , has launched about 200 rockets into southern Israel in the same period in retaliation, injuring more than ten people. Israel announced the draconian closure and collective punishment Thursday to halt the rocket attacks, begun on Tuesday, when eighteen Palestinians, including the son of a Hamas leader, were killed by Israeli forces.

This is not another typical spat between Israelis and Palestinians. This is the final, collective strangulation of the Palestinians in Gaza. The United Nations Relief and Works Agency's (UNRWA's) decision to block shipments of food means that two-thirds of the Palestinians who rely on relief aid will no longer be able to eat when UN stockpiles in Gaza run out. Reports from inside Gaza speak of gasoline stations out of fuel, hospitals that lack basic medicine, and a shortage of clean water. Whole neighborhoods were plunged into darkness when Israel cut off its supply of fuel to Gaza's only power plant. The level of malnutrition in Gaza is now equal to that in the poorest sub-Saharan nations.

Israeli Prime Minister Ehud Olmert uses words like *war* to describe the fight to subdue and control Gaza. But it is not war. The Palestinians have little more than old pipes fashioned into primitive rocket launchers, AK-47s, and human bombs with which to counter the assault by one of the best-equipped militaries in the world. Palestinian resistance is largely symbolic. The rocket attacks are paltry, especially when pitted against Israeli jet fighters, attack helicopters, unmanned drones, and the mechanized units that make regular incursions into Gaza. A total of twelve Israelis have been killed over the past six years in rocket attacks. Suicide bombings, which once rocked Jerusalem and Tel Aviv, have diminished, and the last one inside Israel that was claimed by Hamas took place in 2005. Since the current uprising began in September 2000, 1,033 Israelis and 4,437 Palestinians have died in the violence, according to the Israeli human rights organization B'Tselem. B'Tselem noted in a December 2007 report that the dead included 119 Israeli children and 971 Palestinian children.

The failure on the part of Israel to grasp that this kind of brutal force is deeply counterproductive is perhaps understandable given the demonization of Arabs, and especially Palestinians, in Israeli society. The failure of Washington to intervene—especially after President Bush's hollow words about peace days before the new fighting began—is baffling. Collective abuse is the most potent recruiting tool in the hands of radicals, as we saw after the indiscriminate Israeli bombing of Lebanon and the American occupation of Iraq. The death of innocents and collective humiliation are used to justify callous acts of indiscriminate violence and revenge. It is how our own radicals, in the wake of 9/11, lured us into the wars in Afghanistan and Iraq.

Israel has been attempting to isolate and punish Gaza since June when Hamas took control after days of street fighting against its political rival, Fatah. The Palestinian Authority president, Mahmoud Abbas, a Fatah leader, dissolved the unity government. His party, ousted from Gaza, has been displaced to the Israeli-controlled West Bank. The isolation of Hamas has been accompanied by a delicate dance between Israel and Fatah. Israel hopes to turn Fatah into a Vichy-style government to administer the Palestinian territories on its behalf, a move that has sapped support for Fatah among Palestinians and across the Arab world. Hamas's stature rises with each act of resistance.

I knew the Hamas leader Dr. Abdel Aziz al-Rantissi, who was assassinated by Israel in April 2004. Rantissi took over Hamas after its founder, Sheik Ahmed Yassin, was assassinated by the Israelis in March of that year. Rantissi was born in what is now Israel and driven from his home in 1948 during the war that established the Jewish state. He, along with more than 700,000 other Palestinian refugees, grew up in squalid camps. As a small boy, he watched the Israeli army enter and occupy the camp of Khan Younis in 1956 when Israel invaded Gaza. The Israeli soldiers lined up dozens of men and boys, including some of Rantissi's relatives, and executed them. The memory of the executions marked his life. It fed his lifelong refusal to trust Israel and stoked the rage and collective humiliation that drove him into the arms of the Muslim Brotherhood and later Hamas. He was not alone. Several of those who founded the most militant Palestinian organizations witnessed the executions in Gaza carried out by Israel in 1956 that left hundreds dead.

Rantissi was a militant. But he was also brilliant. He studied pediatric medicine and genetics at Egypt's Alexandria University and graduated first in his class. He was articulate and well read and never used in my presence the crude, racist taunts attributed to him by his Israeli enemies. He reminded me that Hamas did not target Israeli civilians until February 25, 1994, when Dr. Baruch Goldstein, dressed in his Israeli army uniform, entered a room in the Cave of the Patriarchs, which served as a mosque, and opened fire on Palestinian worshipers. Goldstein killed 29 unarmed people and wounded 150. Goldstein was rushed caught by the survivors and beaten to death.

"When Israel stops killing Palestinian civilians we will stop killing Israeli civilians," Rantissi told me. "Look at the numbers. It is we who suffer most. But it is only by striking back, by making Israel feel what we feel, that we will have any hope of protecting our people."

The drive to remove Hamas from power will not be accomplished by force. Force and collective punishment create more Rantissis. They create more outrage, more generations of embittered young men and women who will dedicate their lives to avenging the humiliation, perhaps years later, they endured and witnessed as children. The assault on Gaza, far from shortening the clash between the Israelis and Palestinians, ensures that it will continue for generations. If Israel keeps up this attempt to physically subdue Gaza, we will see Hamas-directed suicide bombings begin again. This is what resistance groups that do not have tanks, jets, heavy artillery and attack helicopters do when they want to fight back and create maximum terror. Israeli hawks such as Ephraim Halevy (a former head of Mossad), Giora Eiland (who was national security adviser to Ariel Sharon), and Shaul Mofaz (a former defense minister) are all calling for some form of dialogue with Hamas. They get it. But without American pressure, Prime Minister Olmert will not bend.

Israel, despite its airstrikes and bloody incursions, has been unable to halt the rocket fire from Gaza or free Cpl. Gilad Shalit, an Israeli soldier captured in the summer of 2006. Continued collective abuse and starvation will not break Hamas, which was formed, in large part, in response to Israel's misguided policies and mounting repression. There will, in fact, never be Israeli-Palestinian stability or a viable peace accord now without Hamas's agreement. And the refusal of the Bush administration to intercede, to move Israel toward the only solution that can assure mutual stability, is tragic not only for the Palestinians but also, ultimately, for Israel.

And so it goes on. The cycle of violence that began decades ago, that turned a young Palestinian refugee with promise and talent into a militant and, finally, a martyr, is turning small boys today into new versions of what went before them. Olmert, Bush's vaunted partner for peace, has vowed to strike at Palestinian militants "without compromise, without concessions and without mercy," proof that he and the rest of his government have learned nothing. It is also proof that we, as the only country with the power to intervene, have become accessories to murder.

CHAPTER FOUR

# This Brutal Siege of Gaza Can Only Breed Violence

## KAREN KONING ABUZAYD

(1-23-2008)

Palestinian suffering has reached new depths. Peace cannot be achieved by reducing 1.5 million people to a state of abject destitution. Gaza is on the threshold of becoming the first territory to be intentionally reduced to a state of abject destitution, with the knowledge, acquiescence, and—some would say—encouragement of the international community. An international community that professes to uphold the inherent dignity of every human being must not allow this to happen.

Across this tiny territory, twenty-five miles long and no more than six miles wide, a deep darkness descended at 8 p.m. on January 21, 2008, as the lights went out for each of its 1.5 million Palestinian residents. A new hallmark of Palestinian suffering had been reached. There have been three turns of the screw on the people of Gaza, triggered in turn by the outcome of elections in January 2006, the assumption by Hamas of de facto control last June, and the Israeli decision in September 2008 to declare Gaza a "hostile territory." Each instance has prompted ever-tighter restrictions on the movement of people and goods in and out of Gaza. Each turn of the screw inflicts deeper indignity on ordinary Palestinians, breeding more resentment toward the outside world.

Gaza's border closures are without precedent. Palestinians are effectively incarcerated. The overwhelming majority cannot leave or enter Gaza. Without fuel and spare parts, public health conditions are declining steeply as water and sanitation services struggle to function. The electricity supply is sporadic and has been reduced further along with fuel supply in these past days. UNICEF reports that the partial functioning of Gaza City's main pumping station is affecting the supply of safe water to some 600,000 Palestinians. Medication is in short supply, and hospitals are paralyzed by power failures and the shortage of fuel for generators. Hospital infrastructure and essential pieces of equipment are breaking down at an alarming rate, with limited possibility of repair or maintenance as spare parts are not available. It is distressing to see the impact of closures on patients who need to travel outside Gaza to get medical treatment. The demand for such treatment is rising as medical standards fall inside Gaza, yet the permit regime for medical referrals has become more stringent. Many have had their treatment delayed or denied, worsening their medical conditions and causing preventable deaths.

Living standards in Gaza are at levels unacceptable to a world that promotes the elimination of poverty and the observance of human rights as core principles: 35 percent of Gazans live on less than two dollars a day; unemployment stands at around 50 percent; and 80 percent of Gazans receive some form of humanitarian assistance. Concrete is in such short supply that people are unable to make graves for their dead. Hospitals are handing out sheets as funeral shrouds.

As the head of a humanitarian and human development agency for Palestinian refugees, I am deeply concerned by the stark inhumanity of Gaza's closure. I am disturbed by the seeming indifference of much of the world as hundreds and thousands of Palestinians are harshly penalized for acts in which they have no part. In discharging its mandate, the United Nations Relief and Works Agency (UNRWA) delivers a variety of services to improve living conditions and prospects for self-reliance. It is impossible to sustain our operations when the occupying power adopts an "on, off, here today, gone tomorrow" policy toward Gaza's borders. To take one example, this week we were on the verge of suspending our food distribution program. The reason was seemingly mundane: plastic bags. Israel blocked entry into Gaza of the plastic bags in which we package our food rations.

In today's Gaza, how can we foster a spirit of moderation and compromise among Palestinians or cultivate a belief in the peaceful resolution of disputes? There are already indications that the severity of the closure is playing into the hands of those who have no desire for peace. We ignore this risk at our peril. What we should be doing now is nurturing moderation and empowering those who believe that Gaza's rightful future lies in peaceful coexistence with its neighbors. We welcome the new efforts to resuscitate the peace process, revive the Palestinian economy, and build institutions. These pillars, on which a solution will be built, are the very ones being eroded.

Yesterday, the people of Gaza received a temporary reprieve when the occupying power allowed fuel and other supplies to enter: 2.2m litres of fuel per week for the Gaza power plant and 0.5m litres a week for industrial usage, hospitals, and clinics. We have been informed that the crossings into Gaza will be partially open, allowing UNRWA and other organizations to bring in about fifty trucks a day. No one knows how long the reprieve will last, as the resumption of Qassam rocket fire—which we ourselves strongly condemn—will lead to further closures.

The people of Gaza have been spared from reaching new depths of anguish—but only for the moment. There has never been a more urgent need for the international community to act to restore normality in Gaza. Hungry, unhealthy, angry communities do not make good partners for peace.

# CHAPTER FIVE

# The Olive Trees of Palestine Weep

## SONJA KARKAR

(9-7-2007)

Universally regarded as the symbol of peace, the olive tree has become
the object of violence. For more than forty years, Israel has uprooted over
1 million olive trees and hundreds of thousands of fruit trees in Palestine with
terrible economic and ecological consequences for the Palestinian people.
Their willful destruction has so threatened Palestinian culture, heritage, and
identity that the olive tree has now become the symbol of Palestinian stead-
fastness because of its rootedness and ability to survive in a land where water
is perennially scarce.

Throughout the centuries, Palestinian farmers have made their living from
olive cultivation and olive oil production; 80 percent of cultivated land in
the West Bank and Gaza is planted with olive trees.[1] In the West Bank alone,
some 100,000 families are dependent on olive sales.[2] Today, the olive harvest
provides Palestinian farmers with anywhere between 25 and 50 percent of
their annual income, and as the economic crisis deepens, the harvest provides
for many their basic means of survival.[3] But despite the hardships, it is the
festivities and traditions that accompany the weeks of harvesting that have
held Palestinian communities together and are, in fact, a demonstration of
their ownership of the land that no occupation can extinguish except by the
annihilation of Palestinian society itself. And that is precisely what Israel has
been doing—through brute force and far more insidious ways.

Under an old law from the Ottoman era, Israel claims as state property land that has been "abandoned" and left uncultivated for a period of four years, and this land is then usually allocated to Israeli settlers. Of course, the land has not been voluntarily abandoned. Because of Israel's closure policy, which imposes the most draconian restrictions on movement, Palestinian farmers cannot reach their agricultural lands to tend and harvest their crops.

Not only are permits required to move about in their own homeland, but farmers are forced to use alternative routes that must be negotiated on foot or by donkey because about 70 percent of these alternative routes—those connected to main or bypass roads—have been closed by the Israeli army with concrete blocks and ditches. And now, for "security reasons," a wall is being built that will permanently separate Palestinian families from their farmlands, except for the gates that allow access at certain times, but more often than not, at the whim of Israeli soldiers who may not even turn up to open them.[4] This makes year-round maintenance of farmers' crops extremely difficult, if not impossible. Hence the "abandonment" of land that Israel uses to justify its land theft.

Since 1967, the Israeli military and illegal settlers have destroyed more than 1 million olive trees, claiming that stone throwers and gunmen hide behind them to attack the settlers.[5] This is a specious argument, because these trees grow deep inside Palestinian territory where no Israeli settler or soldier should be in any case. But Israel is intent on appropriating even the last vestiges of land left to the Palestinians and so turns a blind eye to any methods used by settlers and soldiers alike to terrorize the farmers away from their farms and crops, even if that means razing their land. Farmers are constantly under threat of being beaten and shot at, having their water supplies contaminated (already scarce, because 85 percent of renewable water resources go to the settlers and Israel), their olive groves torched, and their olive trees uprooted.[6]

On a larger scale, the Israeli military brings in the bulldozers to uproot trees in the way of the "security wall's" route and where they impede the development of infrastructure necessary to service the illegal settlements. Some of these threatened trees are 700 to 1,000 years old and are still producing olives. These precious trees are being replaced by roads, sewerage, electricity, running water, and telecommunications networks, Israeli military barracks, training areas, industrial estates, and factories, leading to massive despoliation of the environment. If Israel has its way, neither the trees nor the Palestinians who have cared for them will survive the barbaric ethnic and environmental cleansing of Palestine.

The irony of it all is that Israel's uprooting of olive trees is contrary to the Jewish halakic principle, whose origin is found in the Torah: "Even if you are at war with a city…you must not destroy its trees" (Deut. 20:19). Under the pretext of "redeeming" the land the Jews claim God gave them and the trees they are supposed to preserve, Israel continues to violently expropriate Palestinian land. With each uprooted tree, another slab of concrete is put in place for the wall and the illegal Jewish settlements—the landscape sculpted and changed beyond all recognition and no longer the sacrosanct place that has long given Israel its spurious biblical justification for dispossessing the Palestinians of the land they have nurtured since time immemorial.

The agonizing pain of loss felt by Palestinians for their ravaged land is not expressed in the statistics. Only those who have suffered the same cruel violations or those who seek to protect and preserve the delicate balance of the world's environment can understand what it means for a people to be robbed of their land. International law, although on their side, remains ineffective, as no world government, not even the United Nations, is prepared to pressure Israel to stop its illegal collective punishment of the entire Palestinian population.

Today, there are campaigns all around the world to end the uprooting of trees in Palestine and to replant those that have already been uprooted. And each year, when the Palestinian olive harvest approaches, international volunteers join Palestinians to provide some human protection from the acts of violence visited on Palestinian farmers by Israeli settlers and soldiers who want to stop the harvesting of crops. These wonderful acts of solidarity help to heal the land, but they cannot heal the pain of those who have to watch the uprooting of age-old olive trees and the desecration of their land and their millennia-old heritage. Such heartbreaking reality has led the Palestinian poet Mahmoud Darwish to say, "If the olive trees knew the hands that planted them, their oil would have become tears."[7]

## Notes

1. UN Office for the Coordination of Humanitarian Affairs, "The Olive Harvest in the West Bank and Gaza," October 2006.
2. Applied Research Institute of Jerusalem (ARIJ), "Olive Harvest in Palestine: Another Season, Another Anguish," November 2004.
3. Canaan Fair Trade, www.olivecoop.com/Canaan.html.
4. OXFAM, "Forgotten Villages: Struggling to Survive under Closure in the West Bank," September 9, 2002, 21. http://www.electronicintefada.net/v2/articles56.shtml.
5. ARIJ, "Olive Harvest in Palestine.
6. UN Report of the Special Committee to Investigate Israeli Practices Affecting the Human Rights of the Palestinian People and other Arabs of the Occupied Territory, No. 40, September 2005.
7. Atyaf Alwazir, "Uprooting Olive Trees in Palestine," Inventory of Conflict and Environment (ICE), Case Number: 110, American University, November 2002.

CHAPTER SIX

# Slouching toward a Palestinian Holocaust

RICHARD FALK

(6-29-2007)

"And what rough beast, its hour come round at last, Slouches towards Bethlehem to be born?"
(William Butler Yeats, "The Second Coming")

There is little doubt that the Nazi Holocaust was as close to unconditional evil as has been revealed throughout the entire bloody history of the human species. Its massiveness, unconcealed genocidal intent, and reliance on the mentality and instruments of modernity give its enactment in the death camps of Europe a special status in our moral imagination. This special status is exhibited in the continuing presentation of its gruesome realities through film, books, and a variety of cultural artifacts more than six decades after the events in question ceased. The permanent memory of the Holocaust is also kept alive by the existence of several notable museums devoted exclusively to the depiction of the horrors that took place during the period of Nazi rule in Germany.

Against this background, it is especially painful for me, as an American Jew, to feel compelled to portray the ongoing and intensifying abuse of the Palestinian people by Israel through a reliance on such an inflammatory metaphor as "holocaust." The word is derived from the Greek *holos* (meaning "completely") and *kaustos* (meaning "burnt"), and was used in ancient Greece to refer to the complete burning of a sacrificial offering to a divinity. Because such a background implies a religious undertaking, there is some inclination in Jewish literature to prefer the Hebrew word *shoah,* which can be translated roughly as "calamity," and was the name given to the 1985 epic nine-hour narration of the Nazi experience by the French filmmaker Claude Lanzmann. The Germans themselves were more antiseptic in their designation, officially naming their undertaking the "Final Solution of the Jewish Question." The label is, of course, inaccurate, as a variety of non-Jewish identities were also targets of this genocidal assault, including the Roma and Sinti (Gypsies), Jehovah's Witnesses, gays, disabled persons, and political opponents.

Is it an irresponsible overstatement to associate the treatment of Palestinians with this criminalized Nazi record of collective atrocity? I think not. The recent developments in Gaza are especially disturbing because they express so vividly a deliberate intention on the part of Israel and its allies to subject an entire human community to life-endangering conditions of utmost cruelty. The suggestion that this pattern of conduct is a holocaust in the making represents a rather desperate appeal to the governments of the world and to international public opinion to act urgently to prevent these current genocidal tendencies from culminating in a collective tragedy. If ever the ethos of "a responsibility to protect," recently adopted by the UN Security Council as the basis of "humanitarian intervention," is applicable, it would be to act now to start protecting the people of Gaza from further pain and suffering. But it would be unrealistic to expect the UN to do anything in the face of this crisis, given the pattern of U.S. support for Israel and taking into account the extent to which European governments have lent their weight to recent illicit efforts to crush Hamas as a Palestinian political force.

Even if the pressures exerted on Gaza were to be acknowledged as having genocidal potential, and even if Israel's impunity under America's geopolitical umbrella is put aside, there is little assurance that any sort of protective action in Gaza will be taken. There were strong advance signals in 1994 of a genocide to come in Rwanda, and yet nothing was done to stop it; the UN and the world watched while the 1995 Srebrenica massacre of Bosnians took place, an incident that the World Court described as "genocide" only 3 years ago;[1] similarly, there have been repeated allegations of genocidal conduct in Darfur over the course of the last several years, and hardly an international finger has been raised, either to protect those threatened or to resolve the conflict in some manner that shares power and resources among the contending ethnic groups.

But the situation in Gaza is morally far worse, although mass death has not yet resulted. It is far worse because the international community is watching the ugly spectacle unfold while some of its most influential members actively encourage and assist Israel in its approach to Gaza. Not only the United States, but also the European Union, are complicit, as are such neighbors as Egypt and Jordan, apparently motivated by their worry that Hamas is somehow connected with the rising strength of the Muslim Brotherhood within their own borders. It is helpful to recall that the liberal democracies of Europe paid homage to Hitler at the 1936 Olympic Games, and then turned away tens of thousands of Jewish refugees fleeing Nazi Germany. I am not suggesting that this comparison should be taken literally, but rather that a pattern of criminality associated with Israeli policies in Gaza has actually been supported by the leading democracies of the twenty-first century.

To ground these allegations, it is necessary to consider the background of the current situation. For over four decades, ever since 1967, Gaza has been occupied by Israel in a manner that turned this crowded area into a cauldron of pain and suffering for the entire population on a daily basis, with more than half of Gazans living in miserable refugees camps and even more dependent on humanitarian relief to satisfy basic human needs. With great fanfare, under Ariel Sharon's leadership, Israel supposedly ended its military occupation and dismantled its settlements in 2005. The process was largely a sham as Israel maintained full control over borders, air space, and offshore seas, and also asserted its military control of Gaza, engaging in violent incursions, sending missiles to Gaza at will on assassination missions that themselves violate international humanitarian law, and managing to kill more than 300 Gazan civilians since its supposed physical departure from the area.

As unacceptable as is this earlier part of the story, a dramatic turn for the worse occurred when Hamas prevailed in the January 2006 national legislative elections. It is a bitter irony that Hamas was encouraged, especially by Washington, to participate in the elections to show its commitment to a political process (as an alternative to violence) and then was badly punished for having the temerity to succeed. These elections were internationally monitored under the leadership of the former American president Jimmy Carter, and pronounced as completely fair. Carter has recently termed this Israeli/American refusal to accept the outcome of such a democratic verdict as itself "criminal." The refusal to accept Hamas's election victory is also deeply discrediting of the Bush presidency's campaign to promote democracy in the region, an effort already under a dark shadow in view of the policy failure in Iraq.

After winning the Palestinian elections, Hamas was castigated as a terrorist organization that had not renounced violence against Israel and had refused to recognize the Jewish state as a legitimate political entity. In fact, the behavior and outlook of Hamas is quite different. From the outset of its political victory, Hamas was ready to work with other Palestinian groups, especially Fatah and Mahmoud Abbas, to establish a "unity" government. More than this, their leadership revealed a willingness to move toward an acceptance of Israel's existence if Israel would in turn agree to move back to its 1967 borders, implementing, finally, the unanimous Security Council Resolutions 242 and 338.

Even more dramatically, Hamas proposed a ten-year truce with Israel and went so far as to put in place a unilateral cease-fire that lasted for eighteen months, and was broken only to engage in rather pathetic strikes mainly taking place in response to violent Israeli provocations in Gaza. As Efraim Halevi, the former head of Israel's Mossad was reported to have said, "What Israel needs from Hamas is an end to violence, not diplomatic recognition." And this is precisely what Hamas offered and what Israel rejected.

The main weapons available to Hamas—and other Palestinian extremist elements—were Qassam missiles that resulted in no more than twelve Israeli deaths in six years. While each civilian death is an unacceptable tragedy, the ratio of death and injury for the two sides is so unequal as to call into question the security logic of continuously inflicting excessive force and collective punishment on the entire beleaguered population of Gaza, which is accurately regarded as the world's largest "prison."

Instead of trying diplomacy and respecting democratic results, Israel and the United States used their leverage to reverse the outcome of the 2006 elections by organizing a variety of international efforts designed to make Hamas fail in its attempts to govern in Gaza. Such efforts were reinforced by the related unwillingness of the defeated Fatah elements to cooperate with Hamas in establishing a government that would be representative of Palestinians as a whole. The main anti-Hamas tactic relied upon was to support Abbas as the sole legitimate leader of the Palestinian people, to impose an economic boycott on the Palestinians generally, to send in weapons for Fatah militias, and to enlist neighbors in these efforts, particularly Egypt and Jordan. The U. S. government appointed a special envoy, Lt. Gen. Keith Dayton, to work with the Abbas forces and helped channel 40 million dollars to build up the Presidential Guard, which were the Fatah forces associated with Abbas.

This was a particularly disgraceful policy. Fatah militias, especially in Gaza, had long been wildly corrupt and often used their weapons to terrorize their adversaries and intimidate the population in a variety of thuggish ways. It was this pattern of abuse by Fatah that was significantly responsible for the Hamas victory in the 2006 elections, along with the popular feelings that Fatah, as a political actor, had neither the will nor capacity to achieve results helpful to the Palestinian people, whereas Hamas had managed resistance and community service efforts that were widely admired by Gazans.

The latest phase of this external/internal dynamic was to induce civil strife in Gaza that led to a complete takeover by Hamas forces. With standard irony, a set of policies adopted by Israel in partnership with the United States once more produced exactly the opposite of their intended effects. The impact of the refusal to honor the election results has, after eighteen months, made Hamas much stronger throughout the Palestinian territories and put it in control of Gaza. Such an outcome is reminiscent of a similar effect of the 2006 Lebanon War that was undertaken by the Israel/United States strategic partnership to destroy Hezbollah, but had the actual consequence of making Hezbollah a much stronger, more respected force in Lebanon and throughout the region.

Israel and the United States seem trapped in a faulty logic that is incapable of learning from mistakes and, consequently, they take every setback as a sign that instead of shifting course, the faulty undertaking should be expanded and intensified; that failure results from doing too little of the right thing, rather than, as is often the case, doing the wrong thing. So instead of taking advantage of Hamas's renewed call for a unity government, its clarification that it is not against Fatah, but only that "[w]e have fought against a small clique within Fatah" (Abu Ubaya, Hamas military commander), Israel seems more determined than ever to foment civil war in Palestine, to make the Gazans pay with their well-being and lives to the extent necessary to crush their will, and to separate once and for all the destinies of Gaza and the West Bank.

The insidious new turn of Israeli occupation policy is as follows: to push Abbas to rely on a hard-line, no-compromise approach toward Hamas, high-lighted by the creation of an unelected "emergency" government to replace the elected leadership, and the emergency designation of Prime Minister Salam Fayyad, appointed to replace the Hamas leader, Ismail Haniya, as the head of the Palestinian Authority. It is revealing to recall that when Fayyad's party was on the 2006 election list, its candidates won only 2 percent of the vote. Israel is also reportedly ready to ease some West Bank restrictions on movement in such a way as to convince Palestinians that they can have a better future if they repudiate Hamas and place their bets on Abbas, by now a most discredited political figure who has substantially sold out the Palestinian cause to gain favor and support from Israel/United States, as well as to prevail in the internal Palestinian power struggle.

To promote these goals it is conceivable, although unlikely, that Israel might release Marwan Barghouti, the only credible Fatah leader, from prison, provided Barghouti is willing to accept the Israeli approach of Sharon/Olmert to the establishment of a Palestinian state. This latter step is doubtful, as Barghouti is a far cry from Abbas, and would be highly unlikely to agree to anything less than a full withdrawal of Israel to the 1967 borders, including the elimination of West Bank and East Jerusalem settlements.

This latest turn in policy needs to be understood in the wider context of the Israeli refusal to reach a reasonable compromise with the Palestinian people since 1967. There is widespread recognition that the achievement of such a compromise would depend on Israeli withdrawal, establishment of a Palestinian state with full sovereignty on the West Bank and Gaza and with East Jerusalem as capital, and sufficient external financial assistance to give the Palestinians the prospect of economic viability. The truth is that there is no Israeli leadership with the vision or backing to negotiate such a solution, and so the struggle will continue with violence on both sides.

The Israeli approach to the Palestinian challenge is based on isolating Gaza and cantonizing the West Bank, leaving the settlement blocs intact, and appropriating the whole of Jerusalem as the capital of Israel. For years, this sidestepping of diplomacy has dominated Israeli behavior, including during the Oslo peace process that was initiated on the White House lawns in 1993 by the famous handshake between Yitzhak Rabin and Yasser Arafat.

While talking about peace, the number of Israeli settlers doubled, huge sums were invested in settlement roads linked directly to Israel, and the process of Israeli settlement and Palestinian displacement from East Jerusalem was moving ahead at a steady pace. Significantly, also, the "moderate" Arafat was totally discredited as a Palestinian leader capable of negotiating with Israel, being treated as dangerous precisely because he was willing to accept a reasonable compromise. Interestingly, until recently, when he became useful in the effort to reverse the Hamas electoral victory, Abbas was treated by Israel as too weak and too lacking in authority to act on behalf of the Palestinian people in a negotiating process, which gave Israel one more excuse for persisting with its preferred unilateralist course.

These considerations also make it highly unlikely that Barghouti will be released from prison unless there is some dramatic change of heart on the Israeli side. Instead of working toward some kind of political resolution, Israel has built an elaborate and illegal security wall on Palestinian territory, expanded the settlements, made life intolerable for the 1.4 million people crammed into Gaza, and pretends that such unlawful "facts on the ground" are a path leading toward security and peace.

On June 25, 2007, leaders from Israel, Egypt, Jordan, and the Palestinian Authority met in Sharm El Sheik on the Red Sea to move ahead with their anti-Hamas diplomacy. Israel proposes to release 250 Fatah prisoners (of 9,000 Palestinians being held at the time) and to hand over Palestinian revenues to Abbas on an installment basis, provided none of the funds is used in Gaza, where a humanitarian catastrophe unfolds day by day. These leaders agreed to cooperate in this effort to break Hamas and to impose a Fatah-led Palestinian Authority on an unwilling Palestinian population. Remember that Hamas prevailed in the 2006 elections, not only in Gaza, but in the West Bank as well. To deny Palestinians their right to self-determination is almost certain to backfire in a manner similar to other efforts, producing a radicalized version of what is being opposed. As some commentators have expressed, getting rid of Hamas means establishing al Qaeda.

Israel is currently stiffening the boycott on economic relations that has brought the people of Gaza to the brink of collective starvation. This set of policies, carried on for more than four decades, has imposed a subhuman existence on a people that have been repeatedly and systematically made the target of a variety of severe forms of collective punishment. The entire population of Gaza is treated as the "enemy" of Israel, and little pretext is made in Tel Aviv of acknowledging the innocence of this long-victimized civilian society.

To persist with such an approach under present circumstances is indeed genocidal and risks destroying an entire Palestinian community that is an integral part of an ethnic whole. It is this prospect that makes appropriate the warning of a Palestinian holocaust in the making and should make the world mindful of the famous post-Nazi pledge of "Never Again."

## Note

1. "UN Court Rules Srebrencia Massacre Was Genocide," *Global Policy Forum*, April 19, 2004. www.globalpolicy.org/component/content/article/163/29298.html.

CHAPTER SEVEN

# *Gaza Is a Jail: Gaza Is Dying*

## Patrick Cockburn

### (9-8-2006)

Gaza is dying. The Israeli siege of the Palestinian enclave is so tight that its people are on the edge of starvation. Here on the shores of the Mediterranean a great tragedy is taking place that is being ignored because the world's attention has been diverted by wars in Lebanon and Iraq. A whole society is being destroyed. There are 1.5 million Palestinians imprisoned in the most heavily populated area in the world. Israel has stopped all trade. It has even forbidden fishermen to go far from the shore, so they wade into the surf to try vainly to catch fish with hand-thrown nets.

Many people are being killed by Israeli incursions that occur every day by land and air. A total of 262 people have been killed and 1,200 wounded, of whom 60 had arms or legs amputated since June 25, 2006, says Dr. Juma al-Saqa, the director of the al-Shifa Hospital in Gaza City, which is fast running out of medicine. Of these, sixty-four were children and twenty-six women. This bloody conflict in Gaza has so far received only a fraction of the attention given by the international media to the war in Lebanon.

It was on June 25, 2006, that the Israeli soldier Gilad Shalit was taken captive and two other soldiers were killed by Palestinian militants who used a tunnel to get out of the Gaza Strip. In the aftermath of this, writes Gideon Levy in the daily *Ha'aretz,* the Israeli army "has been rampaging through Gaza—there's no other word to describe it—killing and demolishing, bombing and shelling, indiscriminately." Gaza has essentially been reoccupied, since Israeli troops and tanks come and go at will. In the northern district of Shajhayeh, Israeli troops took over several houses last week and stayed five days. By the time they withdrew, twenty-two Palestinians had been killed, three houses were destroyed, and groves of olive, citrus, and almond trees had been bulldozed.

Fuad al-Tuba, the sixty-one-year-old farmer who owned a farm here, said: "They even destroyed twenty-two of my bee-hives and killed four sheep." He pointed sadly to a field, its brown, sandy earth churned up by tracks of bulldozers, where the stumps of trees and broken branches with wilting leaves lay in heaps. Nearby, a yellow car was standing on its nose in the middle of a heap of concrete blocks that had once been a small house.

His son Baher al-Tuba described how for five days Israeli soldiers confined him and his relatives to one room in his house, where they survived by drinking water from a fish pond. "Snipers took up positions in the windows and shot at anybody who came near," he said. "They killed one of my neighbors called Fathi Abu Gumbuz who was fifty-six years old and just went out to get water."

Sometimes the Israeli army gives a warning before a house is destroyed. The sound that Palestinians most dread is an unknown voice on their cell phone saying they have half an hour to leave their home before it is hit by bombs or missiles. There is no appeal. But it is not the Israeli incursions alone that are destroying Gaza and its people. In the understated prose of a World Bank report published last month (August 2006), the West Bank and Gaza face "a year of unprecedented economic recession. Real incomes may contract by at least a third in 2006 and poverty to affect close to two thirds of the population." Poverty in this case means a per capita income of under two dollars (£1.06) a day.

There are signs of desperation everywhere. Crime is increasing. People do anything to feed their families. Israeli troops entered the Gaza industrial zone to search for tunnels and kicked out the Palestinian police. When the Israelis withdrew they were replaced not by the police but by looters. On one day this week there were three donkey carts removing twisted scrap metal from the remains of factories that once employed thousands.

"It is the worst year for us since 1948 [when Palestinian refugees first poured into Gaza]," says Dr. Maged Abu-Ramadan, a former ophthalmologist who is the mayor of Gaza City. "Gaza is a jail. Neither people nor goods are allowed to leave it. People are already starving. They try to live on bread and falafel and a few tomatoes and cucumbers they grow themselves."

The few ways that Gazans had of making money have disappeared. Dr Abu-Ramadan says the Israelis "have destroyed 70 percent of our orange groves in order to create security zones." Carnations and strawberries, two of Gaza's main exports, were thrown away or left to rot. An Israeli air strike destroyed the electric power station, so 50 percent of power was lost. Electricity supply is now becoming almost as intermittent as in Baghdad.

The Israeli assault over the past two months struck a society already hit by the withdrawal of EU subsidies after the election of Hamas as the Palestinian government in March. Israel is withholding taxes owed on goods entering Gaza. Under U.S. pressure, Arab banks abroad will not transfer funds to the government. Two-thirds of people are unemployed, and the remaining third who mostly work for the state are not being paid. Gaza is now by far the poorest region in the Mediterranean. Per capita annual income is $700, compared with $20,000 in Israel. Conditions are much worse than in Lebanon, where Hezbollah liberally compensates war victims for the loss of their houses. If Gaza did not have enough troubles this week, there were protest strikes and marches by unpaid soldiers, police, and security men. These were organized by Fatah, the movement of the Palestinian president Mahmoud Abbas (also known as Abu Mazen), which lost the election to Hamas in January. His supporters marched through the streets waving their Kalashnikovs in the air. "Abu Mazen you are brave," they shouted. "Save us from this disaster." Sour-looking Hamas gunmen kept a low profile during the demonstration, but the two sides are not far from fighting it out in the streets.

The Israeli siege and the European boycott are a collective punishment of everybody in Gaza. The gunmen are unlikely to be deterred. In a bed in Shifa Hospital was a sturdy young man called Ala Hejairi with wounds to his neck, legs, chest, and stomach. "I was laying an anti-tank mine last week in Shajhayeh when I was hit by fire from an Israeli drone," he said. "I will return to the resistance when I am better. Why should I worry? If I die I will die a martyr and go to paradise." His father, Adel, said he was proud of what his son had done, adding that three of his nephews were already martyrs. He supported the Hamas government: "Arab and Western countries want to destroy this government because it is the government of the resistance."

As the economy collapses there will be many more young men in Gaza willing to take Ala Hejairi's place. Untrained and ill-armed, most will be killed. But the destruction of Gaza, now under way, will ensure that no peace is possible in the Middle East for generations to come.

CHAPTER EIGHT

# The Shame of Being an American

PAUL CRAIG ROBERTS

(7-22-2006)

Gentle reader, do you know that Israel is engaged in ethnic cleansing in
southern Lebanon? Israel has ordered all the villagers to clear out. Israel then
destroys their homes and murders the fleeing villagers. That way, no one
can come back, and there is nothing to which to return, making it easier for
Israel to grab the territory, just as Israel has been stealing Palestine from the
Palestinians.

Do you know that one-third of the Lebanese civilians murdered by Israel's
attacks on civilian residential districts are children? That is the report from Jan
Egeland, the emergency relief coordinator for the United Nations.[1] He says
that it is impossible for help to reach the wounded and those buried in rubble
because Israeli air strikes have blown up all the bridges and roads. Considering
how often (almost always) Israel misses Hezbollah targets and hits civilian
ones, one might think that Israeli fire is being guided by U.S. satellites and
U.S. military GPS. Don't be surprised at U.S. complicity. Why would the
puppet be any less evil than the puppet master?

Of course, you don't know these things, because the U.S. print and TV
media do not report them. Because Bush is so proud of himself, you do know
that he has blocked every effort to stop the Israeli slaughter of Lebanese civilians. Bush has told the UN "No." Bush has told the European Union "No."
Bush has told the pro-American Lebanese prime minister "No." Twice. Bush
is very proud of his firmness. He is enjoying Israel's rampage and wishes he
could do the same thing in Iraq.

Does it make you a proud American that President Bush gave Israel the green light to drop bombs on convoys of villagers fleeing from Israeli shelling, on residential neighborhoods in the capital of Beirut and throughout Lebanon, on hospitals, on power plants, on food production and storage, on ports, on civilian airports, on bridges, on roads, on every piece of infrastructure on which civilized life depends? Are you a proud American? Or are you an Israeli puppet?

On July 20, 2006, "your" House of Representatives voted 410–8 in favor of Israel's massive war crimes in Lebanon.[2] Not content with making every American complicit in war crimes, "your" House of Representatives, according to the Associated Press, also "condemns enemies of the Jewish state." Who are the "enemies of the Jewish state"?

They are the Palestinians whose land has been stolen by the Jewish state, whose homes and olive groves have been destroyed by the Jewish state, whose children have been shot down in the streets by the Jewish state, whose women have been abused by the Jewish state. They are Palestinians who have been walled off into ghettos, who cannot reach their farm lands or medical care or schools, who cannot drive on roads through Palestine that have been constructed for Israelis only. They are Palestinians whose ancient towns have been invaded by militant Zionist "settlers" under the protection of the Israeli army who beat and persecute the Palestinians and drive them out of their towns. They are Palestinians who cannot allow their children outside their homes because they will be murdered by Israeli "settlers."

The Palestinians who confront Israeli evil are called "terrorists." When Bush forced free elections on Palestine, the people voted for Hamas. Hamas is the organization that has stood up to Israel. This means, of course, that Hamas is evil, anti-Semitic, un-American, and terrorist. The U.S. and Israel responded by cutting off all funds to the new government. Democracy is permitted only if it produces the results Bush and Israel want. Israelis never practice terror. Only those who are in Israel's way are terrorists.

Another enemy of the Jewish state is Hezbollah. Hezbollah is a militia of Shi'ite Muslims created in 1982 when Israel first invaded Lebanon. During this invasion, the great moral Jewish state arranged for the murder of refugees in refugee camps. The result of Israel's atrocities was Hezbollah, which fought the Israeli army, defeated it, and drove it out of Lebanon. Today, Hezbollah not only defends southern Lebanon but also provides social services such as orphanages and medical care.

To cut to the chase, the enemies of the Jewish state are any Muslim country not ruled by an American puppet friendly to Israel. Egypt, Jordan, Saudi Arabia, and the oil emirates have sided with Israel against their own kind because they are dependent either on American money or on American protection from their own people. Sooner or later these totally corrupt governments that do not represent the people they rule will be overthrown. It is only a matter of time.

Indeed, Bush and Israel may be hastening the process in their frantic effort to overthrow the governments of Syria and Iran. Both governments have more popular support than Bush has, but Bush doesn't know this. He thinks Syria and Iran will be "cakewalks" like Iraq, where ten proud divisions of the U.S. military are tied down by a few lightly armed insurgents.

If you are still a proud American, consider that your pride is doing nothing good for Israel or for America.

On July 20, 2006, when "your" House of Representatives, following "your" U.S. Senate, passed the resolution in support of Israel's war crimes, the most powerful lobby in Washington, the American Israeli Public Affairs Committee (AIPAC), quickly issued a press release proclaiming, "The American people overwhelming support Israel's war on terrorism and understand that we must stand by our closest ally in this time of crisis."

The truth is that Israel created the crisis by invading a country with a pro-American government. The truth is that the American people do not support Israel's war crimes, as the CNN quick poll results make clear and as was made clear by callers into C-Span. Despite the Israeli spin on news provided by U.S. "reporting," a majority of Americans do not approve of Israeli atrocities against Lebanese civilians. Hezbollah is located in southern Lebanon. If Israel is targeting Hezbollah, why are Israeli bombs falling on northern Lebanon? Why are they falling on Beirut? Why are they falling on civilian airports? On schools and hospitals?

Now we arrive at the main point. When the U.S. Senate and House of Representatives pass resolutions in support of Israeli war crimes and condemn those who resist Israeli aggression, the Senate and House confirm Osama bin Laden's propaganda that America stands with Israel against the Arab and Muslim world. Indeed, Israel, which has one of the world's largest per capita incomes, is the largest recipient of U.S. foreign aid. Many believe that much of this "aid" comes back to AIPAC, which uses it to elect "our" representatives in Congress.

This perception is no favor to Israel, whose population is declining, as the smart ones have seen the writing on the wall and have been leaving. Israel is surrounded by hundreds of millions of Muslims who are being turned into enemies of Israel by Israel's actions and inhumane policies. The hope in the Muslim world has always been that the United States would intervene on behalf of compromise and make Israel realize that Israel cannot steal Palestine and turn every Palestinian into a refugee. This has been the hope of the Arab world. This is the reason our puppets have not been overthrown. This hope is the reason America still has some prestige in the Arab world.

The House of Representatives resolution, bought and paid for by AIPAC money, is the final nail in the coffin of American prestige in the Middle East. It shows that America is, indeed, Israel's puppet, just as Osama bin Laden says, and as a majority of Muslims believe. With hope and diplomacy dead, henceforth America and Israel have only tooth and claw. The vaunted Israeli army could not defeat a rag-tag militia in southern Lebanon. The vaunted U.S. military cannot defeat a rag-tag, lightly armed insurgency drawn from a minority of the population in Iraq, insurgents, moreover, who are mainly engaged in civil war against the Shi'ite majority.

What will the United States and its puppet master do? Both are too full of hubris and paranoia to admit their terrible mistakes. Israel and the United States will either destroy from the air the civilian infrastructure of Lebanon, Palestine, Syria, and Iran so that civilized life becomes impossible for Muslims, or they will use nuclear weapons to intimidate Muslims into acquiescence to Israel's desires.

Muslim genocide in one form or another is the professed goal of the neoconservatives who have total control over the Bush administration. The neocon godfather Norman Podhoretz has called for World War IV (in neocon thinking, World War III was the Cold War) to overthrow Islam in the Middle East, deracinate the Islamic religion, and turn it into a formalized, secular ritual.

Donald Rumsfeld's neocon Pentagon has drafted a new U.S. war doctrine that permits preemptive nuclear attacks on nonnuclear states. Neocon David Horowitz says that by slaughtering Palestinian and Lebanese civilians, "Israel is doing the work of the rest of the civilized world," thus equating war criminals with civilized men. Neocon Larry Kudlow says that "Israel is doing the Lord's work" by murdering Lebanese civilians, a claim that should give pause to Israel's Christian evangelical supporters. Where does the Lord Jesus say, "Go forth and murder your neighbors so that you may steal their lands"?

The complicity of the American public in these heinous crimes will damn America for all time in history.

## Notes

1. See www.un.org for listing of reports and www.un.org/News/briefings/docs/2006/060830_ Egeland.doc.html.
2. "House Passes Pro-Israel Resolution," CBS News, July 20, 2006. www.cbsnews.com/ stories/2006/07/20/politics/main1820193.shtml. America's support ran counter to the opinions of most peoples throughout the world, who demonstrated against Israel's excessive force, as noted above, forcing a UNSC-brokered cease-fire.

# CHAPTER NINE

# Israeli Immunity for Genocide

## ANDREA HOWARD

### (7-15-2006)

Having no concept of the rule of law and no sense of humanity or morality, Israel continues its genocidal adventure in Palestine. Violating every crime of war and human rights known to man with the tacit approval and complicity of the international community, the military might of Israel collectively targets a civilian population and the infrastructure of a nation.

This is an army, complete with warplanes and missiles, tanks and munitions, armored vehicles, landmines, rocket-propelled grenades (RPGs), and a multitude of automatic weapons, targeting a civilian population.

Israel has collectively targeted, and is collectively punishing, 1.4 million Palestinian civilians in the Gaza Strip. The most densely populated place on the planet, the Gaza Strip has 1.4 million people crowded into a mere 146 square miles, that is, 9,712 people per square mile. The unemployment rate is approximately 50 percent, with 81 percent of the population in poverty.

Israel initially invaded the Gaza Strip under the guise of a "search and rescue mission" after the June 25, 2006, Palestinian strike on an Israeli army post, during which two Israeli occupation soldiers were killed and one was taken captive by Palestinian resistance. Approximately sixteen days later, Israel has reoccupied the Gaza Strip, in the process killing more than 74 Palestinians and injuring more than 200. Israel has invaded villages and towns in the West Bank, arresting Palestinian citizens, and has kidnapped sixty-four Palestinian government officials—democratically elected by the people of Palestine.

Israel sent its warplanes, on June 28, 2006, into the sovereign nation of Syria in a blatant attempt at intimidation and psychological terror. Israeli warplanes simulated a low-altitude attack on the home of President Assad, diving sharply toward it and then rapidly accelerating, creating a window-shattering sonic boom. Israel has now commenced (July 2006 as this article was being written) bombing the sovereign nation of Lebanon after two Israeli soldiers were taken captive. As in the Gaza Strip Israeli forces are targeting the infrastructure in Lebanon, bombing all three runways at the only international airport, bridges, and power plants, killing 55 and wounding more than 103 people. Israel has initiated a full naval blockade, virtually taking control of Lebanese sea, air, and border space.

The June 26, 2006, Palestinian strike, in which an Israeli soldier was taken captive, is the Israeli excuse for unleashing the current invasions and bombings. That strike was against an Israeli army base. This is in contrast to Israeli strikes, which target densely populated civilian areas, national infrastructure, schools, power plants, charity organizations, and civilian homes and vehicles. Israel, armed by the United States and subsidized with billions from the American taxpayer, uses Lockheed Martin F-16 Fighting Falcons, Boeing F-15s, Caterpillar bulldozers, and various U.S. munitions against the Palestinians.

The Palestinians, in glaring contrast, launch Qassam "rockets" toward Israeli territory and throw stones at Israeli occupation soldiers and Israeli tanks/vehicles during regular invasions of villages and towns. The Palestinians have no army, no form of self-defense, and are relegated to using whatever means of resistance is at their disposal. Suicide bombings, sometimes used by the Palestinian resistance, killed twenty-two Israelis in 2005; by contrast, 235 Palestinians died in 2005 because of Israeli forces and settler violence.

Far from existing in a vacuum, the Palestinian strike against the Israeli army post occurred within the context of the occupation; to deny or obfuscate the facts of living under Israeli occupation, especially since the 2005 Palestinian elections, is absurd and serves to propagandize reality. In the months prior to the June 26 operation that captured the Israeli occupation soldier, Israel did the following:

- 26 January–24 February: seven people killed, fifty-five wounded by Israeli occupation forces; fifty-eight Israeli incursions into Palestinian communities, with 252 civilians arrested, including 32 children; Israeli forces turned twenty-two Palestinian homes into military outposts; Israeli forces shelled an apartment building in the Gaza Strip

- 23 March–29 March: five Palestinians killed; eighteen wounded by Israeli gunfire; Israel continues shelling Gaza Strip; twenty-seven Israeli incursions into Palestinian communities, with at least forty-four civilians arrested, including four children; Israeli forces turned six Palestinian homes into military outposts; Israel conducted an extrajudicial execution

- 6 April–12 April: nineteen Palestinians killed, ninety-four wounded by Israeli gunfire; Israeli forces conducted twenty-seven incursions in the West Bank and arrested seventy people, including six children; Israeli forces turned seven Palestinian homes into military outposts; Israeli forces raided a hospital and arrested injured Palestinians; Israel conducted an extrajudicial execution in which ten Palestinians died

- 8 June–14 June: twenty-eight people killed, seventy-six wounded; Israeli forces conducted forty incursions into Palestinian communities with forty-nine civilians, including twelve children, arrested; Israeli forces turned two Palestinian homes into military outposts; extrajudicial executions killed nineteen people; Israeli forces continue closing borders in the Gaza Strip. (On July 9, 2006, Israel slammed a Gaza beach with artillery shells, killing eight people as they were picnicking, including two women and three children, and wounding more than thirty [there are no words to describe this incident; please watch the video "The Aftermath of the Killing."])[1]

On July 4, 2006, the Palestinian resistance fired a Qassam "rocket" into the Israeli town of Ashkelon. the Israeli prime minister Olmert responded that the rocket was a "grave escalation" for which there will be "far-reaching ramifications." Israel has the entire Gaza Strip within its military stranglehold, and while bombing civilian infrastructure and government buildings, Israel continues to employ the reactionary "national security-self-defense" model in rationalizing its criminal actions.

Reviewing the weekly "Humanitarian Briefing Notes" produced by the United Nations Office for Coordination of Humanitarian Affairs (OCHA) shows the complete absurdity of Israeli officials' assertions that Palestinians have been "escalating" aggression. Between March 29, 2006, and June 13, 2006, Israel fired 4,748 shells and 107 missiles into Gaza. OCHA conducted further review for this time frame and concluded that in total, 7,986 Israeli missiles and shells had actually been launched at the Gaza Strip. During that same time period, 455 Palestinian Qassams were fired toward Israel. In the thirty-four days between April 29 and May 1, 2006, Israel fired 3,068 shells and missiles into Gaza compared to 162 Palestinian Qassams launched toward Israel. Between September 12, 2005, and March 28, 2006, Israel fired 1161 artillery shells and surface-to-air missiles into Gaza, while 686 Palestinian Qassams were fired toward Israel.[2]

In the last three years, eight Israelis have been killed by Palestinian Qassams, while in one week's time, Israeli forces have killed anywhere from five to twenty-eight Palestinians. In one twenty-four-hour period, Israel launched more than 500 missiles into northern Gaza. Given this data, it is obvious who is escalating the aggression.

Three weeks prior to the Gaza beach massacre, a failed Israeli assassination attempt in Gaza left a three-year-old girl paralyzed, a ventilator doing her breathing for her, and killed her mother (aged twenty-seven), brother (aged seven), grandmother (aged forty-six) and injured her father and other brother (aged two). The missile, fired by Israel's warplanes, also injured another family whose vehicle just happened to be too close to the targeted area. The target was a "militant" on his way to the hospital to visit his wife and newborn baby; he was executed along with his two brothers while en route to the hospital.

This is not an anomaly. Israel's attempts at extrajudicial liquidation kill and injure innocent Palestinian civilians on a regular basis. For a glimpse at how routine, illegal, and deadly these assassinations are, consider that Israel's assassination attempts and air strikes regularly kill and injure innocent civilians when these missiles "miss" their intended targets. On June 23, 2006, a twenty-five-year-old Palestinian woman, seven months pregnant, gave birth to a stillborn baby girl in an emergency caesarean section after shrapnel injured the woman in a botched Israeli air raid.

An Israeli occupation force spokeswoman addressed the deaths of the baby and other deaths and injuries by stating, "The missile simply missed." Israeli prime minister Olmert, in a rare moment, provided an honest assessment of the extensive deaths of Palestinian civilians by stating that the lives of Israelis were "more important" than the lives of Palestinians.

Israel conducts mass home demolishing when Palestinians do not have the proper "permits," while Israel builds illegal Israeli-only colonies on Palestinian lands and, in the process, clears vast swaths of farm/agricultural land upon which families' lives depend. Israel has created "Jewish-only" roads, for which one has to have the correct color license plate to travel, and has cornered Palestinians into ghettos by constructing a giant apartheid wall, larger and more fortified than the Berlin Wall. Permission to cross the hundreds of military checkpoints to go to work, school, the doctor, or to visit family in other areas is arbitrarily granted by Israeli occupation forces guarding the crossings.

Palestinians endure arbitrary arrests, humiliation, intimidation, beatings, and purposefully long waits at checkpoints simply because some Israeli occupation soldier is having a bad day. Palestinian resistance fighters, who have faced no arrest or trial and no form of due process, face extrajudicial executions through missile strikes by Israeli warplanes, and while bystanders are killed for inadvertently being in the way of an Israeli "operation." Palestinian cities and villages are invaded, and extended curfews are imposed during which people are not allowed to leave their homes for work, school, doctor visits, and so on. Twenty-four-hour curfews have sometimes been in effect for days on end.

Israel began its most current rampage using warplanes to bomb a Gaza Strip power plant, destroying all six transformers and knocking out power to half of the population, immediately leaving some 700,000 people as well as two primary hospitals in the dark and with no running water. On June 29, 2006, Israel used its warplanes to target the second power plant in Gaza. The hospitals are now rationing electricity and water for critical patients such as babies in incubators, those on ventilators, and those undergoing or recovering from emergency surgery. Lutfi Halawa has a nine-month-old daughter on a ventilator in a Gaza hospital and contemplates what no father would ever want to: "Without electricity my daughter will die."

No electricity means relying on generators, which take fuel, fuel that has to be brought in from outside the Gaza Strip now that supplies are running out. Since Israeli occupation forces control Palestinian borders, they decide when supplies are allowed into the Gaza Strip.

In addition, the Gaza Strip relies on electricity to pump water, leaving half of the population to go without or use water from other sources such as wells and unsanitary storage tanks. The lack of electricity will also cause raw sewage to back up and eventually flood throughout the area. Plant officials report that it will take four to five months to make repairs to the power plant. To pump water, Palestinians are relying on generators for which the UN will assist with fueling, using its own thirty-day supply of fuel earmarked for the delivery of emergency food. With Israel continuing the blockade of border routes, it will not be possible for Palestine to obtain urgently needed fuel.

Gaza City, with approximately 600,000 residents, has halted garbage collection, leaving roughly 400 metric tons of trash per day in Palestinian communities. Throughout the Gaza Strip electricity is now rationed, and with generators being used to pump water, Palestinians manage a six-hour-on/six-hour-off water supply to some of their communities.

Eliminating electricity—for light, refrigeration, hospital/health needs, water pumps, sewage treatment, and water for bathing—in an area with a population of 1.4 million people is nothing more than collective punishment. Eliminating water for bathing, washing clothes, cleaning, cooking, drinking, pumping water, and sewage treatment is collective punishment. Eliminating fuel for cooking and driving is collective punishment. Collective punishment is a war crime.

The spokesman for the Israeli Foreign Ministry submitted that the power plant was "targeted to make it more difficult for militants holding Shalit [the Israeli occupation soldier held by the Palestinian resistance] to move around." The statement itself is absurd; the siege on Palestine obviously has great political motivations. It is not a coincidence that Israel increased its aggression once the new, democratically elected, Hamas-led government was sworn in on March 29, 2006. Clearly, Israel did not approve of the democratic election that took place in Palestine and has therefore chosen to use its arsenal to ensure that government is eliminated.

In addition to eliminating the basic services in Gaza, Israel's "operation" has targeted charity agencies, which provide the bulk of social services for Palestinians. Last Friday, the Palestinian Society for the Speech Impaired was bombed; it is the only organization working with the speech impaired in Gaza; notably, the agency worked mostly with children.

Israel kidnapped sixty-four Palestinian cabinet members and parliamentarians in an egregious violation of any notion of the sovereignty and independence of the Palestinian government. The illegal arrests attest to the mentality, and intention, of the Israeli leadership in doing whatever it can to ultimately destroy the Palestinian government. Attesting to this fact is an article published by *Ha'aretz* that stated, "The detention of Hamas parliamentarians had been planned several weeks ago."[3] The Israelis planned the kidnapping of government officials weeks prior to any taking of the Israeli occupation soldier, making clear that this current offensive was not in retaliation for any Palestinian strike or captive soldier.

While the focus has been on the siege of the Gaza Strip, the kidnapping of Palestinian government officials took place throughout West Bank areas including Ramallah, Qalqilyah, Hebron, Jenin, and East Jerusalem. In addition, regular incursions by Israeli occupation forces have taken place in the West Bank since the siege on Gaza began. Regarding Palestine's Hamas-led government, Israel's national infrastructure minister stated that "no one is immune. This is not a government. It is a murderous organization," and then proceeded to directly threaten to kill the democratically elected Palestinian prime minister. Israeli hypocrisy has finally matched the level of its own genocidal intent.

Israel states that the Hamas-led government is a "terror" organization, which is ironic, since in the sixteen months preceding the Israeli escalation of violence, beginning shortly after Hamas was democratically elected and sworn in, Hamas had honored a truce against attacks on Israel. Israel complains that there is no "negotiating partner" in the Palestinian government. However, in truth, no matter whom the Palestinians democratically elect, those officials will not be accepted by Israel either. Whether it was Arafat, Abbas, Hamas, or any other individual or party, Israel will refuse to participate in any dialogue with a Palestinian official seeking independence and sovereignty for Palestine. Israel has one agenda and that is to force the Palestinians to submit to Israeli rule whether willingly, by force, or in death.

Israel, once again, has the residents of the Gaza Strip under siege, physically by sealing the Palestinians within Gaza through the blockade or closure of border crossings, stranding many residents of Gaza on the Egyptian side of the border; and psychologically, using intimidation and repeated sonic booms over the densely populated area. The unrelenting fear for any Palestinian man, woman, child, "militant," or civilian is the reality that anyone can be killed in an Israeli assassination attempt or subjected to arrest by Israeli occupation forces; the alternative is to stay locked away in their homes. While in their homes Palestinian children and their families, are bombarded with the sounds of gunfire, warplanes, tanks, and sonic booms reverberating though their homes shattering windows and causing children to scream in utter terror. But then, this is what Israeli leaders want; this is precisely the campaign they are waging against an entire civilian population: a physical, psychological, and genocidal war of terror.

Operation "Summer Rains," the name for the current illegal invasion and siege of the Gaza Strip, attests to the fact that nothing is sacred to Israel, nothing except the ultimate elimination of their "demographic problem," the mere existence of the Palestinian people. As the international community calls for "restraint," diplomats and leaders continue to spout rhetoric, making "demands" that Israel observe the law while the regional Arab governments take no action to defend their neighbors, and Israel continues its genocidal "operation." While the United States continues to assert Israel's "right to self-defense," finances and provides Israel with the military hardware used to commit international crimes, ignores Israel as the primary nuclear nation in the region that refuses to adhere to the Nuclear Non-Proliferation Treaty, and punishes the Palestinians for their choice of government,

- Israel collectively punishes 1.4 million civilians by bombing power plants and destroying essential infrastructure;
- Israel violates the sovereignty of other nations, continues to threaten other nations, and flies warplanes over the home of the Syrian president;
- Israel closes border crossings, preventing urgently needed humanitarian relief from reaching civilians;
- Israel bombs government buildings;
- Israel targets charity agencies which provide the bulk of social services to the population;
- Israel targets university and school buildings;

- Israel raids hospitals;
- Israel destroys businesses in air raids;
- Israel executes government officials;
- Israel actively plans the kidnapping of democratically elected government officials;
- Israel kidnaps sixty four democratically elected government officials;
- Israel threatens to assassinate a democratically elected prime minister;
- Israel sends its warplanes on assassination missions in densely populated civilian areas, killing and injuring innocent people who just happen to be nearby;
- Israel uses dozens of bulldozers to raze Palestinian homes and vast swaths of agricultural land;
- Israel arrests and imprisons thousands of Palestinians, including hundreds of children, as political prisoners.

The above is not a list of Israeli crimes specific to this latest siege of the Gaza Strip. The list, quite incomplete, is a mere sample of what the civilians of Palestine have been managing to live with for years, and years, and years. Israel has made an absolute mockery of human rights law and its own "Proclamation of Israel's Independence." The basic concepts codified within the Nuremberg Principles have not only been ignored but have been repeatedly violated by Israel with impunity.

Israel has obligations, to which it has committed, in protecting Palestinians under its control. Israel has violated the Fourth Hague Convention, the Fourth Geneva Convention, the First Additional Protocol to the Geneva Convention, the Universal Declaration of Human Rights, and the International Covenant on Civil and Political Rights. Civilians, regardless of where they live, and the infrastructure that supports them, can never be targeted unless, of course, the nation that does the targeting is Israel. The international community, responding to these blatant and absolute violations of the law, collectively tells the Palestinian population to "deal with it."

During World War II, the world watched as Nazi Germany enacted discriminatory laws; isolated specific populations based on religion and ethnicity; created and imprisoned those people in ghettos; invaded, destroyed, and expropriated public and private property; arbitrarily arrested and imprisoned thousands of people, carried out extra-judicial executions, and undertook a campaign to eradicate an entire people. Today, in Israel proper and in the Israeli-occupied territories of Palestine, Israel is undertaking a campaign strikingly like that undertaken by the Nazis.

Israel's ingenuity as the occupying force ensures that Palestinians have no chance at success in any undertaking, least of which is building a strong Palestine. As long as Palestinians are fighting to survive, they will not be able to undertake community building, obtain political stability, or, most importantly, establish a sovereign and self-determined Palestine. This is Israel's intention. When people's entire lives are controlled by military forces, when individuals live in a constant state of fear and anxiety, when people have been relegated to ghettos, when 96 percent of a population's children have seen a friend or relative killed by occupation forces and exhibit symptoms of trauma, when the world has turned a blind eye to genocide and apartheid for so long, does one expect that people will not rise up to defend themselves in a struggle for self-determination? Does one expect that those people would sit idly by, and allow Israeli actions to continue, in silence? Should one expect a different response than striking back in any way one can to subjugation? Absolutely not.

Does one not think that the Palestinians realize what they face when striking against the massive military force that is destroying them? They know best what retaliations will occur when fighting against the occupation, but they press on using the means available to them. Having no military forces, the Palestinians fight against Israeli military forces, garnered in large part due to U.S financing, with homemade "rockets" and stones, yes, stones. The Palestinians have the legally protected right to defend themselves against Israeli terrorism, and they have the right to fight for self-determination and their own independence against the occupiers. History has shown that a people oppressed will throw off the oppressors. It is only a matter of time and steadfast commitment.

It is absolutely unconscionable to remain silent and allow Israeli leadership, and the massive might of the Israeli military apparatus, to commit genocide in Palestine. It is unconscionable to allow an army to target and wage a full-scale war against a civilian population. I know, you are busy and have children to care for, you have car and mortgage payments to make, and you have sleep to catch up on. Every day, as you go about your daily lives, you are providing financial and military assistance to fund the Israeli occupation through your tax dollars. The United States continues to absurdly define genocide as Israeli self-defense, and a blind eye continues to be turned to the systematic subjugation and the slaughter of innocent people. The world has seen genocide before. For the war crimes committed under Hitler's reign the United States played a central role in the trials of those who committed and assisted in the commission of crimes against humanity. The Nuremberg Tribunal mandated every individual to stand in defense of those targeted, by any nation, for genocide and take action to stop it:

> Individuals have international duties which transcend the national obligations of Obedience and therefore have the duty to violate domestic laws to prevent crimes against peace and humanity from occurring.
> (Nuremberg Tribunal, 1950).[4]

The mandate to intervene is clear. Do something; get involved and act now. Your silence is not only betrayal; it is support for Israel's policy of genocide.

## Notes

1. Details provided in this commentary can be found in the reports provided by the following organizations: the Palestine Council for Human Rights (PCHR) ( www.pchrgaza.org/PCHR/docs.html) publishes position papers to track current events and a number of regular reports on various aspects of the human rights situation in the Occupied Palestinian Territory (OPT), and regularly produces in-depth studies on various aspects of the human rights situation in the OPT, dealing with violations by Israeli forces, the Palestinian National Authority, or the state of democratic institutions and the rule of law in the OPT. See also www.amnesty.org/en/contact/Israel+/+occupied+Palestian+territory.
2. www.un.org/en/humanitarian.
3. Avi Issacharoft and Amos Harel, "IDF forces Arrest Palestinian Cabinet Ministers, Lawmakers," *Ha'aretz*, June 29, 2006.
4. www.heartsandmindsredux.wordpress.com/international-law/nuremberg-trials-openingaddress-for-the-us.

CHAPTER TEN

# Palestinian Misery in Perspective

PAUL DE ROOIJ

(6-3-2004)

The media usually focus on the latest casualty and quickly forget those who died even a few days before. The American media, in particular, have a Dracula-like predilection for warm bodies and no interest in cases where blood has already dried. Unfortunately, this ahistoric focus on the last victim hides the scale of mass crimes and the responsibility of various perpetrators. Whether in Iraq, Palestine, Colombia, or Haiti, it is necessary to locate human rights abuses in a wider context to appreciate the scale of what is occurring on the ground.

In the case of Palestinian casualties, it is all too evident that CNN, BBC, and other major media are mostly interested in today's casualties; they seem to studiously ignore precedents, and above all, they will not refer to the pattern of killings as systematic in nature. Of course, admitting that such killings are systematic would imply that Israel is committing "crimes against humanity," a precursor to genocide. When the media seeks to whitewash "friendly" mass crimes, there is a tendency to fixate on specific instances to the exclusion of broad patterns. Even when a pattern of killings and other abuses is chronic and systematic, the BBC or CNN will tend to focus on specific cases without reference to broader trends. When referring to Palestinian conditions, what we find is that reports of casualties, house demolitions, and dispossession in these media outlets pertain to specific cases and not to general patterns.[1] Incidentally, the opposite is true when there is an incident of Palestinian violence; here, lists and charts are available to highlight their context.

The chosen context can be used to obfuscate the reality on the ground. The tools at the media's disposal can be likened to an instrument of variable magnification, ranging from a wide-angle lens to a telescope. Informative journalism requires using the most appropriate level of magnification for the story under investigation. On the other hand, propaganda requires contextual blurring and the use of inappropriate tools. Thus, it is best to use a telescope to view the stars, and clearly, a wide-angle lens is the wrong tool. In the case of Palestinian casualties, it is evident that the mainstream media are intent on presenting news using a telescope (preferably out of focus), when a wide-angle lens should be used.

The tables and graphs below put the Palestinian casualty toll into perspective over the course of the second intifada. These graphs speak for themselves, revealing a pattern that is all too evident. These graphs are meant to fill a gap in the available data pertaining to the casualty toll during the second intifada.

## Average Death Tolls and an Interpretation

During the course of the second intifada, the average number of Palestinians killed stands at 2.26 per day. The total killed between September 29, 2000, and May 31, 2004, is 3,023. To interpret these numbers, one must scale these figures to make them comparable to understand what they would mean in the context of our own countries. This is the purpose of table 10.1.

An average daily fatality rate of 2.26 would proportionally equate to 177 deaths per day in the United States. Similarly, the total Palestinian fatalities

**Table 10.1**  Average and total Palestinian fatalities during Intifada II, September 29, 2000–May 31, 2004

|  | *Actual and Population Scaled Numbers* | | | |
|---|---|---|---|---|
|  | *Average fatalities/day* | *Total fatalities* | *Scale factor* | *Population size(m)* |
| Palestine | 2.26 | 3,023 | 1 | 3.7 |
| US | 177 | 236,938 | 78 | 290.0 |
| UK | 37 | 49,022 | 16 | 60.0 |
| Spain | 25 | 32,844 | 11 | 40.2 |

*Explanation:*
Column (1) The average fatalities per day for the Palestinians is an actual number. The numbers below this have been scaled using the scale factor in column #3.
Column (2) is analogous to column #1, but refers to the total fatalities.
Column (3) is the scaling factor derived from the population numbers in column #4.

of 3,023 would equate to 236,938 in the United States. One wonders how Americans would react if they experienced such a fatality rate, that is, if they suffered a 9/11 death toll every two weeks. One suspects that there would be a level of mass hysteria, and rightly so. Actually, Americans are prone to suffer from mass hysteria with far less provocation. The Washington, D.C., snipers killed ten and wounded three during a three-week "killing spree"; this is relatively minuscule when compared with the Palestinian experience. However, the media stoked a level of mass hysteria about these killings; Americans were even afraid to fill up their SUVs at the gas station—heavens! Americans are entitled to their hysteria about sniper killings, but then they should be aware that they finance the Israel military machine and support Ariel Sharon to the hilt, and therefore they have direct responsibility in the killing of 2.26 Palestinians per day. While in the United States, such numbers would be abhorrent, when it comes to Palestine, Americans even provide the bullets and untold billions of dollars in funding. While the United States justifies "preventive" wars, the abrogation of democracy, and so on, after suffering 3.000 fatalities during 9/11, it lambasts and demonizes a brutalized Palestinian population that is suffering a death toll several orders of magnitude higher in terms of a scaled fatality rate.

Before anyone objects to the use of these scaled numbers, consider that Israel has frequently used such statistics for its own ends—referring exclusively to Israeli casualties.[2]

## Average Fatalities per Month

Graph 10.1 plots the average death toll per month during the second intifada. It has fluctuated depending on Sharon's willingness to play along with "peace processes" and temporarily alternating with his proclivities to demolish Palestinian hopes for an independent state. Thus, during the attack on the West Bank in April 2002, about eight Palestinians were killed every day.[3] While it was convenient for Sharon to play along with the Aqaba peace negotiation appearances, only 0.3 Palestinians were killed per day—the lowest level during the intifada.

What is also evident is the escalation of the fatality rate after July 2003. After the Aqaba summit, it was not possible to obtain any meaningful negotiations because of the inexorable building of the land-grab wall. Inevitably, the ongoing ethnic cleansing and dispossession gave rise to an increasing death toll. From the graph it seems that the Israeli military increase the level of dispossession or killings in a gradual fashion. If they can get away with

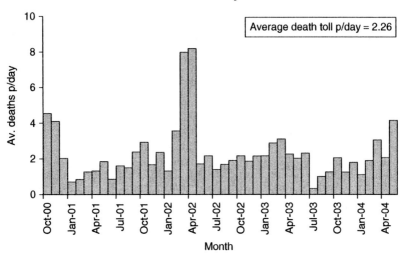

**Graph 10.1**   Average number of Palestinians killed per day during Intifada II

killing four Palestinians per day now, then we can expect a gradual increase in the following months. While killings, destruction, and dispossession remain under a magic threshold level, the media will not consider this to be "news." Even human rights organizations aren't much bothered if the killings remain below this threshold. Of course, if some egregious killings take place, then Amnesty International, the Mother Teresa of human rights organizations, will suggest that the killings "were not proportionate," and occasionally it will utter a condemnation. Killings under the magic threshold are presumably "proportionate" and thus can be ignored.

## And the Wounded

Even when the mainstream media will say something about fatalities, the wounded are mostly ignored. However, consider that Israel uses heavy-duty battlefield weaponry against a mostly defenseless population in densely populated civilian neighborhoods, where the effect of these weapons on their victims is devastating. Even the so-called nonlethal bullets create harrowing wounds; even tear gas can be fatal or cause permanent lung damage. There are tens of thousands of wounded with permanent disabilities,

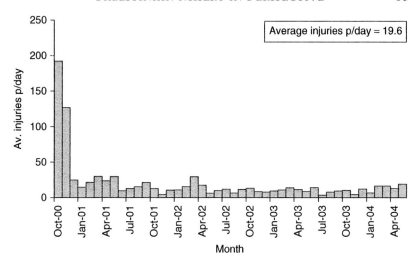

**Graph 10.2**    Average number of Palestinians wounded per day during Intifada II

such as blindness, paraplegia, and loss of limbs. As Graph 10.2 shows, these numbers are staggering, and a tremendous burden for a society already on the edge.

The average number of injured Palestinian victims stands at 19.6 per day (the U.S. scaled equivalent would be 1,540). This number includes victims shot with military high-velocity bullets, the so-called plastic or rubber bullets, tear gas, and other unidentified gases with neurological effects, helicopter gunfire, and other large military ordnance. One must also remember that at the beginning of the intifada, 193 Palestinians were injured on average every day. The Israeli army used millions of bullets during the first month of the intifada—and their effects were all too evident.[4]

## The Nature of the Wounds

While at the beginning of the intifada a significant percentage of the casualties were shot with so-called nonlethal bullets, the ratio of casualties caused by this type of weaponry has fallen significantly. It is increasingly rare to find Israeli soldiers using "plastic bullets" (in reality, plastic-coated bullets); the predilection today is to use "high-velocity bullets." Graph 3 shows

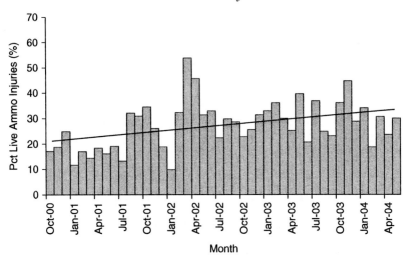

**Graph 10.3**　Live ammo injuries/total injuries

that the percentage of injuries caused by "live ammunition" has increased steadily. In other words, this implies that the use of "nonlethal" bullets and weapons has fallen over time. However, the graph hides some increasing trends. Someone wounded by a missile fired by an Apache helicopter enters the "other" category, and hence it doesn't register as "live ammunition." The reason why the "live ammo" ratio has fallen during the past few months is directly attributable to wounds caused by helicopter or tank fire. Graph 10.3 with the "other" category as a ratio of total injuries shows a steady increase.

## Injuries and Deaths

Graph 10.4 shows the number of injuries in relation to deaths over the same period. Thus, at the beginning of the intifada, there were a large number of injuries for each fatality, and this ratio has fallen steadily. The reason behind the dropping trend is the changing nature of the confrontation. Whereas at the beginning there were many popular demonstrations with a large number of ensuing wounded victims, this has steadily given way to sniper fire or

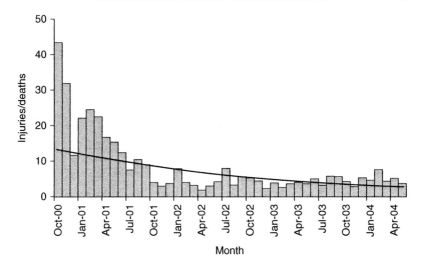

**Graph 10.4**  Injuries vs. deaths ratio

helicopter or tank fire. The latter is more lethal, and the resulting ratio of injuries to fatalities tends to be lower. A reduction in this ratio sometimes implies an increase in the lethality of the Israeli tactics: they are increasingly shooting to kill.

A clear crime committed against Palestinians is the destruction of ambulances, abuse of ambulance staff, and the impediment of access to medical treatment. The summary statistics during the intifada are presented in table 10.2.

The Palestine Red Crescent Society keeps meticulous statistics, and it is worth studying this graph (www.palestinercs.org). If one found that most of the damage occurred during the April 2002 attack, then maybe this would be understandable. However, the recurrent pattern is a steady interference and destruction of Palestinian ambulances; the graph makes this very clear. Even though a so-called peace process was kicked off in July 2003, the level of ambulance destruction continued unabated. One could easily imagine the howls of indignation and disgust if Palestinians were to shoot up an Israeli ambulance or just impede its access. However, destruction of these increasingly important vehicles or even their commandeering by the Israeli military is a media nonevent.

**Table 10.2**   Obstruction and destruction of ambulances in Palestine

| | |
|---|---|
| Attacks on ambulances to date | 302 |
| Total ambulances damaged | 126 |
| Total ambulance personnel injured | 198 |
| Total ambulance personnel killed | 12 |
| Denial of access to ambulances (recorded instances) | 1,376 |
| Number of ambulances damaged beyond repair | 28 |

*Note:* Data refers to the second intifada up to May 28, 2004.
*Source:* Palestine Red Crescent Society.

## Is It Genocide?

It is evident that Israel under Ariel Sharon is pursuing a relentless campaign that aims to drive the Palestinians off the land and dispossess an ever-greater number of people. The construction of the wall is proof that this policy is being implemented. Driving armored Caterpillar bulldozers through refugee camps obviously entails a casualty toll. Similarly, the usually violent suppression of the demonstrations against this policy conjures its own grim statistics. From the graphs we detect a pattern: the repression is systematic, and the severity of its methods is gradually increasing—this is especially apparent after July 2003. In Ariel Sharon's calculus, and with America's blessing, the dispossession and repression of the Palestinians can continue as long as it is performed gradually with a slowly increasing rate. So mass abuses are occurring in the occupied territories today; these are chronic, and indeed systematic. When the scale, intent, and period are taken into account, then one can only conclude that Israel's policy is genocidal.[5] Please note that this is not a conclusion that could only have been reached recently. In December 2, 2000, Francis Boyle, a professor of International Law at the University of Illinois, Urbana-Champaign, stated:

I am sure we can all agree that Israel has indeed perpetrated the international crime of genocide against the Palestinian People.[6]

So who will take responsibility for blowing the whistle and classifying Israeli actions as genocide? Unfortunately, this has to be determined by the UN Commission on Human Rights or the General Assembly, and the legal basis for the classification of genocide is the UN convention against Genocide.[7] There are numerous obstacles before the UN will take any action because of this arrangement. Via a private communication with senior UN personnel, we discover that there has been no movement whatsoever at the UN to determine whether Israel's policies are genocidal, confirming that the UN's role in preventing genocide is hopeless. It is very likely that the UN will not move at all regarding Palestine.

The explanation for the UN's inaction has much to do with the United States' role at the UN; this has been less than constructive, and it will pressure member countries to avoid issuing a "genocide" warning.[8] One only has to remember the United States' efforts prior to February 2004 to block the International Court of Justice's hearings on the land-grab wall; to defend its client it attempted to obstruct this international legal body. Furthermore, the UN Convention against Genocide is very narrowly defined, and it is almost the case that genocide can only be determined after the fact. The convention almost guarantees that there will be no action to prevent genocide or stem an ongoing genocide. Finally, the insufferable Kofi Annan is known for his callousness and inaction in the face of mass slaughter. As the head of UN peacekeeping forces during the Rwandan genocide, he was instrumental in delaying and obstructing UN action. As Michael Hourigan, a UN war crimes investigator in Rwanda, stated, "Consistently, repeatedly people like Kofi Annan failed to act." And the UN's Carlson Commission, an internal inquiry about the Rwandan genocide, actually blamed Kofi Annan and the unit he led.[9] Annan's record of inaction bodes ill for the UN to engage in any action to lend international protection to the Palestinians.

## Data Sources

The data used in this article originate from the Palestinian Red Crescent Society (PRCS)—with one small modification discussed below. This is a high-quality database, and the data originate from the PRCS hospitals and medical staff. The numbers are conflict-related deaths and injuries, which includes all Palestinian killed or injured irrespective of cause. PRCS numbers are closely related to the Health Ministry numbers, but they are not the same. The Palestine Authority (PA) is now publishing its numbers on its website, and data quality has improved over time. The PA's statistics can be found here.[10] Finally, the *Palestine Monitor* also publishes good-quality data and can be found here.[11] The total casualty numbers of these three sources are not equal, yet there is only a minor discrepancy. Part of the reason for the discrepancy has to do with the reported numbers during the April 2002 attack. In many instances, there was no access to hospitals, victims were buried without adequate record keeping, or victims were removed by the Israeli army.

PRCS's approach has been to zero out most of the entries of this period, and thus understates the total casualty figures. The *Palestine Monitor* has imputed some numbers to this period based on interviews with residents and victim exhumations. The approach taken in this article was to use *Palestine Monitor* data for the months that were zeroed out by PRCS. This makes a difference of nineteen fatalities.

## Notes

1. The opposite also happens. That is, if confronted by a particularly egregious Israeli crime, this can be whitewashed by placing it in a wider context. Alternatively, Israeli actions can be juxtaposed with Palestinian violence (suggesting that Israel is only responding to Palestinian action). Thus, the Israelis are only responding.
2. See Israel's "Campaign of Misinformation," *Palestine Monitor*, January 14, 2004.
3. Please note that the statistical record during the April 2002 military assault on the West Bank is incomplete. For example, notwithstanding the UN or Amnesty International reports, it is not known how many people were killed in Jenin or the West Bank during this month. NB: Because the investigation was vetoed by the United States, there was no in-depth investigation of the killings in Jenin.
4. Raji Sourani, lawyer and director of the Palestinian Center for Human Rights in Gaza. Data provided during his "The Worst Yet to Come from Occupied Palestine" lecture in London, October 11, 2002.
5. Mass killings don't need to occur before mass abuses can be classed as genocide. See Ward Churchill, *A Little Matter of Genocide* (San Francisco: City Lights Books, 1997), 399–444.
6. Francis Boyle, "Palestine Should Sue Israel for Genocide before the International Court of Justice," *MediaMonitors*, December 2, 2000.
7. The official name of the convention is the International Convention on the Prevention and Punishment of the Crime of Genocide, UN, 1948.
8. In the late 1940s, the United States sought to wreck and postpone the UN convention on Genocide. It managed to have the principal architect of the convention (Raphael Lemkin) removed; it then reduced the scope of the convention, thereby eliminating its effectiveness in preventing future genocides. Even after wrecking the convention, the United States didn't ratify it but delayed until 1988, when it gave a conditional ratification and ratified it only after adding many provisos that rendered the convention toothless. For an excellent discussion of the American machinations surrounding the convention, see Churchill, *A Little Matter of Genocide*, 363–393.
9. Judi Mcleod, "One Minute for 100 Days of Rwandan Hell," Canada Free Press.com, April 5, 2004. Also important: is Per Ahlmakr, "UN Chief's Career Concluded," *The Australian*, May 3, 2004. The following article also contains important information: Max Teichman, "UN: Kofi Annan and the Rwanda Genocide," *NewsWeekly*, April 24, 2004.
10. Negotiations Affairs Department. www.nad-plo.org.
11. www.palestinemonitor.org.

# CHAPTER ELEVEN

# A Slow, Steady Genocide

## TANYA REINHART

## (INTERVIEWED BY JON ELMER)

## (9-11-2003)

**Jon Elmer, FromOccupiedPalestine.org:**
I would like to begin the discussion with the topic of September 11, given the coming of the second anniversary. In *The Crisis of Islam*, Bernard Lewis writes of September 11: "There are few acts of comparable deliberate and indiscriminate wickedness in human history."[1] Can you comment on this assertion with a view from the Middle East?

**Tanya Reinhart:**
Well, just with a general view, obviously this was an indiscriminate and wicked act, but I don't think it is unprecedented. If you look at the types of things the United States has been doing for years—the atrocities in Vietnam, or of the previous Iraq war where the Iraqi army, after being defeated, was bombarded by the United States as its soldiers were withdrawing.

You could also look at the number of civilians who died in Iraq both from the bombardments and the starvation imposed on them for ten years, which is clearly much more in scope [than the September 11 attacks]. So in terms of scope, there are really many acts comparable in history, many of which the United States itself is responsible for.

What I think is new here is that it wasn't done by an army. We are used to the fact that those killing civilians are military airplanes with sophisticated weapons—then it is a conceivable act. But when it is done not by an army, but by a group with no military means, by a group driven by despair and determination to fight, this is shocking. It also exposed the vulnerability of the strongest power in the world—it turned out that having the most sophisticated military machine was not going to generate security. I think this is the biggest shock of the event for the United States, and for other states.

**Elmer:**
Israeli officials were quick to co-opt and align themselves with American grief and rage after 9/11 to justify escalating the war on the Palestinians. In fact, Netanyahu—the same man who thought that Tiananmen Square provided the perfect cover for the expulsion of Palestinians from Greater Israel back in 1989—was infamously quoted in the *New York Times* on September 12, 2001, saying: "It's very good...well, not very good, but it will generate immediate sympathy."[2] How significant was September 11 for the Israel/Palestine conflict, and specifically for the Palestinians?

**Reinhart:**
Yes, it is true, Israel immediately seized the opportunity opened, from its perspective, by September 11. The Israeli cabinet, Sharon, and the ministers immediately labeled the Palestinian struggle as an instance of global terror, and Israel's oppression of the Palestinians as part of the war against terror. The September 11 attack came a year after Israel launched its own attack on the Palestinians. At that time, military circles, Barak, and later Sharon—figures who were against the Oslo agreements from the start—were working on a grand scale to undo all the arrangements of Oslo, destroy the Palestinian society, and shrink it into smaller and smaller enclaves. They were ready, right from the start, to use the full scale of the military machine against the Palestinians. They got some support from the Clinton administration, but apparently not as much as they had hoped—there were some conflicting views in the U.S. administration. After September 11, Israel succeeded in depicting its project of destroying Palestinian society as part of the war against terror and the Palestinians terrorists. The consequence, at least in the Israeli propaganda, has been that the same means the United States uses in fighting its own terror, Israel can also use in fighting the Palestinians. For the Palestinians, this has had very grave consequences—Operation Defensive Shield [in April 2002, Israel's largest escalation since the 1982 war on Lebanon], in which Israel

invaded all of the West Bank, and the Jenin horrors that came afterward. Ever since, Israel has used all of the U.S. methods, including economic strangulation. Under the pretext of fighting terror, they are freezing all sorts of funds to the Palestinian society. Many of the Hamas funds go to support families that are affected by the siege, the blockades, and the lack of work. The only funds that are still supporting the social infrastructure of the Occupied Territories are often these charity funds, and they are being frozen—all in the name of the war against terror.

**Elmer:**

Gideon Levy wrote in *Ha'aretz* recently: "Every day of quiet in Israel is another day of crass disregard for what is going on in our backyard. If there is no terrorism there are no Palestinians."[3] What is your feeling on that statement?

**Reinhart:**

It is true that the Israelis view the Palestinians only through their effect on Israeli society. It is really amazing how life in Tel Aviv goes on normally when there is no terror. People go about their life, their work, their studies, their coffee shops, while just a few kilometers away, a whole society is dying. What is happening in the Territories is a process of slow and steady genocide. People die from being shot and killed, many die from their wounds—the number of wounded is enormous, it is in the tens of thousands. Often, people cannot get medical treatment, so someone with a heart attack will die at a road block because they cannot get to the hospital. There is a serious shortage of food, so there is malnutrition of children. The Palestinian society is dying—daily—and there is hardly any awareness of this in Israeli society.

The established Israeli peace camp actually collapsed in the Oslo years. From their perspective, they were fully willing to accept that in the Oslo Accords, Israel had in fact given the Palestinians back their land. There were a few technicalities to still go over in the coming years, but essentially the occupation was over. No facts on the ground—like the fact that the number of settlers doubled since Oslo, that the confiscated Palestinian land increased in size, and that the 1 million Palestinians in Gaza were locked in a prison surrounded by massive electronic fences, with the Israeli army guarding the prison from outside—were actually perceived by the Israeli peace camp. So the reaction at the beginning of the Palestinian uprising [September 28, 2000] and its repression was that we Israelis gave the Palestinians everything. We peaceniks were against the occupation, we had agreed to end it, and the Palestinians were extremists who were not willing to accept our offers. Although this has changed somewhat by now, there are still many who view whatever we do in the Territories as self-defense: we have no choice, and, in war there are victims.

But it is important to mention that there are also many Israelis who do see what is happening, and there is a growing group of draft resisters who keep reporting on what they have seen during their reserve service in the Territories, and declare that they will never do this again. There are groups of young Israelis who are going to the Territories and are trying to fight the [separation] wall. The Mas'ha Camp, which is very much grassroots, is a joint project with Palestinians, Israelis, and internationals from the International Solidarity Movement. Together with the villagers who are losing their land to the wall, they built a camp and they stayed for about three months. The camp was dismantled by the army recently, but they are in the process of rebuilding it. And so Palestinians are not transparent to all Israelis. There is some awareness, but it is not in the mainstream.

**Elmer:**
I want to talk to you about the political uses of anti-Semitism. Tel Aviv University has published a report entitled "Anti-Semitism Worldwide" wherein it claims: "The barriers between anti-Semitism and anti-Zionism have been lifted and the two merged."[4] What are your thoughts on conflating anti-Semitism and anti-Zionism?

**Reinhart:**
I haven't seen the specific report, but the claim is of course very widespread. Usually the source of this claim that anti-Zionism is anti-Semitism is Israeli propaganda and its very well-oiled branches of the pro-Israel lobby across the world. The supposition in this claim is that if you look at Israel's behavior, it is essentially all right: it is a country defending itself, and it is doing what is necessary to defend itself—there isn't anything peculiar about it. Therefore there must be some hidden reason why people criticize Israel and object to Israel's acts in the Territories, and what could that reason be if not anti-Semitism? The reason that it is picked on is because it can work—given that there was, and is, anti-Semitism, given the horrible history of the Jewish people, people do have fears of anti-Semitism. But I don't like the term "anti-Zionism" to define opposition to Israeli policies, because Zionism—the way it is perceived by most Israelis—is that Jews are entitled to a state of their own. It is the liberation and self-determination of the Jewish people motivated by the Holocaust and their fate in exile. The

trouble is not exactly with Zionism, but with the Israeli leadership
and the way Zionism has been executed, based on ethnic cleansing
from the very start. I believe it was possible to reach the same goal [of
Jewish self-determination] with much less loss and sacrifice for the
Palestinian people. It is not part of having your own state that it must
be based on striving to grab more and more of your neighbor's land, or
depriving minorities of their rights—this is the Israeli military system's
implementation of the idea of Zionism. So I believe what we should
say is that we are against Israel—meaning Israel's acts and the policy
of its leadership, and against the Occupation, and leave the question of
Zionism aside.

**Elmer:**

In an article in the *Guardian* this past week a British police commissioner said that suicide bombings were "inevitable" in the UK. He
cited the two Britons who carried out the May bombing in Tel Aviv as
a "leap" that was "all about people prepared to give their lives in relation to their causes." He asks: "Why are they created? What motivates
them? The old way of doing things...just doesn't work any more.
They are totally dedicated to their cause. It is quite chilling."[5] On the
other hand, a front-page story in the *Jerusalem Post* on Sunday featured
an Israeli naval commando killed in Nablus. The story spoke of how
"he was ready to die for the state of Israel." His primary goal in life
was to be a naval commando; he worked overtime to pay for the laser
eye surgery he needed to qualify and "he didn't sleep or eat well until
he was accepted." At his funeral, his commander said of him, "You
defended us with your body...[His was] a full life of a warrior of
twenty-three years who finished his task in this world and did it with
honour."[6] Is the commitment and willingness of a Palestinian martyr
to die for his or her cause really a unique phenomenon from that of an
Israeli soldier such as this naval commando?

**Reinhart:**

The willingness to die for your community, for what you believe in,
for your struggle, is really not new and it is really not different from
people dying on the battlefield. So I don't think it is necessarily the
willingness to die that is under consideration. I think that the difference between dying in battle and dying in a terror attack is that
the latter is still a real act of despair—this is something you do when
you are convinced that there is no other channel open to you. Battles
have been organized throughout history to have rules, conventions, a
determined end, means to decide the rights of prisoners...the battle

of the despaired is not subject to any rules or conditions or protections. The best explanation for this growing wave of terrorism is that the present power system closes all other means of struggle that were open to people throughout history. There is no country in the Middle East that could defeat Israel—it has atomic and chemical weapons, it has the best air force in the area—so there is no room anymore for any conventional war with Israel. That is why for Israel, the biggest danger is terror. So the major thing in thinking about terror is thinking about whether there are options left for struggle. If we look at the Palestinian perspective, that is exactly the situation: there is not a thing the Palestinians could do that would satisfy Israel—Israel wants their land, and wants them essentially out of this land. The Palestinians lived quietly under the Israeli occupation during the Oslo years—there was hardly any terror. They accepted essentially the Israeli occupation with some form of self-rule. But that wasn't good enough for the military wing of Israel, whose goal was getting more Palestinian land, and getting them out of even the little they still had.

This is not just an abstract struggle for their land—the Palestinians have impossible life conditions. In history, colonists and occupiers have at times learned to create conditions that enable people to still survive, and to have some reason to live. Israel hasn't been doing that—there are really very few motivations for a young, unemployed person who cannot support his family to want to live. That said, I still believe that not just terror (which is, obviously, profoundly morally wrong), but even armed struggle against the occupying army is the wrong choice, and should not be taken by Palestinian society. The only hope under these conditions, with all other options closed, is still the slow, painful and patient road of civil disobedience—the struggle of the whole of society.

**Elmer:**

With the death of the Road Map, another peace proposal has fallen by the wayside. Is there really a legitimate "peace process?"

**Reinhart:**

Well, legitimate is what the United States decides. But legitimate or not, there is no peace process. There actually never has been. The ceremony of "renewing the peace process" happens periodically—the last time was in March 2002, when the U.S. envoy [Anthony Zinni] was sent to the area to talk about cease-fire. The ceremony ended with the Israeli Operation Defensive Shield and the horrors of Jenin. So I am afraid this latest round, the Road Map, is only the preparation for the next round of bloodshed. If you look at the details of the Road Map, there were a few concrete steps that had to be taken by the Israeli side in the first round. For example, it said that Israel should with-draw immediately to the lines it held in September 2000, when the Palestinian uprising started. Israel made it completely clear that it was not accepting this—which did not stop anybody from presenting Israel as the side that accepted the cease-fire. Same with the dismantling of settlement outposts that was supposed to take place. So it was com-pletely clear that Israel was not fulfilling any of its obligations. It said instead that it would ease conditions in the Occupied Territories, like lift roadblocks. Even that it didn't do. Throughout the whole period of the cease-fire, it was one-sided; Palestinians declared it and kept it, but Israel kept violating it. [In mid-August 2003], there was a big escalation in Israel's aggression and they resumed their assassination policy. It was completely obvious that with these intensive assassina-tions, there would be Palestinian revenge. Israel was doing everything it could to provoke terror. Israel tried to assassinate [Sheikh Ahmed] Yassin, the major spiritual leader of Hamas, who is viewed as such by many Muslims regardless of their organization. Such a direct provoca-tion can only be interpreted as trying to explode the whole situation. But the Israeli understanding is that the perception of the world will again be that Israel tried to obtain peace, and the Palestinians refused to take it.

**Elmer:**
To close, Professor Reinhart, how do we end the war of 1948?[7]

**Reinhart:**
The most obvious way is the one that somehow no one happens to think about: the only way to end an occupation is to get out of the Occupied Territories. In fact, this can be done immediately, within a month or two. The majority of Israeli settlers are concentrated in relatively small settlement blocks. The forty Israeli settlements that are scattered within the Palestinian Territories have very few resi-dents. Despite controlling the land, Israel hasn't actually managed to settle large areas of the West Bank. The majority of these settlers are willing—even begging—to get out and back into Israel, with com-pensation for what they invested. If you ask Israelis, if you pose the idea of immediate unilateral withdrawal in polls—and this is not often done—the answer you get is up to 60 percent support, so it is very easy to convince the Israelis to do this. The only problem is that the Israeli elite, the government, and the army, are still motivated by greed

of land. They want the Palestinian land, and so they have to invent ways of postponing the idea of withdrawal by either the Oslo model— endless negotiations—or by keeping Israeli fears alive, fear that the Jewish state will not survive, and provoking terror. A simple solution like unilateral withdrawal is still possible, and after Israel gets out of most of the territories and the Palestinians get back most of their land, they will start to rebuild their society, democratize, settle, and return refugees. Then there can be a long process of the two people discussing how they want to build the future, together, or side by side, in this one land with two people.

## Notes

1. Bernard Lewis, *The Crisis of Islam* (New York: Modern Library, 2003).
2. James Bennet, "Spilled Blood Is Seen as Bond That Draws Nations Closer," *New York Times*, September 12, 2001.
3. Gideon Levy, "The Empty Square," *Ha'aretz*, September 7, 2003.
4. The Stephen Roth Institute for the Study of Contemporary Anti-Semitism and Racism, "Anti-Semitism Worldwide 2001/2002" (Tel Aviv: Tel Aviv University, 2003).
5. Owen Bowcott, "Recruiting by al-Qaida 'Means Bombs in UK,'" *Guardian*, September 4, 2003.
6. *Jerusalem Post*, September 7, 2003.
7. Tanya Reinhart, *Israel-Palestine: How to End the War of 1948* (New York: Open Media, 2002).

# PART 2

## *Propaganda, Perception, and Reality*

"By way of deception, thou shalt do war."

(Mossad slogan, pre-2007)[1]

"Great is truth, and it prevails."

(3 Esdras, 4:41)

Perception is all too often the stepchild of ignorance and deception. The Mossad's Department of Psychological Warfare understands this as it feeds its global media contacts disinformation and lies to discredit and destroy the Palestinians—and the Arab nations that support them—and elicit sympathy for Israel's elimination of Palestinians. "Nobody speaks the truth when there is something they must have," notes Elizabeth Bowen, who lived during the years of the Israeli theft of Palestine. Yet the Prophet Ezra teaches that truth will prevail. Perhaps its time has come and the veil of deceit regarding Israel can be rent asunder.

What is the true nature of this state of Israel that commands the allegiance of the American people?

- It is a state without mercy, a state without morals, a state premised on racism, a state built on deception and lies;
- a state defiant of international law, the Universal Declaration of Human Rights, and the Geneva Conventions that apply to occupying powers;
- a state, unlike North Korea or Iran, the other identified Axis of Evil states, that has invaded neighboring states and occupies them;
- a state, unlike all nations in the Mid-East, that possesses weapons of mass destruction, including hundreds of nuclear weapons, and refuses to sign the Nuclear Non-Proliferation Treaty;

- a state that uses cluster bombs, white phosphorus, and other internationally banned weapons of warfare, not only against the innocent people of Lebanon, but also against the defenseless people of Palestine;
- a state that proclaims itself above the law as it executes individuals without arrest, without charges brought, without counsel, without habeas corpus, and without trial by jury;
- a state that imprisons over 10,000 Palestinians without charge and without due process;
- a state that tortures those it imprisons;
- a state that constructs a wall, in defiance of the International Court of Justice and the United Nations, that encircles the Palestinians with full intention of decimating their economy and hence their livelihood as well as their chance to create a state of their own, while inflicting a psychological humiliation that is inhumane and in defiance of every principle of the Universal Declaration of Human Rights;
- a state that has systematically confiscated, appropriated, annexed, and assimilated virtually all land belonging to the Palestinians in a sixty-year period of time, leaving them approximately 14 percent of their original land, making it the greatest visible land theft known to human kind in our day;
- a state whose laws protect a group that belongs to a religion and denies equality of citizenship to all others including the indigenous people of the land;
- a state that has defied more than 160 UNGA and 39 UNSC resolutions, demanding it act as a civilized state abiding by international law and protocol;
- a state that will not tolerate interference by the UN in its calculated genocide of the Palestinian people;
- a state that, through its Zionist supporters in America, particularly through the American Israel Public Affairs Committee (AIPAC), influences U.S. policy in the Mid-East that has resulted in the unlawful invasion of Iraq and irrational economic and political procedures against Syria and Iran;
- a state that has convinced our Congress that it provide billions of dollars to ensure that the state of Israel continues this genocide of the Palestinian people;
- a state that proclaims itself a democracy but is not and, with malicious intent, confiscates the money belonging to a democratically elected government in Palestine and arrests their representatives without charge or trial;
- a state that proclaims peace but creates conditions that prevent peace;

- a state that, like the United States under Bush, has reached the nadir of the civilized state, a return to lawless barbarism inflicted on the weak by the strong, the imposition of the will of the few on the many;
- and, finally, in all brazen hypocrisy, a state that cries to the world that it is the victim of unspeakable cruelty and in constant peril of obliteration by forces within and without. And we wonder why the United States is castigated throughout the world when it supports this rogue state, this state without mercy.

Great is truth, sayeth the Prophet, and it shall prevail, if not for those now living perhaps for the dead who have suffered the consequence of this deceit; it is to them, "to the dead," says Voltaire, "we owe only truth."

# CHAPTER TWELVE

## *Gaza's Holocaust*

### Dr. Elias Akleh

### (3-20-2008)

Holocaust is the genocidal crime against people based on their ethnicity. This genocide could be perpetrated through different means such as poison gas, guns, tanks, air raids, biological warfare, economical siege, starvation, destruction of vital natural resources, eviction into desert, and deprivation of basic vital materials, among others, to produce the same result: mass deaths. For the last sixty years Palestinians have been victims of all these methods in a deliberate programmed holocaust. The perpetrators are not Nazis, but those who claim to be survivors (and their descendents) of the Nazi-caused holocaust: Zionist Jewish Israelis.

The threat of the Israeli deputy defense minister, Metan Vinai, to inflict *"bigger Shoah"* (Holocaust) [British Telegraph 2/29] on Gaza's Palestinians reflects the adopted policy of the Israeli government towards Palestinians.[2] Encircled by an eight-meter-high cement wall on three sides and a sea filled with hostile Israeli gun boats on the fourth, Gaza, with a dense population of 1.5 million people, has become the largest concentration camp ever on this globe. The Israeli army acts as the prison guards of this concentration camp. Controlling all sea and air borders, the Israeli army controls and restricts all vital materials going into Gaza. Life in Gaza is dependent on the whims of the Israeli army guarding all crossings into Gaza. They close these crossings whenever they want, for long periods of time, to starve Palestinians. UN reports warn that the majority of Gazans live under the poverty line. To make things worse Israel turned Gaza into a military exercise theatre for its snipers shooting children in the streets, for their special forces conducting offensive operations within civilian areas, for long range artillery practice, for tanks offensive exercises, for navy gun boats shooting exercises, and for air raid targeting. Starting Wednesday February 27th Israeli terrorist army started their "bigger *Shoah*" against Gaza.

This holocaust did not target only Gaza (although Gaza is now suffering its main assault) but also targeted every Palestinian community in the West Bank. There has been a sharp escalation of Israeli military operations averaging at least five operations a day within these communities. Between February 21st and 27th the Israeli terrorist army conducted thirty six military operations, according to Palestinian Human Rights Center. With tanks and armored personnel carriers randomly shooting at everything, the Israeli army attacked Palestinian cities such as Bethlehem, Hebron (Al-Khalil), Nablus, Yatta, Beit Ummar, Dura, Taffuh and others, turning civilian homes into military headquarters and schools into temporary prisons; stealing valuables, destroying properties, demolishing homes, raiding Islamic charity institutions and Young Men Islamic Associations and confiscating their contents, money and records, and sealed them shut. During those seven days the Israeli army kidnapped sixty seven Palestinians, making a total of 499 hostages since the beginning of this year.

Fearing the angry reactions of huge Arab and Islamic populations and indignation from the international community, Israel is perpetrating a graduated Palestinian holocaust, where murdering Palestinians has become a daily occurrence in an attempt to desensitize world opinion. Yet this Palestinian holocaust has all the ugly features of the European Jewish holocaust. Where European Jews suffered from a social racial superiority ideology of the pure Aryan race, the Palestinians are suffering from a more extreme religious superiority ideology of God's chosen people. Where Nazis confiscated Jewish properties, Zionist Israel has confiscated Palestinian properties, homes, farm land and valuables. Where Nazis murdered Jews (including women and children) for no reason except for being a Jew, Israelis are now murdering Palestinians, especially women and children, for no reason except for being Palestinian. Israel has massacred hundreds of whole Palestinian communities and wiped their towns off the map. Where Nazis had imprisoned Jews in concentration camps, Israel is imprisoning all Palestinians in larger concentration camps enclosed within an eight meter high by 760 km long concrete wall that divides Palestinian territories into separate, small concentrations camps, with Gaza Strip being the largest concentration camp ever in the whole world. Where Nazis transferred thousands of European Jews, making them refugees in foreign countries, Israel has transferred thousands of Palestinians out of their own country, making them refugees in desert refugee camps. Where the, then, unorganized international community had blamed Nazi Germany for the Jewish holocaust and allowed Jewish massacres to go on for a long time, the present more organized and supposedly more civilized international community is blaming the Palestinian victims for their own massacres by denying them the basic human right of self defense against Israeli military occupation, and is allowing the murdering Israeli occupation forces to continue the Palestinian holocaust under the guise of self defense. Where Nazis starved their Jewish prisoners, Israel is now starving all Palestinian populations by cutting off food stuff, inflicting economic and financial siege to the territories, and cutting off all energy supplies.

The sad and unfortunate fact about this holocaust is that the political figures and humanitarian organizations who appointed themselves to defend the victims are the same people who implicitly approved, encouraged and allowed the holocaust to continue, either through cooperation with the enemy or by overlooking the genocide. Zionist Jewish leaders and Jewish organizations openly withheld support, financial and otherwise, to save European Jews from death. In 1938 the Jewish Agency headed by Golda Meir ignored the German offer to transfer German Jews to other countries for the price of $250 a head.[3] In February 1940 Henry Montor, executive vice-president of the United Jewish Appeal refused to rescue a shipload of Jews stranded on the Danube River because they were old. He wanted healthy young Jews, instead, to enslave them in establishing the Israeli terror state in the heart of the Arab World.[4] Zionist Jewish leaders rejected German offers in 1941–42 to transfer European Jews to Spain for deportation to the US or to the British colonies, as well as the 1944 offer to safely deport Hungarian Jews to any country except Palestine, knowing very well that such rejection would cause the death of hundreds of thousands of Jews. Yitzhak Greenbaum, chairman of the Rescue Committee of the Jewish Agency expressed such rejection policy in his famous statement "One cow in Palestine is worth more than all the Jews in Europe."[5] The Jewish Agency and Zionist leaders sabotaged the efforts of Rabbi Michael Ber Weissmandl, who pleaded for help from the World Jewish Congress and the Jewish Agency to pay the sum of $50,000 to save the lives of forty thousand Slovakian Jews in 1943[6] (see TV documentary *Among Blind Fools* trilogy by Verafilm).

Despite the imprisonment and death of thousands of their German Jewish brothers, the terrorist military organization "Fighters for Freedom of Israel"— better known as the *Lehi* or *Stern* headed then by Avraham Stern—offered Hitler a proposal in January 1941 to join Germany in its war against Britain in return for German support to establish Israel. (Original document in German

Auswertiges Amt Archiv, Bestand 47–59, E224152 & 234155–58).[7] All these
Zionist Jewish agencies and organizations betrayed their Jewish brothers.

On the Arab side, the first and most prominent traitor to the Palestinians
is their current President Mahmoud Abbas and his gang, who hijacked and
abused the Fatah movement for their own political and financial gains.
Since his appointment as Palestinian Prime Minister in March 2003, Abbas
has shown inclinations towards American and Israeli policies even when
they were harmful to his people, as had been forced on Arafat. He exhibited opposition to Palestinian resistance groups, which became more prominent after his election as President through the help of Israel and the US.
He routinely described Palestinian resistance, especially that of Hamas, as
harmful and silly, and clamped down on them. Through his chief of security, Mohammad Dahlan, Abbas tried to cripple the democratically elected
Hamas government and to sabotage its work, which led to Hamas' purging
of Gaza Strip. Abbas dissolved the Hamas government and appointed a new
one, severing Gaza Strip from the West Bank. He refused to negotiate with
the Hamas government and negotiated instead with Israel, hoping for the
downfall of Hamas. When Hamas survived and gained more popularity,
Abbas recently accused Hamas of harboring Al-Qaeda elements, thus giving Israel an open invitation and a justification to attack Gaza to get rid of
Hamas.

Other Arab leaders, notably from Gulf States, Jordan and Egypt, openly
supported Abbas and overlooked the Israeli genocidal crimes against Gaza.
Many Arab leaders are ready to feed Palestine to the Israeli government in the
hope of stopping its expansionist ambitions. They are either politically naive
or stupid to ignore the Zionist grand plan of Greater Israel. The bitter fact is
that the Palestinian resistance they are conspiring against has blocked Israeli
expansion into more Arab land. Through their silence, and by ignoring the
Palestinian plight, Arab leaders have become partners to Israel in its economic
siege against Gaza, hoping for Gazans to revolt against the Hamas government. This policy has backfired, and despite the Egyptian forces' attempt to
stop them, starving Gazans blew down the border walls separating them from
their Egyptian brothers, and in crashing waves, rushed in to stock up on food
for their families. Ignoring the fact that Palestinians are their brothers, official
Jordanian and Egyptian media and officials portrayed this spontaneous move
as a threat to their national security. Instead of threatening his enemies (the
Israelis) the Egyptian Foreign Minister Ahmad Aboul Gheit threatened to
break the legs of every Palestinian who crosses the border. It seems that he
forgot that those Gazans he is threatening had once been Egyptian citizens,
and many of them still carry Egyptian passports. The pro American/Israeli

policies of many Arab leaders regarding the Palestinian cause are totally opposite to the sentiments of their people, who are becoming increasingly critical of these leaders.

Successive American administrations, specifically the present Bush neoconservative administration, bear a direct responsibility for the Palestinian holocaust due to their unconditional financial, political, and military support to Israel. The American military aid to Israel includes Boeing F-15 and Lockheed F-16 fighter jets, attack Boeing Apaches and Cobra Bells, and missiles manufactured by American corporations such as Hughes/Raytheon, General Dynamics, and Lockheed Martin. All these weapons are paid for by American tax payers.

This military aid to Israel is illegal and immoral. Its illegality stems from the fact that Israel uses these weapons in violation of the American Arms Export Control Act and the Foreign Assistance Act to bolster its occupation of Palestine and to commit genocidal crimes against resisting Palestinians. It is also immoral because such acts are in violation of international laws. Israel uses these weapons to enforce its inhumane collective punishments and economic siege against Palestinians that cause this humanitarian crisis, thus making every single American tax payer an accessory to Israel's crimes. The unconditional American political support to Israel is also immoral and criminal. The Bush administration has hijacked the UN institution, and using its "war against global terror" and its claimed economic assistance as tools in its stick and carrot policy to twist the arms of other countries to adopt the American protection and support of Israel.

Emboldened by the American support and by Arabs' adoption of the peace option, Israel defiantly continues its genocidal and expansion policies. Israel arrogantly rejects any mediation by the international community into what Ehud Olmert called Israel's right to defend itself—ignoring the fact that Israel is the occupational power—and denying Palestinians every basic human right including the right to defend themselves and to resist occupation.

Israeli expansion policy is a twin sister of Nazi "Lebenraum" policy of creating what they called more living space for God's chosen people. Using Hitler's own words this policy was expressed by the Israeli President, Shimon Peres, stating: "We need more room to breathe," of course, at the expense of Palestinians. Zionism is Nazism incarnate.

The Zionist leaders' justification for allowing the Jewish holocaust to continue was that "The European Jews must accede to suffering and death greater in measure than the other nations in order that the victorious allies agree to a Jewish state at the end of the war." I wonder what the Arab leaders' justification is for allowing the Palestinian holocaust to continue?

## Notes

1. Victor Ostrovsky, *By Way of Deception* (St. Martin's Press: New York 1990).
2. *Telegraph*, February 29, 2008. www.telegraph.co.uk.
3. www.palestineremembered.com/Articles/JNF/story1513.html.
4. Rabbi Gedalya Liebermann, "The Role of Zionism in the Holocaust," True Torah, Jews against Zionism, *Wall Street Journal*, December 2, 1976. www.jewsagiagainstzionism.com/antisemitism/holocaust/gedalyaliebermann.cfm.
5. Ibid.
6. Michael Dov Weissmandl, "Pleas to Rescue Jews in the Holocaust Ignored by Zionist Leaders," in *Min Ha-Metzar* (New York: Emunch, 1961).
7. David Yisraeli, *The Palestine Problem in German Politics, 1889–1945* (Bar Ilan University, Ramat Gen, Israel, 1947), 315–317. The original document can be viewed in two locations: Mar Weber, "Zionism and the Third Reich." Institute of Historical Review. www.ihr.org/ihr/v13/v13n4p29_Weber.html. Also see "The Solution of the Jewish Question in Europe and the Participation of the NMO in the War on the Side of Germany, (1941)." www.marxistz.de/middleeast/brenner/urgunazi.htm.

CHAPTER THIRTEEN

# Big Bang or Chaos: What's Israel Up To?

## RAMZY BAROUD

### (3-20-2008)

Why did Israel attack Gaza with such brutality? (Jonathan Cook. "Nakba Again." *Al-Ahram Weekly*. March 6, 2008.) Did Israeli officials think, even for a fleeting moment, that their army's attacks could halt, as opposed to intensify, Palestinian rockets or retaliatory violence? Indeed, was Palestinian violence at all relevant to the Israeli action? Was the Israeli bloodletting in Gaza solely relevant to the Gaza/Hamas context, or is there a regional dimension that is largely being overlooked?

In an *Al-Jazeera* English TV discussion, the Israeli journalist Gideon Levy and the *al-Quds al-Arabi* editor-in-chief Abd al-Bari Atwan attempted to decipher Israel's actions in Gaza, which have, since February 27, 2008, killed more than 120 Palestinians and 4 Israeli soldiers. These attacks were followed by incursions and further violence, including an attack on a Jewish seminary school in Jerusalem.

Levy explained that the Israeli defense minister Ehud Barak wanted to demonstrate to the Israeli public that he was "doing something" about the regular launching of rockets from Gaza. Although Levy wasn't justifying the Israeli government's inhumane and misguided logic, he disagreed with Atwan over the use of terminology. The latter (who is also an outstanding journalist) had asserted that the killings in Gaza represented a form of "genocide" and "ethnic cleansing."

Arab intellectuals, often wary of the use of certain terminology—since Western sensibilities don't accept associating Israel with genocide and ethnic cleansing—became less hesitant after the Israeli deputy defense minister Matan Vilnai warned Palestinians in a radio interview to expect a "bigger Holocaust." But terminology aside, are we to really believe that the wanton killing in Gaza—a major violation of international and humanitarian laws— was meant to send a message to the Israeli public, as Prime Minister Barak claimed, or to carry out genocide for its own sake?

Initially, albeit unsurprisingly, the Palestinian Authority of Mahmoud Abbas seemed oblivious—then, at best, neutral—to the carnage. First, it asked both Israel and Hamas to cease their violence, and then it accused Israel of attempting to "derail" the peace process (what peace process?). Finally, and only after the Vatican thankfully decried the Israeli killings, Abbas announced the halt of all contacts with Israel. A few days later, following a trip by the U.S. secretary of state Condoleezza Rice to the region, Abbas reversed his position. Nabil Abu Rudeineh, spokesman of the presidency, quoted Abbas as stating that "we intend to resume the peace talks with Israel which reserve the aim of ending the occupation."

Considering the heavy toll Palestinians endured by a deliberate Israeli attempt to cause a "bigger holocaust," Abbas's agreement to resume futile chats with the same men who ordered the death of scores of his people is a mockery, to say the least.

While Palestinian, Israeli, and international responses to violence remain predictable, this view still doesn't explain the timing or the underlying objectives of the Gaza attack. Historically, in my view, Israel's behavior—regardless of its outcome—is always politically motivated, and it never fails to keep a regional picture in mind. There are two lines of military logic that Israel resorts to. One is motivated by the "chaos theory," the idea that seemingly minor events accumulate to have complex and massive effects on dynamic natural systems. For example, Gaza might have been attacked with the hope of provoking a streak of suicide bombings that would eventually be blamed on Syrian planning and Iranian financing—thus provoking a major showdown in Lebanon. The history of Israeli-Arab conflicts demonstrates how many major invasions are justified by seemingly irrelevant events, such as the 1982 Lebanon War. But is Israel capable of sustaining another conflict in Lebanon after its miserable—and costly—failure in July–August 2006?

That's when the United States becomes even more relevant. Just as Israeli attacks occupied major headlines around the world, the USS *Cole* and two additional ships—including one amphibious assault vessel—were quietly making their way from Malta to the shores of Lebanon. The ships were dispatched as a "show of support for regional stability," according to U.S. Navy officials.

With the Bush administration's time in office coming to an end and waning public enthusiasm for war against Iran, Israel cannot afford to allow the regional setup to be stacked in the following way: Hezbollah dominating south Lebanon, Hamas dominating Gaza, and Iran becoming an increasingly formidable regional power.

This leads to the other line of Israeli military logic, the "big bang" theory. The self-explanatory logic of this theory is applicable in the sense that a regional war—accompanied by mini civil wars in Palestine and Lebanon, along with other attempts at destabilizing Iran and Syria—could work in Israel's favor.

Under no condition would the United States be able to stay out of such a conflict (considering its regional interests, allies, and own war in Iraq). Revelations of the sinister role played by the Bush administration in organizing and provoking a civil war among Palestinians shows the extent to which Bush is willing to go to achieve Israel's objectives. More, it shows the willingness of various Arab and Palestinian players to readily participate in the bloody and costly U.S.-Israeli ventures.

With all due respect to Levy and Atwan, I think Israel's main aim was neither to send a message to its public nor to commit genocide—though these are not unreasonable possibilities. Indeed, the majority of the Israeli public, according to a Tel Aviv University poll, wished that their government would negotiate a cease-fire with Hamas, as bombs were falling atop the hapless Gaza residents.[1]

The facts—as demonstrated by the U.S.-Israeli role in the turmoil in Lebanon, the consistent attempt to arraign Iran, and the Israeli provocations and bombings in Syria—all indicate that Israel's plans are regional, with Gaza being a testing ground, and the least costly target to isolate and brutalize. Already a massive concentration camp with a largely starving population, Gaza has provided Israel with a perfect opportunity to start sending stern messages to the other players in the region.

## Note

1. E. and Hermann T. Yaar, "Peace Index November 2007," Tel Aviv University and Tami Steinmetz Center for Peace Research (Tel Aviv). http://www.tau.ac.il/peace.

# CHAPTER FOURTEEN

## Israel Plots Another Palestinian Exodus

### JONATHAN COOK

### (3-10-2008)

The Israeli deputy defense minister Matan Vilnai's much publicized remark last week[1] about Gaza facing a *shoah*—the Hebrew word for the Holocaust—was widely assumed to be unpleasant hyperbole about the army's plans for an imminent full-scale invasion of the Gaza Strip. More significantly, however, his comment offers a disturbing indication of the Israeli army's longer-term strategy toward the Palestinians in the Occupied Territories.

Vilnai, a former general, was interviewed by Army Radio as Israel was in the midst of unleashing a series of air and ground strikes on populated areas of Gaza that killed more than 1,000 Palestinians, at least half of whom were civilians and 25 of whom were children, according to the Israeli human rights group B'Tselem. The interview also took place in the wake of a rocket fired from Gaza that killed a student in Sderot and other rockets that hit the center of the southern city of Ashkelon. Vilnai stated: "The more Qassam fire intensifies and the rockets reach a longer range, they [the Palestinians of Gaza] will bring upon themselves a bigger shoah because we will use all our might to defend ourselves." His comment, picked up by the Reuters wire service, was soon making headlines around the world.

Presumably uncomfortable with a senior public figure in Israel comparing his government's policies to the Nazi plan to exterminate European Jewry, many news services referred to Vilnai's clearly articulated threat as a "warning," as though he was prophesying a cataclysmic natural event over which he and the Israeli army had no control. Nonetheless, officials understood the damage that the translation from Hebrew of Vilnai's remark could do to Israel's image abroad. And sure enough, Palestinian leaders were soon exploiting the comparison, with both the Palestinian president Mahmoud Abbas and the exiled Hamas leader Khaled Meshaal stating that a "holocaust" was unfolding in Gaza.

Within hours, the Israeli Foreign Ministry was launching a large *hasbara* (propaganda) campaign through its diplomats, as the *Jerusalem Post* reported. In a related move, a spokesman for Vilnai explained that the word shoah also meant "disaster"; this, rather than a holocaust, was what the minister had been referring to. Clarifications were issued by many media outlets. However, no one in Israel was fooled. Shoah was long ago reserved for the Holocaust, much as the Arabic word *nakba* (or "catastrophe") is nowadays used only to refer to the Palestinians' dispossession by Israel in 1948. Certainly, the Israeli media in English translated Vilnai's use of shoah as "holocaust."

But this is not the first time that Vilnai has expressed extreme views about Gaza's future. Last summer, he began quietly preparing a plan on behalf of his boss, the defense minister Ehud Barak, to declare Gaza a "hostile entity" and dramatically reduce the essential services supplied by Israel—as longtime occupier—to its inhabitants, including electricity and fuel. The cuts were finally implemented late last year after the Israeli courts gave their blessing. Vilnai and Barak, both former military men, like so many other Israeli politicians, have been "selling" this policy—of choking off basic services to Gaza— to Western public opinion ever since.

Under international law, Israel, as the occupying power, has an obligation to guarantee the welfare of the civilian population in Gaza, a fact forgotten when the media reported Israel's decision to declare Gaza a hostile entity. The pair has therefore claimed tendentiously that the humanitarian needs of Gazans are still being safeguarded by the limited supplies being allowed through and that therefore the measures do not constitute collective punishment. Last October, after a meeting of defense officials, Vilnai said of Gaza: "Because this is an entity that is hostile to us, there is no reason for us to supply them with electricity beyond the minimum required to prevent a crisis."

Three months later, Vilnai went further, arguing that Israel should cut off "all responsibility" for Gaza, though, in line with the advice of Israel's attorney general, he has been careful not to suggest that this would punish ordinary Gazans excessively. Instead, he said that disengagement should be taken to its logical conclusion: "We want to stop supplying electricity to them, stop supplying them with water and medicine, so that it would come from another place." He suggested that Egypt might be forced to take over responsibility. Vilnai's various comments are a reflection of the new thinking inside the defense and political establishments about where next to move Israel's conflict with the Palestinians.

After the occupation of the West Bank and Gaza in 1967, a consensus in the Israeli military quickly emerged in favor of maintaining control through a colonial policy of divide and rule, by factionalizing the Palestinians and then keeping them feuding. As long as the Palestinians were too divided to resist the occupation effectively, Israel could carry on with its settlement program and "creeping annexation" of the occupied territories, as the defense minister of the time, Moshe Dayan, called it. Israel experimented with various methods of undermining the secular Palestinian nationalism of the PLO, which threatened to galvanize a general resistance to the occupation. In particular, Israel established local anti-PLO militias known as the Village Leagues and later backed the Islamic fundamentalism of the Muslim Brotherhood, which would morph into Hamas.

Rivalry between Hamas and the PLO, controlled by Fatah, has been the backdrop to Palestinian politics in the occupied territories ever since (c. 1967) and has moved center stage since Israel's disengagement from Gaza in 2005. Growing antagonism fueled by Israel and the United States, as an article in *Vanity Fair* confirmed this week, culminated in the physical separation of a Fatah-run West Bank from a Hamas-ruled Gaza last summer.[2] The leaderships of Fatah and Hamas are now divided not only geographically but also by their diametrically opposed strategies for dealing with Israel's occupation. Fatah's control of the West Bank is being shored up by Israel because its leaders, including President Mahmoud Abbas, have made it clear that they are prepared to cooperate with an interminable peace process that will give Israel the time it needs to annex yet more of the territory.

Hamas, on the other hand, is under no illusions about the peace process, having seen the Jewish settlers leave, but Israel's military control and its economic siege only tighten from arm's length. In charge of an open-air prison, Hamas has refused to surrender to Israeli dictates and has proven invulnerable to Israeli and U.S. machinations to topple it. Instead, it has begun advancing the only two feasible forms of resistance available: rocket attacks over the fence surrounding Gaza and popular mass action. And this is where the concerns of Vilnai and others emanate from. Both forms of resistance, if Hamas remains in charge of Gaza and improves its level of organization and the clarity of its vision, could over the long term unravel Israel's plans to annex the occupied territories—once their Palestinian inhabitants have been removed.

First, Hamas's development of more sophisticated and longer-range rockets threatens to move its resistance to a much larger canvas than the backwater of the small development town of Sderot. The rockets that landed last week (March 3–9, 2008) in Ashkelon, one of the country's largest cities, could be the harbingers of political change in Israel. Hezbollah proved in the 2006 Lebanon war that Israeli domestic opinion quickly crumbled in the face of sustained rocket attacks. Hamas hopes to achieve the same outcome. After the strikes on Ashkelon, the Israeli media was filled with reports of angry mobs taking to the city's streets and burning tires in protest at their government's failure to protect them. That is their initial response. But in Sderot, where the attacks have been going on for years, the mayor, Eli Moyal, recently called for talks with Hamas. A poll published in the *Ha'aretz* daily showed that 64 percent of Israelis now agree with him. That figure may increase further if the rocket threat grows. The fear among Israel's leaders is that "creeping annexation" of the occupied territories cannot be achieved if the Israeli public starts demanding that Hamas be brought to the negotiating table.

Second, Hamas's mobilization last month (February 2008) of Gazans to break through the wall at Rafah and pour into Egypt has demonstrated to Israel's politician-generals such as Barak and Vilnai that the Islamic movement has the potential, as yet unrealized, to launch a focused, peaceful, mass protest against the military siege of Gaza. Meron Benvenisti, a former deputy mayor of Jerusalem, noted that this scenario "frightens the army more than a violent conflict with armed Palestinians." Israel fears that the sight of unarmed women and children being executed for the crime of trying to free themselves from the prison Israel has built for them may give the lie to the idea that the disengagement ended the occupation.

When several thousand Palestinians held a demonstration a fortnight ago (February 28, 2008) in which they created a human chain along part of Gaza's fence with Israel, the Israeli army could hardly contain its panic. Heavy artillery batteries were brought to the perimeter, and snipers were ordered to shoot protesters' legs if they approached the fence. As Amira Hass, *Ha'aretz's* veteran reporter in the Occupied Territories, observed, Israel has so far managed to terrorize most ordinary Gazans into a paralyzed inactivity on this front. In the main, Palestinians have refused to take the "suicidal" course of directly challenging their imprisonment by Israel, even peacefully: "The Palestinians do not need warnings or reports to know the Israeli soldiers shoot the unarmed as well, and they also kill women and children."

But that may change as the siege brings ever greater misery to Gaza. As a result, Israel's immediate priorities are to provoke Hamas regularly into violence to deflect it from the path of organizing mass peaceful protest; to weaken the Hamas leadership through regular executions; and to ensure that an effective defense against the rockets is developed, including technology such as Barak's pet project, Iron Dome, to shield the country from attacks.

In line with these policies, Israel broke the latest period of "relative calm" in Gaza by initiating the executions of five Hamas members last Wednesday (March 5, 2008). Predictably, Hamas responded by firing into Israel a barrage of rockets that killed the student in Sderot, in turn justifying the bloodbath in Gaza. But a longer-term strategy is also required and is being devised by Vilnai and others. Aware that the Gaza prison is tiny and its resources scarce, and that the Palestinian population is growing at a rapid rate, Israel needs a more permanent solution. It must find a way to stop both the growing threat posed by Hamas's organized resistance and the social explosion that will come sooner or later from the Strip's overcrowding and inhuman conditions. Vilnai's remark hints at that solution, as do a series of comments from cabinet ministers over the past few weeks (of February 2008) proposing war crimes to stop the rockets. Prime Minister Ehud Olmert, for example, has said that Gazans cannot be allowed "to live normal lives"; Internal Security Minister Avi Dichter believes that Israel should take action "irrespective of the cost to the Palestinians"; and Interior Minister Meir Sheetrit suggests that the Israeli army should "decide on a neighborhood in Gaza and level it" after each attack.

This week (March 3, 2008), Barak revealed that his officials were working on the last idea, finding a way to make it lawful for the army to direct artillery fire and air strikes at civilian neighborhoods of Gaza in response to rocket fire. They are already doing this covertly, of course, but now they want their hands freed by making it official policy, sanctioned by the international community. At the same time, Vilnai proposed a related idea, of declaring areas of Gaza "combat zones" in which the army would have free rein and from which residents would have little choice but to flee. In practice, this would allow Israel to expel civilians from wide areas of the Strip, herding them into ever smaller spaces, as has been happening in the West Bank for some time. All these measures—from the intensification of the siege to prevent electricity, fuel, and medicines from reaching Gaza to the concentration of the population into even more confined spaces, as well as new ways of stepping up the violence inflicted on the Strip—are thinly veiled excuses for targeting and punishing the civilian population. They necessarily preclude negotiation and dialogue with Gaza's political leaders. Until now, it had appeared, Israel's plan was eventually to persuade Egypt to take over the policing of Gaza, a return to its status before the 1967 war. The view was that Cairo would be even more ruthless in cracking down on the Islamic militants than Israel.

But increasingly, Vilnai and Barak look set on a different course. Their ultimate goal appears to be related to Vilnai's shoah comment: Gaza's depopulation, with the Strip squeezed on three sides until the pressure forces

Palestinians to break out again into Egypt. This time, it may be assumed, there will be no chance of return.

## Notes

1. Reuters, "Israel Warns Gaza of 'Shoah'...," February 29, 2008.
2. David Rose, "The Gaza Bombshell," *Vanity Fair*, April 2008.

# CHAPTER FIFTEEN

## America's Armageddonites

### JON BASIL UTLEY

### (10-11-2007)

Utopian fantasies have long transfixed the human race. Yet today, a much rarer fantasy has become popular in the United States. Millions of Americans, the richest people in history, have a death wish. They are the new "Armageddonites," fundamentalist evangelicals who have moved from forecasting Armageddon to actually trying to bring it about.

Most journalists find it difficult to take seriously that tens of millions of Americans, filled with fantasies of revenge and empowerment, long to leave a world they despise. These Armageddonites believe that they alone will get a quick, free pass when they are "raptured" to paradise, no good deeds necessary, not even a day of judgment. Ironically, they share this utopian fantasy with a group that they often castigate, namely, fundamentalist Muslims who believe that dying in battle also means direct access to heaven. For the Armageddonites, however, there are no waiting virgins, but they do agree with Muslims that there will be "no booze, no bars," in the words of a popular Gaither Singers song.

These end-timers have great influence over the U.S. government's foreign policy. They are thick with the Republican leadership. At a recent conference in Washington, D.C.,[1] the congressional leader Roy Blunt, for example, said that their work is "part of God's plan." At the same meeting, where speakers promoted attacking Iran, the former House majority leader Tom DeLay glorified "end times." Indeed, the Bush administration often consults with them on Mid-East policies. The organizer of the conference, Rev. John Hagee, is often welcomed at the White House, although his ratings are among the lowest on integrity and transparency by Ministry Watch, which rates religious broadcasters. He raises millions of dollars from his campaign supporting Israeli settlements on the West Bank, including much for himself. Erstwhile presidential candidate Gary Bauer is on his board of directors. Jerry Falwell and Pat Robertson also both express strong end-times beliefs.

American fundamentalists strongly supported the decision to invade Iraq in 2003. They consistently support Israel's hard-line policies. And they are beating the drums for war against Iran. Thanks to these end-timers, American foreign policy has turned much of the world against it, including most Muslims, nearly a quarter of the human race.

## The Beginning of End Times

The evangelical movement originally was not focused around "end times." Rather, it was concerned with the "moral" decline inside America. The Armageddon theory started with the writings of a Scottish preacher, John Nelson Darby (1800–1882). His ideas then spread to America with the publication in 1917 of the *Scofield Reference Bible*, foretelling that the return of the Jews to Palestine would bring about the end times. The best-selling book of the 1970s, *The Late, Great Planet Earth*, further spread this message. The movement did not make a conscious effort to affect foreign policy until Jerry Falwell went to Jerusalem and the *Left Behind* books became best sellers.

Conservative Christian writer Gary North estimates the number of Armageddonites at about 20 million. Many of them have an ecstatic belief in the cleansing power of apocalyptic violence. They are among the more than 30 percent of Americans who believe that the world is soon coming to an end. Armageddonites may be a minority of the evangelicals, but they have vocal leaders and control 2,000 mostly fundamentalist religious radio stations.

Although little focused on in America, Armageddonites attract the attention of Muslims abroad. In 2004, for instance, I attended Qatar's Fifth Conference on Democracy with Muslim leaders from all over the Arabian Gulf. There, the uncle of Jordan's king devoted his whole speech to warning of the Armageddonites' power over American foreign policy.

## Armageddonite Foreign Policy

The beliefs of the Armageddon Lobby, also known as Dispensationalists, come from the Book of Revelation, which Martin Luther relegated to an appendix when he translated the Bible because its image of Christ was so contrary to the image of Christ in the rest of the New Testament. The Armageddonites worship a vengeful, killer-torturer Christ. They also frequently quote a biblical passage that says that God favors those who favor the Jews. Based on this biblical interpretation, the Armageddonites vehemently argue that America must protect Israel and encourage its settlements on the West Bank to help God fulfill His plans. The return of Jews to Palestine is central to the prophetic vision of the Armageddonites, who see it as a critical step toward the final battle, Armageddon, and the victory of the righteous over Satan's minions. But they only praise Jews who make war, not those who are peacemakers. For example, they vigorously opposed Israel's murdered premier Yitzhak Rabin, who promoted the Oslo Peace Accords.

There are a couple of internal inconsistencies in this prophecy, such as the presence of Christians already living in the Holy Land and the role of Jews in the final dispensation. In the first case, Jerry Falwell, Pat Robertson, and other religious Right leaders tried to pretend that Christians already in the Holy Land simply didn't exist. As for Jews, they needed to become "born again" Christians to avoid God's wrath (or, according to some Armageddonites, a separate Jewish covenant with God will gain them a separate paradise). Everyone else—Buddhists, Muslims (of course), Hindus, atheists, and so on—are then slated to die in the tribulation that comes with Armageddon. As described in the bestselling *Left Behind* series, this time of human misery ends with Christ then ruling a paradise on earth for a thousand years.

Armageddonites know little about the outside world, which they think of as threatening and awash with satanic temptations. They are big supporters of Bush's "go it alone" foreign policies. For example, they love John Bolton. They were prime supporters for attacking Iraq. And, with very few exceptions, they were noticeably quiet about, if not supportive, of torturing prisoners of war (only with a new leadership did the National Association of Evangelicals finally condemn torture in May, 2007). Their support of Senator Joseph Lieberman (I-CT) and former New York mayor Rudy Giuliani shows that they consider aggressively prosecuting Mid-East war (to help speed up the apocalypse) more important than the domestic programs of these socially liberal politicians. On other foreign policy issues, they are violently against the pending Law of the Seas Treaty, indeed any treaty that possibly circumscribes U.S. power to go it alone. They want illegal immigrants expelled and oppose more immigration. They fear China's growth. They despise Europeans for not being more warlike. The UN figures prominently in their fears, and the *Left Behind* books present its secretary general as the Antichrist. Domestically, they strongly support the USA PATRIOT Act and all of President Bush's actions, legal or illegal.

## Armageddonites and Fascism

Author and former *New York Times* reporter Christopher Hedges argues that the worldview and reasoning of the Armageddonites tend toward fascism. In his book *American Fascists*, Hedges focuses on their obedience to leadership, their feelings of humiliation and victimhood, their alienation, their support for authoritarian government, and their disinterestedness in constitutional limits on government power. Theirs was originally a defensive movement against the liberal democratic society, particularly abortion, school desegregation, and now globalization, which they saw as undermining their communities and families, their values, and livelihood. Their fundamentalism is very fulfilling and, Hedges writes, "They are terrified of losing this new, mystical world of signs, wonders and moral certitude, of returning to the old world of despair."[2]

Hedges, a graduate of Harvard Divinity School, also shows that fundamentalists are quite selective. They don't take the Bible literally when it comes to justifying slavery or arguing that children who curse a parent are to be executed. The movement is also very masculine, giving poor men a path to reestablish their authority in what they perceive as an overly feminized culture. Their images of Jesus often show Him with thick muscles, clutching a sword. Christian men are portrayed as powerful warriors.

The overwhelming power and warmongering of the Armageddonites has inspired some resistance from other fundamentalists, but they are a minority. Theologian Richard Fenn writes, "Silent complicity (by mainline churches) with apocalyptic rhetoric soon becomes collusion with plans for religiously inspired genocide."[3] Their death-wishing "religion" is actually anti-Christian and should be challenged openly by traditional Christians.

The next election will likely loosen their grip on the White House. However, their growing ties to the military industrial complex will remain. Exposure of their war mongering as a major threat to America and the world may well become as destructive for them as was the famous Scopes trial in the 1920s. But that will only happen if Americans become as concerned as foreign observers about the influence of the Armageddonites.

## Notes

1. "Christians United for Israel" Conference, hosted by Pastor John Hagee of the Cornerstone Church in San Antonio, TX, May 8, 2007.
2. Chris Hedges, *American Facism* (New York: Simon and Schuster, 2007).
3. Richard Fenn, *Dreams of Glory* (Surrey: Ashgate Publishing, 2006), 60.

# CHAPTER SIXTEEN

## Does It Matter What You Call It?
## Genocide or Erasure of Palestinians?

### KATHLEEN AND BILL CHRISTISON

### (11-27-2006)

During an appearance in late October 2006 on Ireland's Pat Kenny radio show, a popular national program broadcast daily on Ireland's *RTE Radio*, we were asked as the opening question whether Israel could be compared to Nazi Germany. Not across the board, we said, but there are certainly some aspects of Israel's policy toward the Palestinians that bear a clear resemblance to the Nazis' oppression. Do you mean the wall? Kenny prompted, and we agreed, describing the ongoing ghettoization in Palestine and other effects of this monstrosity. Before we could elaborate on other Nazi-like features of Israel's policies, Kenny moved on to another question. Within minutes, while we were still on the air, a producer handed Kenny a note, which we later learned was a request from the newly arrived Israeli ambassador to Ireland to appear on the show, by himself. Several days later, on the air by himself, the ambassador pronounced us and our comparisons of Israeli and Nazi policies "outrageous."

We were not surprised or disturbed by his outrage. We had just spent two weeks in the West Bank witnessing the oppression, and it was a sure bet that, even had he not been fulfilling his role as propagandist for Israel, the ambassador would not have known the first thing about the Palestinian situation in the West Bank because he had most likely not set foot there in any recent year. In retrospect, we regret not having used even stronger language. Having at that point just completed our fifth trip to Palestine since early 2003, we should have had the courage and the insight to call what we have observed Israel doing to the Palestinians by its rightful name: genocide. We have long played with words about this, labeling Israel's policy "ethnocide," meaning the attempt to destroy the Palestinians as a people with a specific ethnic identity. Others who dance around the subject use terms like "politicide" or, a new invention, "sociocide," but neither of these terms implies the large-scale destruction of people and identity that is truly the Israeli objective. "Genocide"—defined by the UN Convention as the intention "to destroy, in whole or in part, a national, ethnical, racial, or religious group"—most aptly describes Israel's efforts, akin to the Nazis', to erase an entire people.[1]

In fact, it matters little what you call it, so long as it is recognized that what Israel intends and is working toward is the erasure of the Palestinian people from the Palestine landscape. Israel most likely does not care about how systematic its efforts at erasure are, or how rapidly they proceed, and in these ways it differs from the Nazis. There are no gas chambers; there is no overriding urgency. Gas chambers are not needed. A round of rockets on a residential housing complex in the middle of the night, a few million cluster bombs, or phosphorous weapons can, given time, easily meet the criteria for genocide according to the UN definition above.

Children shot to death sitting in school classrooms here, families murdered while tilling their land there; agricultural land stripped and burned here, farmers cut off from their land there; little girls riddled with bullets here, infants beheaded by shell fire there; a little massacre here, a little starvation there; expulsion here, denial of entry and families torn apart there; dispossession is the name of the game. With no functioning economy, dwindling food supplies, medical supply shortages, no way to move from one area to another, no access to a capital city, no easy access to education or medical care, no civil service salaries, the people will die, the nation will die without a single gas chamber. Or so the Israelis hope.

## Surrender versus Resistance

A major part of the Israeli scheme—apart from the outright land expropriation, national fragmentation, and killing that are designed to strangle and destroy the Palestinian people—is to so discourage the Palestinians psychologically that they will simply leave voluntarily, if they have the money, or give up in abject surrender and agree to live quietly in small enclaves under the Israeli thumb. You wonder sometimes if the Israelis are not succeeding in this bit of psychological warfare, as they are succeeding in tightening their physical stranglehold on territory in the West Bank and Gaza. Overall, we do not believe they have yet brought the Palestinians to this point of psychological surrender, although the breaking point for Palestinians appears nearer than ever before.

The anger and depression, even despair, in Palestine are palpable these days, far worse than we have previously encountered. We met two Palestinians so discouraged that they are preparing to leave, in one case uprooting their family from a Muslim village where roots go back centuries. The other case is a Christian young person, also from an old family, who sees no prospects for herself or anyone and who feels betrayed by the Catholic Church for having abandoned Palestine's Christians. She would rather just be elsewhere. A Palestinian pollster who has tracked attitudes toward emigration recently reported that the proportion of people thinking about leaving has jumped from about 20 percent, where it has long hovered, to 32 percent in a recent poll, largely because of despair arising from intra-Palestinian factional fighting and from Hamas's inability to govern, thanks to crippling Israeli, U.S., and European sanctions.[2]

Nothing like one-third of Palestinians will ultimately leave or even attempt to leave, but the trend in attitudes clearly points to the kind of despair that is afflicting much of Palestine. One thoughtful Palestinian writer with whom we spent an evening feels so defeated and so oppressed by Israeli restrictions that he thinks Hamas should abandon its principled stand and agree to recognize Israel's right to exist, in the hope that this concession might induce the Israelis to lift some of the innumerable restrictions on Palestinian life, end the military siege on Palestinian territories and the land theft, and in general ease the day-to-day misery that Palestinians endure under occupation. Asked if he thought such a major Hamas concession would actually bring meaningful Israeli concessions, he said no, but perhaps it would ease the misery a little. It was clear he holds out no great hope. His village's land is gradually disappearing underneath the separation wall and expanding Israeli settlements.

We met Westerners who have lived in the West Bank, working on behalf of the Palestinians for various NGOs for a decade and more, who are planning to leave out of frustration at seeing the situation worsen year after year and their own work increasingly go for naught. Many other Western human rights workers and educators, particularly at venerable institutions such as the Friends' School in Ramallah and Bir Zeit University, are being denied visas by the Israelis as part of their deliberate campaign to keep out foreign passport holders, including thousands of ethnic Palestinians who have lived in the West Bank with their families and worked there for years. The Israeli campaign to deny residency and reentry permits is a deliberate attempt at ethnic cleansing, a hope that if a husband or wife is barred, he or she will remove the rest of the family, and Israel will have fewer Palestinians to deal with. In addition, the entry-denial campaign targets in particular anyone, Palestinian or international, who might bring a measure of business prosperity, education, medical assistance, or humanitarian assistance to the Palestinian territories.

The campaign against foreigners who might help the Palestinians or bear witness for them became particularly vicious in mid-November when a nineteen-year-old Swedish volunteer with the International Solidarity Movement escorting Palestinian children to school was brutally attacked by Israeli settlers in Hebron as Israeli soldiers watched. The young woman, Tove Johansson, was walking through an Israeli army checkpoint with several other volunteers when they were set upon by a group of approximately one hundred settlers chanting, "We killed Jesus, we'll kill you too!" A settler hit Johansson in the face with a broken bottle, breaking her cheekbone, and as she lay bleeding on the ground, the settlers cheered and clapped and took pictures of themselves posing next to her. The Israeli soldiers briefly questioned three settlers but made no arrests and conducted no investigation. In fact, they threatened the international volunteers with arrest if they did not leave the area immediately. The assault was so raw and brutal that Amnesty International issued an alert, warning internationals to beware of settler attacks. The U.S. media have not seen fit to report the incident, which was clearly part of a longstanding effort to discourage witnesses to Israeli atrocities and deprive Palestinians of any protection against the atrocities.[3]

Palestinian resistance does figure in this dismal story. In the same small village where one of our acquaintances is uprooting his family, others are building—small homes and multistory apartment buildings—simply as a sign of resistance. International human rights volunteers are still trying to reach the West Bank and Gaza to assist Palestinians. When we told one Palestinian friend about our conversation with the writer who wants Hamas to concede Israel's right to exist, his immediate reaction was "absolutely not." He is himself a secular Muslim, a Fatah supporter, does not like Hamas, and did not vote for Hamas in last January's legislative elections, but he fully supports Hamas's refusal to recognize Israel's right to exist until Israel recognizes the right of the Palestinian people to exist as a nation. "Why should I recognize you until you get out of my garden?" he wondered.

Our friend Ahmad's views reflect the general feeling among Palestinians: a poll conducted in September by a Palestinian polling organization found that 67 percent of Palestinians do not think Hamas should recognize Israel in order to satisfy Israeli and international demands, while almost the same proportion, 63 percent, would support recognizing Israel if this came as part of a peace agreement in which a Palestinian state was established—in other words, if Israel also recognized the Palestinians as a nation. Surrender is not yet on the horizon.[4]

On the possibility of pulling up stakes and leaving Palestine, Ahmad was equally adamant. "Why should I leave and then have to fight to get back later? Empires never last." He mentioned the Turks and the British and the Soviets, adding, "and the Americans and the Israelis won't last either. It may take a long time, but we can wait." He was angrier than we have ever previously seen him, and more uncompromising—and with good reason: the separation wall is now within a few yards of his home, and demolition is threatened. Ahmad and some neighbors have been fighting the wall's advance in court and succeeded in stopping it for over a year, but construction is moving ahead again. He already has to drive miles out of his way to skirt the wall on his way to work and will be able to exit only on foot when the wall is completed—assuming that his house is not demolished altogether. But he is not giving up. He thinks suicide bombers are "a piece of shit," but he believes the Palestinians have to resist in some way, if only by throwing stones, and he sees some kind of explosion in the offing. If Palestinians do nothing at all, he said, "the Israelis will just relax" and will feel no pressure to cease the oppression.

Palestinians everywhere are keeping up the pressure. *Ha'aretz* correspondent Gideon Levy described a cloth banner displayed in Beit Hanoun immediately after Israel's devastation of that small Gaza city during the first week in November 2006. "Kill, destroy, crush—you won't succeed in breaking us," declared the banner.[5]

Palestinians in Beit Hanoun, as well as throughout Gaza and the West Bank, have been putting up resistance to their own incompetent, quisling leadership, as well as to Israel. It has not escaped the notice of the Palestinian man in the street that, while Israel slaughters men, women, and children in Beit Hanoun and continues its march across the West Bank, Palestinian Authority president Mahmood Abbas has been cooperating with the United States and Israel to undermine the democratically elected Hamas government. The United States is arming and training a militia that will protect Abbas's and Fatah's narrow factional interests against Hamas's fighters, in what can only be termed an open coup attempt against the legally constituted Palestinian government.[6]

Few Palestinians, even Fatah supporters, condone this U.S. interference or Abbas's traitorous acquiescence. "Fatah are thieves," a local leader who is a Fatah member himself told us. "Hamas won because we wanted to get rid of the thieves." He thinks that if there were an election today, "ordinary people"—by which he means people not associated with either

Fatah or Hamas—would win. In each house, he said, "we find one son with Hamas, another son with Fatah, so how is a father going to support one or the other?" It is perhaps this knowledge that they cannot fight each other without destroying the nuclear and the broader Palestinian family, and that they must not succumb to Israeli and U.S. schemes to fragment Palestinian society, that has motivated intensive Palestinian efforts to achieve some kind of unity in government.

## Around the West Bank

In Bil'in, the small town west of Ramallah that has seen a nonviolent protest against the wall by Palestinians, Israelis, and internationals every Friday for almost two years, the village leader, Ahmad Issa Yassin, talked about the lesson his youngest son learned after being arrested last year at age fourteen in an Israeli raid. "He is more courageous now, more ready to resist," Yassin said. "So am I." We first met this boy, a particularly friendly young man with a sweet smile, a few months before his arrest. He greeted us again this year with another warm smile and bantered with us as we took his picture. He gave no hint of having spent two months in one of Israel's worst prisons or of the horror of having been arrested in a Nazi-style middle-of-the-night raid. Perhaps he threw stones at the Israeli soldiers who converged on his village at least once a week and responded to nonviolent Palestinian protests with live ammunition, rubber bullets, teargas, concussion grenades, and batons. This boy was no terrorist. However, the Israelis may have turned him into a young man willing to fight terror with terror a few years from now.

Yassin walked us to his olive grove, half destroyed, on the other side of the wall. The Israelis allow the villagers access to lands that now lie on Israel's side of the wall, but there is only one gate, manned by Israeli soldiers who may or may not bestir themselves to open it. The villagers' names are all on a list of Palestinians authorized to pass through the gate. At this particular village, one of many whose lands have been cut off from the village, protesters have established an outpost or, as they call it, a "settlement," on the Israeli side to stake a claim to the land for the village even though it now lies on Israel's side in the path of an expanding Israeli settlement. The Palestinian "settlement" consists of a small building, a tent where a couple of activists maintain a constant vigil, and a soccer field for a bit of normality.

Yassin took us uphill on a dirt path running alongside the wall, which in this rural area consists of an electronic fence, a dirt patrol road on each side where footprints can be picked up, a paved patrol road on the Israeli side, and coils of razor wire on each side—encompassing altogether an area about fifty meters wide, where olive groves once stood. We waited at the gate in the electronic fence while Yassin called several times to the Israeli soldiers, whom we could see lounging under a tent canopy on a nearby hillside. When they finally came to the gate, they checked Yassin's name against their list of permitees, recorded our names and passport numbers, and officiously warned us against taking pictures in this "military zone." As we made our way cross-country to the Bil'in outpost, Yassin pointed out olive trees burned and uprooted by Israelis and, at the outpost right next to the stump of a tree that had been cut down, a new tree sprouting from the old one.

We talked for a while with a Palestinian activist from the village and a young British activist, both of whom had been sleeping late into the morning, after enjoying a Ramadan meal, the *Iftar,* late the night before. When we returned to the gate, the Israeli soldiers were even slower arriving to open it, obviously totally bored with their duty. The following Friday at the weekly protest, they enjoyed a little more excitement as protesters managed to erect ladders to scale the fence. The soldiers responded with batons and teargas.

The resistance goes on, but so does the Israeli encroachment. We took away with us two striking impressions: the little olive tree being carefully nurtured as a sign of renewal and resistance and, in the near distance, the constant sound of bulldozers and earth-clearing equipment working on the Israeli settlement of Modiin Illit, being built on the lands of Bil'in and other neighboring villages.

Elsewhere, signs of the Israeli advance override the continuing signs of Palestinian resistance. In the small village of Wadi Fuqin southwest of Bethlehem, a beautiful village sitting in a narrow, fertile valley between ridge lines that is being squeezed on one side by the wall, still to be constructed, and on the other by the already large and rapidly expanding Israeli settlement of Betar Illit, we saw more destruction. The settlement is dumping vast tonnages of construction debris down onto the village, so that its fields are gradually being swallowed. This was more evident this year than when we visited last year. The settlement's sewage often overflows onto village land through sewage pipes evident high up on the hillside. Israeli settlers swagger through the village increasingly, as if it were theirs, swimming in the many irrigation pools that are fed by natural springs dating back to Roman times.

In the village of Walaja, not far away to the north, nearer Jerusalem, Ahmad took us to visit friends of his. The village is scheduled to be surrounded completely by the wall because it sits near the Green Line in the midst of a cluster of Israeli settlements. We sat in a garden of fruit trees with a family whose house is on a hill overlooking a spectacular valley and hills beyond. Jerusalem sits on another hill in the distance. We commented that, except for the Israeli settlements across the valley, the place is like paradise, but our host responded with a cynical laugh that actually it is hell. Even beautiful scenery loses its appeal when one is trapped and surrounded.

In another encircled village that we visited last year, Nu'man, the approximately two hundred residents are also trapped between the wall, now completed, on one side and the advancing settlement of Har Homa, which covets the village land, on the other. Although last year, with the wall incomplete, we could drive in, this year we were denied entry at the one gate in. With Ahmad, we tried to talk to four obviously intimidated young Palestinian men waiting across the patrol road from the gate to gain entry to their homes, but the Israeli soldiers told them not to talk to us; one of them said a few words to Ahmad but never took his eyes off the Israeli guard post. We drove off and left them to their plight. We could have tried to get to the village with an arduous cross-country walk, but we did not.

## "Grand" Terminals

With the near completion of the separation wall, the Israelis have systematized the West Bank prison. Since August 2005, the number of checkpoints throughout the West Bank has risen 40 percent, from 376 to 528, according to the UN Office for the Coordination of Humanitarian Affairs (OCHA), which carefully tracks the numbers and types of Israeli checkpoints, as well as other aspects of the Israeli stranglehold on the Palestinians.[7] As part of the systematization, a series of elaborate terminals now manages the humiliation of Palestinians at major checkpoints, particularly around Jerusalem. The terminals are huge cages resembling cattle runs, which direct foot traffic in snaking lines that double back and forth. At the end of the line is a series of turnstiles, x-ray machines, conveyor belts, and other accoutrements of heavy security. Any Palestinian entering Jerusalem from the West Bank to work, to visit family, to pray at al-Aqsa Mosque or the Church of the Holy Sepulchre, to go to school, or to seek medical treatment must have a hard-to-obtain permit from Israel. The turnstiles and other security barriers are controlled remotely by Israeli soldiers housed behind heavy bullet-proof glass.

The cages are currently painted a bright, cheerful blue, but it's a fair bet that when they are older and worn, the paint job will not be renewed. Adding to the false cheer, the Israelis have erected incongruous welcoming signs at the terminals. Most egregious is the giant sign at the Bethlehem terminal. "Peace be with you," it proclaims in three languages to travelers leaving Jerusalem for Bethlehem. This is on a giant pastel-colored sign erected by the Israeli Ministry of Tourism, as if travel through this terminal were the ordinary tourist lark. At the Qalandiya terminal between Ramallah and Jerusalem, a large cartoon-like red rose welcomes Palestinians with a sign in Arabic. When the terminal was first opened, the rose was on a sign that proclaimed, in three languages, "The hope of us all." Apparently embarrassed at being caught so red-handed in their hypocrisy, the Israelis removed the sign, preserving only the rose, after a Jewish activist stenciled over it the words that once graced the entrance to Auschwitz, "*Arbeit Macht Frei*" (work makes you free). There is still a sign saying in three languages, "May you go in peace and return in peace." The Israelis still don't really get it.

Nor do the Americans. The terminals, advertised as a way to "ease life" for Palestinians by prettying up the checkpoints of old and making passage more efficient, were paid for out of U.S. aid monies designated originally for the Palestinian Authority (before the Hamas election) but diverted to Israel's terminal-building enterprise—helping Israel make Palestinian humiliation more efficient. Steven Erlanger in the *New York Times*, among others, fell for the scam, noting when the Bethlehem terminal opened in December last year that the terminals were aimed at "easing the burden on Palestinians and softening international criticism." He labeled the Bethlehem terminal a "grand" gateway for Christians visiting Jesus' birthplace—not acknowledging that Christians had been visiting for two millennia without the benefit of turnstiles and concrete walls.[8]

The burden on Palestinians has not been significantly eased as far as we could tell. We spent some time watching at several of the terminals—feeling like voyeurs of Palestinian misery. At Qalandiya, about one hundred people stood waiting to pass through three locked turnstiles. A young Israeli woman soldier sat in a glassed-in control booth barking commands at them. Our friend Ahmad speaks Hebrew as well as Arabic and could not even make out which language she was speaking in. There was no reason for her anger or for her decision to lock the turnstiles. When she saw us observing, carrying a camera, she shook her finger in an apparent warning against taking pictures. They don't like witnesses. Immediately after this, she unlocked the turnstiles. We walked through after everyone else who had been waiting, and Ahmad took us to the waiting area on the other side, where Palestinians from the West Bank apply for permits to enter Jerusalem. About fifty people were waiting. A middle-aged man walked up to us and began telling his story. He was scheduled for neurosurgery at Maqassad Hospital in East Jerusalem in two days, according to a certificate from the hospital, written in English and clearly intended for Israeli permit authorities. He had already been waiting for six days—three futilely sitting in this waiting area and a previous three when the Israelis had closed the terminal altogether for Yom Kippur. He was beginning to fear he would never get his permit and, as he expressed his frustration and desperation, he began to cry. He asked that we take his picture holding the certificate and tell the world. We did, but we will never know whether he obtained his permit in time, or at all.

At another terminal, leading from al-Azzariyah, the biblical Bethany, into Jerusalem, a soldier screamed at us—quite literally, his face red, blood vessels standing out on his neck—when he saw us taking pictures of his soldier colleagues questioning Palestinians before they entered the terminal area, a prescreening for the screening at the terminal. We told the soldier we thought pictures would be all right; this terminal was run after all by the Ministry of Tourism and so must be a tourist attraction. But our flippancy didn't go over well. He pushed us toward an exit gate, screaming that this was the "Ministry of Gates" and that we had to get out. We managed to remain inside until Ahmad, who was talking to another Israeli soldier, finished and exited with us. Maybe we saved one or two Palestinians from scrutiny by distracting a couple of soldiers—or maybe unfortunately we just delayed them further.

At a third checkpoint, this a makeshift one set up temporarily at an opening in the wall where the concrete barrier is still incomplete, we watched as a growing crowd of Palestinians wanting to enter Jerusalem to pray at al-Aqsa Mosque tried to negotiate with two young Israeli soldiers. It was a Friday in Ramadan and, although these Palestinians had permits to enter Jerusalem, their names were not on the authorized list at this particular checkpoint. They had to go, according to Israel's administrative fiat, to the main terminal from their area into the city. As the crowd gathered, more Israeli soldiers arrived. The crowd included women as well as men, and several children. Being watched by a couple of Americans who probably appeared more patronizing than helpful, clearly did not improve the mood of most of the crowd.

One little boy of about five, dressed neatly in a tie and pressed white shirt, stood looking at the commotion for a few minutes, standing slightly apart from his father, and suddenly burst into tears. A few minutes later, the soldiers exploded a concussion grenade, and most of the crowd dispersed. It's the Israeli way: make them cry, run them off in fear. We left, embarrassed by our own inadequacy.

## Terminology

Is it genocide when a little boy is made to cry because belligerent armed men intimidate him, intimidate his father, and ultimately run them off; when they are forbidden from performing their religious ceremonies because a belligerent government decides they are of the wrong religion; when their town is encircled and cut off because a racist state decides their ethnic identity is of the wrong variety?

You can argue over terminology, but the truth is evident everywhere on the ground where Israel has extended its writ: Palestinians are unworthy and inferior to Jews, and in the name of the Jewish people, Israel has given itself the right to erase the Palestinian presence in Palestine—in other words, to commit genocide by destroying "in whole or in part, a national, ethnical, racial, or religious group."

As we debate about and analyze the Palestinian psyche, trying to determine whether they have had enough and will surrender or will survive by resisting, it is important to remember that the Jewish people, despite unspeakable tragedy, emerged from the Holocaust ultimately triumphant. Israel and its supporters should keep this in mind: empires never last, as Ahmad said, and gross injustice such as the Nazis and Israel have inflicted on innocent people cannot prevail for long.

## Notes

1. William Cook, "The Rape of Palestine," *Counterpunch*, January 1–7/8, 2006.
2. See Ismail Lubbad, "Migration and Refugee Movement in the Mid-East and North Africa," Ph.D. thesis, American University, Cairo. October 23–25, 2007. A draft of Lubbad's unpublished dissertation was made available in 2006.
3. Chez Twosrat, "Jewish Settlers to Christians in Hebron 'We Killed Jesus and We'll Kill You Too.'" www.cheztwosrat.blogspot.com/2006/12/jewish-settlers--to-christians-in.html.
4. "Results of Palestinian Public Opinion Poll No. 23," September 7–9, 2006. www.zajel.org/article_view.asp?newsID=87418cat=17.
5. Gideon Levy, "The Twilight Zone/After the Rain Death," *Ha'aretz*. November 22, 2006.
6. *USA Today*, "Fatah deploys new militia in West Bank," June 3, 2006.
7. UN Office for the Coordination of Humanities Affairs on Israeli Checkpoints 2006. www.ochaonline.un.org/documents_Gaza_Situation_Report_8_Nov_2006_Eng.pdf.
8. Steven Erlanger, "Israel Is Easing the Barrier Borders, But Palestinians Still See a Border," *New York Times*. December 22, 2005.

# CHAPTER SEVENTEEN

## The Problem with Israel

### JEFF HALPER

### (11-23-2006)

Let's be honest (for once): The problem in the Middle East is not the Palestinian people, not Hamas, not the Arabs, not Hezbollah, not the Iranians, and not the entire Muslim world. It's us, the Israelis. The Israeli-Palestinian conflict, the single greatest cause of instability, extremism, and violence in our region, is perhaps the simplest conflict in the world to resolve. For almost twenty years, since the PLO's recognition of Israel within the 1949 Armistice Lines (the "Green Line" separating Israel from the West Bank and Gaza), every Palestinian leader, backed by large majorities of the Palestinian population, has presented Israel with a most generous offer: a Jewish state on 78 percent of Israel/Palestine in return for a Palestinian state on just 22 percent—the West Bank, East Jerusalem, and Gaza. In fact, this is a proposition supported by a large majority of both the Palestinian and Israeli peoples. As reported in *Ha'aretz* (January 18, 2005),

> Some sixty three percent of the Palestinians support the proposal that after the establishment of the state of Palestine and a solution to all the outstanding issues—including the refugees and Jerusalem—a declaration will be issued recognizing the state of Israel as the state of the Jewish people and the Palestinian state as the state of the Palestinian people... On the Israeli side, seventy percent supported the proposal for mutual recognition.

And if Taba and the Geneva Initiative are indicators, the Palestinians are even willing to "swap" some of the richest and most strategic land around Jerusalem and up through Modi'in for barren tracts of the Negev. What about the refugees, supposedly the hardest issue of all to tackle? It's true that the Palestinians want their right of return acknowledged. After all, it is their right under international law. They also want Israel to acknowledge its role in driving the refugees from the country in order that a healing process may begin (I don't have to remind anyone how important it is for us Jews that our suffering be acknowledged). But they have said repeatedly that when it comes to addressing the actual issue, a package of resettlement in Israel and the Palestinian state, compensation for those wishing to remain in the Arab countries, and the possibility of resettlement in Canada, Australia, and other countries would create solutions acceptable to all parties. Khalil Shkaki, a Palestinian sociologist who conducted an extensive survey among the refugees, estimates that only about 10 percent, mainly the aged, would choose to settle in Israel, a number (about 400,000) Israel could easily digest.[1]

With an end to the occupation and a win-win political arrangement that would satisfy the fundamental needs of both peoples, the Palestinians could make what would be perhaps the most significant contribution of all to peace and stability in the Middle East. Weak as they are, the Palestinians possess one source of tremendous power, one critical trump card: they are the gatekeepers to the Middle East. For the Palestinian conflict is emblematic in the Muslim world and encapsulates the "clash of civilizations" from the Muslim point of view. Once the Palestinians signal to the wider Arab and Muslim worlds that a political accommodation has been achieved that is acceptable to them, and that now is the time to normalize relations with Israel, the forces of fundamentalism, militarism, and reaction will be significantly undercut, giving breathing space to those progressive voices that cannot be heard today—including those in Israel. Israel, of course, would also have to resolve the issue of the Golan Heights, which Syria has been asking it to do for years. Despite the neocon rhetoric to the contrary, anyone familiar with the Middle East knows that such a dynamic is not only possible but would progress at a surprisingly rapid pace.

The problem is Israel in both its pre- and poststate forms, which for the past one hundred years has steadfastly refused to recognize the national existence and rights of self-determination of the Palestinian people. Time and again it has said "no" to any possibility of genuine peace making, and in the clearest of terms. The latest example is the Convergence Plan (or Realignment) of Ehud Olmert, which seeks to end the conflict forever by imposing Israeli control over a "sovereign" Palestinian pseudostate. "Israel will maintain control over the security zones, the Jewish settlement blocs, and those places which have supreme national importance to the Jewish people, first and foremost a united Jerusalem under

Israeli sovereignty," Olmert declared at the January 2006 Herzliya Conference. "We will not allow the entry of Palestinian refugees into the State of Israel." Olmert's plan, which he had promised to implement just as soon as Hamas and Hezbollah were dispensed with, would have perpetuated Israeli control over the Occupied Territories. It could not possibly have given rise to a viable Palestinian state. While the "Separation Barrier"—Israel's demographic border to the east—takes only 10 to 15 percent of the West Bank, it incorporates into Israel the major settlement blocs, carves the West Bank into small, disconnected, impoverished "cantons" (Ariel Sharon's word), and removes from the Palestinians their richest agricultural land and one of the major sources of water. It also creates a "greater" Israeli Jerusalem over the entire central portion of the West Bank, thereby cutting the economic, cultural, religious, and historic heart out of any Palestinian state. It then sandwiches the Palestinians between the wall/border and yet another "security" border, the Jordan Valley, giving Israel two eastern borders. Israel would retain control of all the resources necessary for a viable Palestinian state, and for good measure Israel would appropriate the Palestinians' airspace, their communications sphere, and even the right of a Palestinian state to conduct its own foreign policy.

This plan is obviously unacceptable to the Palestinians—a fact Olmert knows full well—so it must be imposed unilaterally, with American assistance. But who cares? Israel refused to talk genuinely with Arafat, refused to speak at all with Abu Mazen, and currently boycotts entirely the elected Hamas government, arresting or assassinating those associated with it. And if "Convergence" doesn't fly this time around, maintaining the status quo while building settlements has been an effective policy for the past four decades and can be extended indefinitely. True, Israel has descended into blind, pointless violence—the Lebanon War of 2006 and, as this is being written, an increasingly violent assault on Gaza. But the Israeli public has accepted Barak's line that there is no "partner for peace." So if there is any discontent among the voters, they are more likely to throw out the "bleeding heart" liberal left and bring in the right with its failed doctrine of military-based security.

Why? If Israelis truly crave peace and security—"the right to be normal" as Olmert put it recently—then why haven't they grabbed (or at least explored) each and every opportunity for resolving the conflict? Why do they continually elect governments that aggressively pursue settlement expansion and military confrontation with the Palestinians and Israel's neighbors even though they want to get the albatross of occupation off their necks? Why, if most Israelis truly yearn to "separate" from the Palestinians, do they offer the Palestinians so little that separation is simply not an option, even if the Palestinians are willing to make major concessions? "The files of the Israeli Foreign Ministry," writes the Israeli-British historian Avi Shlaim in *The Iron*

*Wall,* "burst at the seams with evidence of Arab peace feelers and Arab readiness to negotiate with Israel from September 1948 on."[2] To take just a few examples of opportunities deliberately rejected:

- In the spring and summer of 1949, Israel and the Arab states met under the auspices of the UN's Palestine Conciliation Committee (PCC) in Lausanne, Switzerland. Israel did not want to make any territorial concessions or take back 100,000 of the 700,000 refugees, as demanded by the Arabs. As much as anything else, however, was Ben-Gurion's observation in a cabinet meeting that the Israeli public was "drunk with victory" and in no mood for concessions, "maximal or minimal," according to the Israeli negotiator Elias Sasson.
- In 1949, Syria's leader Husni Zaim openly declared his readiness to be the first Arab leader to conclude a peace treaty with Israel—as well as to resettle half the Palestinian refugees in Syria. He repeatedly offered to meet with Ben-Gurion, who steadfastly refused. In the end, only an armistice agreement was signed.
- King Abdullah of Jordan engaged in two years of negotiations with Israel but was never able to make a meaningful breakthrough on any major matter before his assassination. His offer to meet with Ben-Gurion was also refused. Foreign Minister Moshe Sharett commented tellingly: "Transjordan said—we are ready for peace immediately. We said—of course, we too want peace, but we cannot run, we have to walk." Three weeks before his assassination, King Abdullah said: "I could justify a peace by pointing to concessions made by the Jews. But without any concessions from them, I am defeated before I even start."
- In 1952–1953, extensive negotiations were held with the Syrian government of Adib Shishakli, a pro-American leader who was eager for accommodation with Israel. Those talks failed because Israel insisted on exclusive control of the Sea of Galilee, Lake Huleh, and the Jordan River.
- Nasser's repeated offers to talk peace with Ben-Gurion, beginning soon after the 1952 Revolution, finally ended with the refusal of Ben-Gurion's successor, Moshe Sharett, to continue the process and a devastating Israeli attack (led by Ariel Sharon) on an Egyptian military base in Gaza.
- In general, Israel's postwar inflexibility was due to its success in negotiating the armistice agreements, which left it in a politically, territorially, and militarily superior position. "The renewed threat of war had been pushed back," writes the Israeli historian Benny Morris in his book *Righteous Victims.* "So why strain to make a peace involving major territorial concessions?" In a cable to Sharett, Ben-Gurion stated flatly what would become Israel's long-term policy, essentially valid

until today: "Israel will not discuss a peace involving the concession of any piece of territory. The neighboring states do not deserve an inch of Israel's land... We are ready for peace in exchange for peace." In July 1949, he told a visiting American journalist, "I am not in a hurry and I can wait ten years. We are under no pressure whatsoever." Nonetheless, this period saw the emergence of the image of the Arab leaders as intractable enemies, an image curried so carefully by Israel and representing such a powerful part of the Israeli framing. Morris summarizes it succinctly and bluntly:

> For decades Ben-Gurion, and successive administrations after his, lied to the Israeli public about the post-1948 peace overtures and about Arab interest in a deal. The Arab leaders (with the possible exception of Abdullah) were presented, one and all, as a recalcitrant collection of warmongers, hell-bent on Israel's destruction. The recent opening of the Israeli archive offers a far more complex picture.[3]

- In late 1965, Abdel Hakim Amer, the vice president and deputy commander of the Egyptian army invited the head of the Mossad, Meir Amit, to come to Cairo. The visit was vetoed after stiff opposition from Isser Harel, Eshkol's intelligence adviser. Could the 1967 war have been avoided? We'll never know.
- Immediately after the 1967 war, Israel sent out feelers for an accommodation with both the Palestinians of the West Bank and with Jordan. The Palestinians were willing to enter into discussion over peace, but only if that meant an independent Palestinian state, an option Israel never even entertained. The Jordanians were also ready, but only if they received full control over the West Bank and, in particular, East Jerusalem and its holy sites. King Hussein even held meetings with Israeli officials, but Israel's refusal to contemplate a full return of the territories scuttled the process. The annexation of a "greater" Jerusalem area and immediate program of settlement construction foreclosed any chance for a full peace.
- In 1971 Anwar Sadat sent a letter to the UN Jarring Commission expressing Egypt's willingness to enter into a peace agreement with Israel. Israeli acceptance could have prevented the 1973 war. After the war, Golda Meir summarily dismissed Sadat's renewed overtures of peace talks.
- Israel ignored numerous feelers put out by Yasser Arafat and other Palestinian leaders in the early 1970s expressing a readiness to discuss peace with Israel.

- Sadat's attempts in 1978 to resolve the Palestine issue as a part of the Israel-Egypt peace process were rebuffed by Begin, who refused to consider anything beyond Palestinian "autonomy."
- In 1988 in Algiers, as part of its declaration of Palestinian independence, the PLO recognized Israel within the Green Line and expressed a willingness to enter into discussions.
- In 1993, at the start of the Oslo peace process, Arafat and the PLO reiterated in writing their recognition of Israel within the 1967 borders (again, on 78 percent of historic Palestine). Although they recognized Israel as a "legitimate" state in the Middle East, Israel did not reciprocate. The Rabin government did not recognize the Palestinians' national right of self-determination, but was only willing to recognize the Palestinians as a negotiating partner. Not in Oslo nor subsequently has Israel ever agreed to relinquish the territory it conquered in 1967 in favor of a Palestinian state despite this being called for by the UN (Resolution 242), the international community (including, until Bush, the Americans), and, since 1988, the Palestinians.
- Perhaps the greatest missed opportunity of all was the undermining, by successive Labor and Likud governments, of any viable Palestinian state by doubling Israel's settler population during the seven years of the Oslo "peace process" (1993–2000), thus effectively eliminating the two-state solution.
- In late 1995, Yossi Beilin, a key member of the Oslo negotiating team, presented Rabin with the "Stockholm document" (negotiated with Abu Mazen's team) for resolving the conflict. So promising was this agreement that Abu Mazen had tears in his eyes when he signed off on it. Rabin was assassinated a few days later, and his successor, Shimon Peres, turned it down flat.
- Israel's dismissal of Syrian readiness to negotiate peace, repeated frequently until this day, if Israel will make concessions on the occupied Golan Heights.
- Ariel Sharon's complete disregard for the Arab League's 2002 offer of recognition, peace, and regional integration in return for relinquishing the occupation.
- Sharon's disqualification of Arafat, by far the most congenial and cooperative partner Israel ever had, and the last Palestinian leader who could "deliver," and his subsequent boycott of Abu Mazen.
- Olmert declared "irrelevant" the Prisoners' Document, in which all Palestinian factions, including Hamas, agreed on a political program seeking a two-state solution—followed by attempts to destroy the democratically-elected government of Hamas by force; and on until this

day when in September and October 2006 Bashar Assad made repeated overtures for peace with Israel, declaring in public: "I am ready for an immediate peace with Israel, with which we want to live in peace." On the day of Assad's first statement to that regard, Prime Minister Olmert declared, "We will never leave the Golan Heights"; accused Syria of "harboring terrorists"; and, together with his foreign minister, Tzipi Livni, announced that "conditions are not ripe for peace with Syria."

To all this we can add the unnecessary wars, more limited conflicts, and the bloody attacks that served mainly to bolster Israel's position, directly or indirectly, in its attempt to extend its control over the entire land west of the Jordan: the systematic killing between 1948 and 1956 of 3000–5000 "infiltrators," Palestinian refugees, mainly unarmed, who sought mainly to return to their homes, to till their fields, or to recover lost property; the 1956 war with Egypt, fought partly to prevent the reemergence onto the international agenda of the "Palestine Problem," as well as to strengthen Israel militarily, territorially, and diplomatically; military operations against Palestinian civilians, beginning with the infamous killings in Sharafat, Beit Jala, and, most notoriously, Qibia, led by Sharon's Unit 101. These operations continue in the Occupied Territories and Lebanon until this day, mainly for purposes of collective punishment and "pacification." Others include the campaign, decades old, of systematically liquidating any effective Palestinian leader; the three wars in Lebanon (Operation Litani in 1978, Operation Peace for the Galilee in 1982, and the war of 2006); and more.

Lurking behind all these military actions, be they major wars or "targeted assassinations," is the consistent and steadfast Israeli refusal (in fact extending back to the pre-Zionist days of the 1880s) to deal directly and seriously with the Palestinians. Israel's strategy until today is to bypass and encircle them, making deals with governments that isolate and, unsuccessfully so far, neutralize the Palestinians as players. This was most tellingly shown in the Madrid peace talks, when Israel allowed Palestinian participation only as part of the Jordanian delegation. But it includes the Oslo "peace process" as well. While Israel insisted on a letter from Arafat explicitly recognizing Israel as a "legitimate construct" in the Middle East and later demanded a specific statement recognizing Israel as a Jewish state (both of which it got), no Israeli government ever recognized the collective rights of the Palestinian people to self-determination. Rabin was forthright as to the reason: if Israel recognizes the Palestinians' right to self-determination, it means that a Palestinian state must by definition emerge—and Israel did not want to promise that.[4] So except for vague pronouncements about not wanting to rule over another people and claiming to offer "our hand outstretched in peace," Israel has never allowed the framework for genuine negotiations. The Palestinians must be taken into account, they may be asked to react to one or another of our proposals, but they are certainly not equal partners with claims to the country rivaling ours. Israel's fierce response to the eruption of the second *intifada*, when it shot more than a million rounds, including missiles, into civilian centers in the West Bank and Gaza despite the complete lack of shooting from the Palestinian side during the first five days, can only be explained as punishing them for rejecting what Barak tried to impose on them at Camp David (July 2000), disabusing them of the notion that they are equals in deciding the future of "our" country. We will beat them, Sharon used to say frequently, "until they get 'the message.' " And what is the "message"? That "this is our country and only we Israeli Jews have the prerogative of deciding whether and how we wish to divide it."

## Nonconstraining Conflict Management

The irrelevance of the Palestinians to Israeli policymakers is merely a localized expression of an overall assumption that has determined Israeli policy toward the Arabs since the founding of the state. Israel, prime ministers from Ben-Gurion to Olmert have asserted, is simply too strong for the Arabs to ignore. We therefore cannot make peace too soon. Once we get everything we want, the Arabs will still be willing to sue for peace with us. The answer, then, to the apparent contradiction of why Israel claims it desires peace and security and yet pursues policies of conflict and expansion has four parts.

1. Territory and hegemony trump peace. As Ben-Gurion disclosed years ago, Israel's geopolitical goals take precedence over peace with any Arab country. Since a state of nonconflict is even better than one of peace (Israel has such a relationship with Syria, with whom it hasn't fought for thirty-four years, and is thereby able to avoid the compromises associated with peace that might threaten its occupation of the Golan Heights), Israel makes "peace" only with countries that acquiesce to its expansionist agenda. Jordan gave up all claims to the West Bank, and East Jerusalem and has even ceased to actively advocate for Palestinian rights. Peace with Egypt, it is true, did cost Israel the Sinai Peninsula, but it left its occupation of Gaza and the West Bank intact. Differentiating between those parts of the Arab world with which it wants an actual peace agreement, those with which it needs merely a state of nonconflict, and those that it believes it can control, isolate, and defeat creates a situation of great flexibility and allows Israel to employ the carrot or the stick according to its particular agenda at any particular time.

Israel can pursue this strategy today only because of the umbrella, political, military, and financial, provided by the United States. This is rooted in many different sources, including the influence of the organized Jewish community and the Christian fundamentalists on domestic politics and the Congress most obviously. Bipartisan and unassailable support for Israel, however, arises from Israel's place in the American arms industry and U.S. defense diplomacy. Since the mid-1990s, Israel has specialized in developing hi-tech components for weapons systems, and in this way it has also gained a central place in the world's arms and security industries. One could look at Israel's suppression of the intifadas, its attempted pacification of the Occupied Territories, and occasional combat with the likes of Hezbollah as valuable opportunities in almost laboratory-like conditions to develop useful weaponry and tactics. This has made it extremely valuable to the West. In fact, Israel is among the five largest exporters of arms in the world and is poised to overtake Russia as number two in just a few years.[5] The fact that it has discrete military ties with many Muslim countries, including Iran, adds another layer of rationality to its guiding assumption that a separate peace with Arab states is achievable without major concessions to the Palestinians. If any state significantly challenges Israeli positions, Israel can pull rank as the gatekeeper to American military programs, including, to some degree, the U.S. defense industry, and thus to major sources of hi-tech research and development, a formidable position indeed.

2. A militarily defined security doctrine. Israel's concept of "security" has always been so exaggerated that it leaves no breathing space whatsoever for the Palestinians, thus eliminating any viable resolution of the conflict. This reflects, of course, its traditional reliance on its overwhelming military superiority (the "qualitative edge") over the Arabs. So overwhelming is it perceived to be—despite its near disaster in the 1973 war, its failure to pacify the Occupied Territories, and, most recently, its failure against Hezbollah in Lebanon—that it precludes any need for accommodation or genuine negotiations, let alone meaningful concessions to the Palestinians. Several Israeli scholars, including ex-military officials, have written on the preponderance of the military in formulating government policy. Ben-Gurion's linking the concept of nation building with that of a nation-in-arms, writes Yigal Levy (reviewing Yoram Peri's recent book *Generals in the Cabinet Room: How the Military Shapes Israeli Policy*), made the army an instrument for maintaining a social order that rested on keeping war a permanent fixture.

The centrality of the army depends on the centrality of war...but the moment the political leadership opted to create a "mobilized," disciplined, and inequitable society by turning the army into the "nation builder" and making war a constant, the politicians became dependent on the army. It was not just dependence on the army as an organization, but on military thinking. The military view of political reality has become the main anchor of Israeli statesmanship, from the victory of Ben-Gurion and his allies over Moshe Sharett's more conciliatory policies in the 1950s, through the occupation as a fact of life from the 1960s, to the current preference for another war in Lebanon over the political option (*Ha'aretz*, August 25, 2006).

Ze'ev Maoz, in an article entitled "Israel's Nonstrategy of Peace," argues that Israel has a well-developed security doctrine [but] does not have a peace policy... Israel's history of peacemaking has been largely reactive, demonstrating a pattern of hesitancy, risk avoidance, and gradualism that stands in stark contrast to its proactive, audacious, and trigger-happy strategic doctrine... The military is essentially the only government organization that offers policy options—typically military plans—at times of crisis. Israel's foreign ministry and diplomatic community are reduced to public relations functions, explaining why Israel is using force instead of diplomacy to deal with crisis situations.[6]

Again, this approach to dealing with the Arabs is not recent: It is found throughout the entire history of Zionism and has been dominant in the Yishuv/Israeli leadership from the time of the Arab "riots" and the recommendations for partition from the Peel commission in 1937 until this day, with a few very brief interruptions: Sharett (1954–55), Levi Eshkol (1963–69) and, perhaps, Rabin in his Oslo phase (1992–95). Sharett labeled it the camp of the military "activists," and in 1957 described it as follows:

> The activists believe that the Arabs understand only the language of force... The State of Israel must, from time to time, prove clearly that [it is] strong, and able and willing to use force, in a devastating and highly effective way. If it does not prove this, it will be swallowed up, and perhaps wiped off the face of the earth. As to peace—this approach states—it is in any case doubtful; in any case very remote. If peace comes, it will come only if [the Arabs] are convinced that this country cannot be beaten.... If [retaliatory] operations... rekindle the fires of hatred, that is no cause for fear, for the fires will be fueled in any event.[7]

Feeling that its security is guaranteed by its military power, and that a separate peace (or state of nonconflict) with each Arab state is sufficient, Israel allows itself an expanded concept of "security" that eliminates a negotiated settlement. Thus, Israel defines the conflict with the Palestinians just as the United States defines its war on terror: as an "us-or-them" equation where "they" are fundamentally, irretrievably, and permanently our enemies. It is no longer a political conflict, and thus it has no solution. Israel's security, in this view, can be guaranteed only in military terms, or until each and every one of "them" [the Palestinians] is either dead, in prison, driven out of the country, or confined to a sealed enclave. This is why rational attempts to resolve the conflict based on mutual interests, identifying the sources of the conflict, and negotiating solutions has proven futile all these years. Israel's guiding agenda and principles have nothing whatsoever to do with either the Palestinians or actual peace. They are rooted instead in an uncompromising project of creating a purely Jewish space in the entire Land of Israel, with closed islands of Palestinians. Even Israel's most ardent supporters—organized American Jewry, for instance—do not grasp this (Christian fundamentalists and neo-cons do, and it's just fine with them). The claim made by these "pro-Israel" supporters and, indeed, by Israel itself, that Israel has always sought peace and has been rebuffed by Arab intransigence, is actually the opposite of the case. Again, Israel is seeking a proprietorship and regional hegemony that can only be achieved unilaterally, rendering negotiations superfluous and irrelevant. Like the Zionist ideology itself, Israel's security doctrine is self-contained, a closed circuit. That's why peace-making efforts over the years, Israeli as well as foreign, have failed miserably. If the assumption—encouraged by Israel—is that the conflict can be resolved through diplomatic means, then Israel can justly be accused of acting in bad faith. Israel and its interlocutors are essentially talking past each other.

The prominence (one is tempted to say "monopoly") of the military in political policymaking explains the mystery of why Labor in the post–Ben-Gurion era chose territorial expansion over peace. Uri Savir, the head of Israel's Foreign Ministry under Rabin and Peres, and a chief negotiator in the Oslo peace process, provides a glimpse into this dynamic in his book *The Process*. After the Declaration of Principles between Israel and the Palestinians was signed on the White House lawn in September 1993,

> Rabin chose a new team of negotiators led by Deputy Chief of Staff Gen. Amnon Shahak composed mostly of military officers. When the military grumbled bitterly at having been shut out of the Oslo talks, Rabin did not reject the criticism. That Israel's approach should be dictated by the army invariably made immediate security considerations dominant so that the fundamental political process had been subordinated to short-term military needs. In Grenada, Peres had painstakingly explained to Arafat Israel's stand on security, especially external security and the border passages. "Mr. Chairman, I'm going to give you the straight truth, without embellishment," he said. "We will not compromise on the operational side of controlling the border passages [to

Jordan and Egypt]. We're concerned about the smuggling of weapons. Ten pistols can make for many victims," he stressed. "This is absolutely vital to our security." Arafat, who translated this straight talk into a vision of Palestinians caged in on all sides, replied: "I cannot go for a Bantustan."[8]

In the end, Israel's security doctrine generally prevailed. Would compliance with Arafat's demand for more power and responsibility have improved Israel's security? The truth is, we will never know.

Now the bureaucrats and the officers who ruled the Palestinians had been asked to pass on their powers to their "wards"...Some of these administrators found it almost unbearable to sit down in Eilat with representatives of their "subjects." We had been engaged in dehumanization for so long that we really thought ourselves "more equal"—and at the same time the threatened side, therefore justifiably hesitant. The group negotiating the transfer of civil powers did not rebel against their mandate, but whenever we offered a concession or a compromise, our people tended to begin by saying, "We have decided to allow you." "Security" became ever more constrictive as right-wing soldiers and security advisors began moving into the highest echelons of the military and political establishments during the years of Likud rule. Fourteen of the first fifteen Chiefs of Staff were associated with the Labor Party; the last three—Shaul Mofaz, Moshe Ya'alon and Dan Halutz—are associated with the right wing of the Likud, a mix of ideology and militarism that reinforces a concept of security that, even if sincerely held, cannot create the space needed for a viable Palestinian state.

3. Israel as a self-defined bastion of the West in the Middle East. Israel's European orientation, which leads it to view the Arab world as a mere hinterland offering Israel little of value, explains why Israel does not place more importance on pursuing peace with its neighbors. Israel does not consider itself a part of the Middle East and has no desire whatsoever to integrate into it. If anything, it sees itself as a Middle Eastern variation of Singapore. Like Singapore, it seeks a correct relationship with its hinterland, but views itself as a service center for the West, to which its economy and political affiliations are tied. (Israel, we might note, has built the Singaporean army into what it is today, the strongest military force in Southeast Asia.) That means it lacks the fundamental motivation to achieve any form of regional integration, as evidenced by its off-hand dismissal of the Saudi Initiative of 2002, which, with the backing of the Arab League, offered Israel recognition, peace, and regional integration in return for relinquishing the Occupation. And finally,

4. The immaterial Palestinians. Israel believes that it can achieve a separate peace with countries of the Arab and Muslim worlds (and maintain its overall strong international position) without reference to the Palestinians. Not with the peoples, it is true; that would require a degree of concession to the Palestinians "on the ground" beyond which Israel is willing to go. Knowing this, yet having little interest in either the Palestinian people or the Muslim masses, Israel is willing to limit its state of peace/nonconflict with governments—Egypt, Jordan, an emerging Iraq (although Israel is arming the Kurds), the Gulf states, the countries of North Africa (Libya included), Pakistan, Indonesia, and some Muslim African countries. In the view of Israeli leaders surveying with satisfaction the political landscape, the notion that Israel is too strong to ignore seems to hold true.

Though it has sustained some serious hits in Lebanon, at the moment Israel is flying high with its central place in the American neocon agenda of consolidating American Empire; its key role in what the Pentagon calls "The Long War" to ensure American hegemony remains, despite growing doubts over Israel's ability to "deliver." Whether or not U.S. policy has been "Israelized" or the "strategic alliance" between the two countries merely rests on perceived common interests and services Israel can offer the United States, the Bush administration has provided Israel with a window of opportunity it is exploiting to the hilt. Despite the Lebanese setback, Israeli leaders still believe they can "win," beat the Palestinians, engineer Israel's permanent control over the Occupied Territories, and achieve enough peace with enough of the Arab and Muslim worlds. That is what Olmert's "Convergence Plan" (now temporarily shelved) is all about, and why he has resolved to implement it while Bush is still in office. Israel's security, then, rests in that broad sphere defined by military might, services provided to the U.S. military, the uncritical support of the American Congress, its military diplomacy including arms sales, Israel's central role in the neocon agenda, its ability to parley European guilt over the Holocaust into political support, its ability to manipulate Arab and Muslim governments, and its ability to suppress Palestinian resistance.

So what's wrong with this picture? Nothing, unless one truly wants peace, security, and "the right to be normal," and considerations such as justice and human rights enter into the equation. From a purely utilitarian perspective, Israel is a tremendous success. Perhaps the most hopeful sign of Israel's "normalization" is its acceptance by most of the Arab and Muslim world, best illustrated by the very Saudi Initiative Israel so summarily ignored. But this also pinpoints the problem. The Saudi/Arab League offer was contingent upon Israel's relinquishing the Occupation, something it is not prepared to do. True to form, Israel responded to the offer "on the ground" rather than through diplomatic channels. Sharon carried out his plan of "disengagement" from Gaza explicitly to ensure Israel's permanent and unassailable rule over the West Bank and East Jerusalem, while his successor Olmert vigorously pushed a plan under which the Occupation would be transformed into a permanent state of Israeli control. All this conforms to Israeli policy going back to Ben-Gurion, which asserts that if Israel limits its aim to achieving a modus vivendi with the Arab and Muslim worlds rather than full-fledged peace, it can ensure its security while retaining control over the land west of the Jordan River. To be sure, occasional spats will erupt, such as those in Gaza or with the Hezbollah in Lebanon. Israel might even be called upon to do America's dirty work in Iran, as it played its role (limited as it was) in Iraq. But those (or at least this was the thinking before the Lebanese debacle) are easily contained, American co-opting of Egypt and Jordan providing the necessary cushion.

This Israeli realpolitik rests on an extremely pragmatic approach to the conflict akin to what the British termed "muddling through." If Israel's goal was to resolve the conflict with the Palestinians and seek genuine peace and regional integration, it could easily have adopted policies that would have achieved that, probably long ago. The goal, however, is conflict management, maintaining the "status quo" in perpetuity, and not conflict resolution. Muddling through well suits Israel's attempt to balance the unbalanceable: expanding territorially at the expense of the Palestinians while still maintaining an acceptable level of security and "quiet." It enables Israel to meet each challenge as it arises rather than to lock itself into a strategy or set of policies that fail to take into account unexpected developments. Yesterday we tried Oslo; today we'll hit Gaza and Lebanon; tomorrow, "convergence."

It may not look rational or neat, but conflict management means going with the flow, staying on top of things, knowing where you are going, having contingency plans always at the ready to take advantage of any opening, and dealing with events as they happen. Not long-term strategies but a vision implemented in many often imperceptible stages over time, under the radar so as to attract as little attention or opposition as possible, realized through short-term initiatives such as the Convergence Plan that progressively nail down gains "on the ground."

If this analysis is correct, Israel is willing to settle for peace and quiet rather than genuine peace, for management of the conflict rather than closure, and for territorial gains that may perpetuate tensions and occasional conflicts in the region but do not jeopardize Israel's essential security. Declaring "the right to be normal" becomes a PR move designed to blame the other side and cast Israel as the victim; it is not something that Israeli leaders sincerely expect. Indeed, their very policies are based on the assumption that functional normality—an acceptable level of "quiet," the economy doing well, and a fairly normal existence for an insulated Israeli public most of the time—is a preferred status to the concessions required for a genuine, and attainable, peace.

## What about the Battered and Exhausted Israeli Public?

The Jewish Israeli public only partially buys into all this. It would prefer actual peace and normalization to territorial gains in the Occupied Territories, though it definitely prefers separation from the Arab world to regional integration. If Israelis prefer peace to continued conflict with the Palestinians and their Arab neighbors, why, then, do they vote for governments that pursue the exact opposite, that prefer conflict management and territory to peace? Mystification of the conflict on the part of Israeli leaders plays a large role, just as it does in the "clash of civilizations" discourse in other Western countries. Since Israel's strategy of enduring a certain level of conflict as an acceptable price for territorial expansion would not be tolerated if it was stated in those terms, successive Israel governments from Ben-Gurion to Olmert instead have convinced the public that there is simply no political solution. The Arabs are our intransigent and permanent enemies; we Israeli Jews, the victims, have sought only peace and a normal existence, but in vain. And that's just the way it is, as Yitzhak Shamir put it so colorfully: "The Arabs are the same Arabs, the Jews are the same Jews and the sea [into which the former seek to throw the latter] is the same sea." Israel effectively adopted the clash of civilizations notion years before Samuel Huntington. This manipulative framing of the conflict also fashions discourse in a way that prevents the public from "getting it." Israel's official national narrative supplies a coherent, compelling justification for doing whatever it likes without being held accountable—indeed, it renders all criticism of itself as "anti-Semitism." The self-evident framing that determines the parameters of all political, media, and public discussion goes something like this: The Land of Israel belongs exclusively to the Jewish people; Arabs (the term "Palestinian" is seldom used) reside there by sufferance and not by right. Since the problem is implacable Arab hatred and terrorism and the Palestinians are our permanent enemies, the conflict has no political solution. Israel's policies are based on concerns for security. The Arabs have rejected all our many peace offers; we are the victim fighting for our existence. Israel, therefore, is exempt from accountability for its actions under international law and covenants of human rights.

Any solution, then, must leave Israel in control of the entire country. Any Palestinian state will have to be truncated, nonviable, and semisovereign. The conflict is a win-lose proposition: either we "win" or "they" do. The answer to Israel's security concerns is a militarily strong Israel aligned with the United States.

One of this framing's most glaring omissions is the very term "occupation." Without that, debate is reduced solely to what "they" are doing to us; in other words, to seemingly self-evident issues of terrorism and security. There are no "Occupied Territories" (in fact, Israel officially denies it even has an occupation), only Judea and Samaria, the heart of Israel's historic homeland, or strangely disembodied but certainly hostile "territories." Quite deliberately, then, Israelis are studiously ignorant of what is going on in the Occupied Territories, whether in terms of settlement expansion and other "facts" on the ground or in terms of government policies. One can listen to the endless political talk shows and commentaries in the Israeli media without ever hearing a reference to the Occupation. Pieces of it yes; settlements, perhaps; the separation barrier (called a "fence" in Israel) occasionally; almost never house demolitions or references to the massive system of Israel-only highways that have incorporated the West Bank irreversibly into Israel proper, never the big picture. Although Olmert's Convergence Plan, which is of fundamental importance to the future of Israelis, is based upon the annexation of Israel's major settlement blocs, the public has never been shown a map of those blocs and therefore has no clear idea of what is actually being proposed or its significance for any eventual peace. But that is considered irrelevant anyway. When, very occasionally, Israelis are confronted by the massive "facts on the ground," they invoke the mechanism of minimization: OK, they say, we know all that, but nothing is irreversible, the fence and the settlements can be dismantled, all options continue to be open. In this way they do not have to deal with the enormity of what they have created, one system for two peoples, which, if the status quo cannot be maintained forever, can only lead to a single binational state or to apartheid, confining the Palestinians to a truncated Bantustan. While the official narrative deflects public attention from the sources of the conflict, minimization relieves Israelis of responsibility for either perpetuating or resolving it.

Framing, then, becomes much more than a PR exercise. It becomes an essential element of defense in insulating the core of the conflict—the Occupation itself, the proactive policies of settlement that belie the claims of "security," and Israel's responsibility as the occupying power—from both public scrutiny and public discussion. Defending that framing is therefore tantamount to defending Israel's very claim to the country, the very "moral basis" of Zionism Israelis constantly invoke. No wonder it is impossible to engage even liberal "pro-Israeli" individuals and organizations in a substantive and genuine discussion of the issues at hand.

One result of such discursive processes is the disempowerment of the Israeli public. If, in fact, there is no solution, then all that's left is to hunker down and carve out as much normality as possible. For Israelis, the entire conflict with the Arabs has been reduced to one technical issue: How do we ensure our personal security? Since conflict management assumes a certain level of violence, the public has entered into a kind of deal with the government: You reduce terrorism to "acceptable" levels, and we won't ask how you do it. In a sense the public extends to the government a line of credit. We don't care how you guarantee our personal security. Establish a Palestinian state in the Occupied Territories if you think that will work; load the Arabs on trucks and transfer them out of the country; build a wall so high that, as someone said, even birds can't fly over it. We, the Israeli Jewish public, don't care how you do it. Just do it if you want to be reelected.

This is what accounts for the apparent contradiction between the public will and the policies of the governments it elects. That explains how in 1999 Barak was elected with a clear mandate to end the conflict, and when he failed and the intifada broke out, that same public, in early 2001, elected his mirror opposite, Ariel Sharon, the architect of Israel's settlement policies, who eschewed any negotiations at all. Israelis are willing to sacrifice peace for security—and do not see the contradiction—because true "peace" is considered unattainable. In fact, "peace" carries a negative political connotation among most Israelis. It denotes concessions, weakness, and increased vulnerability. Israel's unique electoral system, in which voters cast their ballots for parties rather than candidates and end up either with unwieldy coalition governments incapable of formulating and pursuing a coherent policy, only adds to the public's disempowerment and its unwillingness to entrust any government with a mandate to arrive at a final settlement with the Arabs.

Because the "situation," as we call it, has been reduced to a technical problem of personal security without political solution, Israelis have become passive, bordering on irresponsible. They have been removed from the political equation altogether. Any attempt to actually resolve the Israel-Palestine conflict (and its corollaries) will have to come from the outside; the Israeli public will simply not make a proactive move in that direction. While the government will obviously oppose such intervention, the Israeli public may actually welcome it—if it is announced by a friend (the United States), pronounced authoritatively with little space for haggling (as Reagan did over the sale of AWAC (Airborne Warning and Control System) surveillance aircraft to Saudi Arabia in the early 1980s), and couched as originating out of concern for Israel's security. Israeli Jews may be likened to the whites of South Africa during the last phase of apartheid. The latter had grown accustomed to apartheid and would not themselves have risen up to abolish it. But when international and domestic pressures became unbearable and de Klerk finally said, "It's over," there was no uprising, even among the Afrikaners who constructed the regime. I sincerely believe that if cowboy Bush would get up one morning and say to Israel: "We love you, we will guarantee your security, but the Occupation has to end. Period," you would hear the sigh of relief from Israelis all the way in Washington.

As it stands, the Israeli leadership thinks it is winning, the people are not so sure but are too disinformed and cowed by security threats (bogus and real) to act, and the peace movement has been reduced to a pariah few crying out in the wilderness. Given the support Israel receives from the United States in return for services rendered to the empire, Europe's quiescent complicity, and Palestinian isolation, the question remains whether Israel's strategy of conflict management has not in fact succeeded—again, considerations of justice, genuine peace, and human rights aside. Say what you will, the realists can point to almost sixty years during which Israel has emerged as a regional, if not global, superpower in firm control of the greater Land of Israel. If Olmert succeeds in implementing his Convergence Plan, the conflict with the Palestinians is over from Israel's point of view—and we've won. Yet so overwhelming is our military might, so massive and permanent have we made our controlling presence in the Occupied Territories, that we have fatally overplayed our hand. Ben-Gurion's formula worked. We now have everything we want—the entire Land of Israel west of the Jordan River—and the Arab governments have sued for peace. But four elements of the equation that Ben-Gurion (or Meir or Peres, or Netanyahu, Barak, Sharon, Olmert, and all the rest) did not take into account have arisen to fundamentally challenge the paradigm of power:

1. Demographics. Israel does not have enough Jews to sustain its control over the greater Land of Israel. (Indeed, whether Israel proper can remain "Jewish" is a question, with the Jewish majority down just under 75 percent, factoring in the Arab population, the non-Jewish Russians, and emigration.) Zionism created a strong state, but it did not succeed in convincing Jews to settle it. The Jewish population of Israel represents less than a third of world Jewry; only 1 percent of American Jews made aliyah. In fact, whenever Jews had a choice—in North Africa, the former Soviet Union, Iraq, Iran, South Africa, and Argentina, not to mention all the countries of Europe and North America—they chose not to come to Israel. And it is demographics that drives Olmert's Convergence Plan. "It's only a matter of time before the Palestinians demand 'one man, one vote' and then, what will we do?" he asked plaintively at the 2004 Herzilya conference. Olmert's scheme retains control of Israel and the Occupied Territories (in his terms, Judea, Samaria, and eastern Jerusalem) while doing the only thing possible with the Palestinians who make up half the population locking them into a truncated Bantustan on a sterile 15 to 20 percent of the country.

2. Palestinians. Israel's historical policy of ignoring and bypassing the Palestinians can no longer work. Palestinians comprise about half the population of the land west of the Jordan River, all of which Israel seeks to control, and will be a clear majority if significant numbers of refugees are repatriated to the Palestinian Bantustan. Keeping that population under control means that Israel must adopt ever more repressive policies, whether prohibiting Israeli Arab citizens from bringing their spouses and children from the Occupied Territories to live with them in Israel, as recent legislation has decreed, or imprisoning an entire people behind twenty-six-foot concrete walls. Despite Olmert's assertion that Israelis have a right to live a normal life, normalcy cannot be achieved unilaterally. Neither an Occupation nor a Bantustan nor any other form of oppression can be normalized or routinized; it will always be resisted by the oppressed. Strong as Israel is militarily, it has not succeeded in pacifying the Palestinians over the last forty years of occupation, sixty years since the *Nakba*, or century since the Zionist movement claimed exclusive patrimony over Palestine and began to systematically dispossess the indigenous population. The Palestinians today possess one weapon that Israel cannot defeat, that it must one day deal with, and that is their position as gatekeepers. Until the Palestinians signal the wider Arab, Muslim, and international communities that they have reached a satisfactory political accommodation with Israel, the conflict will continue, and Israel will fail to achieve either closure or normalcy.

3. The Arab/Muslim peoples. The role of Palestinians as gatekeepers reflects the rise in importance of civil society as a player in political affairs. Israel's lack of concern over the Arab and Muslim "streets" and its reliance solely on peace-making with governments indicate a major failure in Israel's strategic approach to the conflict: underestimation of the power of the people. Sentiments such as "We don't care about making peace with the Arab peoples; correct relations with their governments are enough" ignore the fragile state of Arab governments created by the rise of Muslim fundamentalism, which in turn has been fueled in large part (though not exclusively, of course) by the Occupation. If Hezbollah has the power to create the instability it has, imagine what will happen if the Muslim Brotherhood seizes power in Egypt. The disproportionate bias toward Israel in American and European policies only fuels and sharpens the "clash of civilizations," while Israel's Occupation effectively prevents progressive elements from emerging in the Arab and Muslim worlds. The strategic role played by Palestinians as gatekeepers has a significant effect upon the stability of the entire global system. The Israel-Palestine conflict is no longer a localized one.

4. International civil society. As we have seen, Israeli leaders, surveying the international political landscape as elected officials do, take great comfort. They believe that, with uncritical and unlimited American support, their country is "winning" its conflict over the Palestinians (and Israel's other enemies, real and imagined). Like political leaders everywhere, they don't seriously take "the people" into account. Yet, the people—what is known as international civil society—have some achievements under their belt when it comes to defeating injustice. They forced the American government to enforce the civil rights of black people in the United States and to abandon the war in Vietnam. They played major roles in the collapse of South African apartheid, of the Soviet Union, and of the shah's regime, among many others. Since governments will almost never do the right thing on their own, it was civil society, through the newly established UN, that forced them to accept the Universal Declaration of Human Rights, the Geneva Conventions, and a whole corpus of human rights and international law. With the International Court of Justice and the International Criminal Court at our disposal, as well as other instruments, and as civil society organizes into social forums and other forms of action coalitions, major cases of injustice, such as Israel's Occupation, are becoming less and less sustainable. As the Occupation assumes the proportions of an injustice on the scale of apartheid—a conflict with global implications—Olmert may convince Bush and Blair to support his plan, but the conflict will not be over until two gatekeepers say it is: the Palestinians and the people worldwide.

## The Only Way Out: Forcing Israel to Take Responsibility

Israel has only one way out: it must take responsibility for its actions. No more blaming Arafat and Hamas and the Arabs in general. No more playing the victim. No more denying Occupation or the human rights of a people just as lodged into this land as the Jews, if not more so. No more using the military to ensure "our" security. No more unilateralism. Instead, Israel must work with the Palestinians to create a genuine two-state solution. No Geneva Initiative whereby the Palestinians get a nonviable 22 percent of the country; nor convergence, nor realignment, nor apartheid. Simply an end of Occupation and a return to the 1967 borders (in which Israel still retains 78 percent of the country)—or, if a just and viable two-state solution is in fact buried forever under massive Israeli settlement blocs and highways, then another solution. And a just solution to the refugee issue. Over time, the Palestinians—who are greater friends of Israel than any Israeli realizes—might even use their good offices to eventually enter into a regional confederation with the neighboring states.[9]

This is a tall order, and it will not happen soon. The military's mobilization of Jewish Israelis has created a remarkably high consensus (85 percent support the construction of the separation wall; 93 percent supported the recent war in Lebanon), making it impossible for truly divergent views to penetrate. Some of this is caused by Israel's overpowering feelings of self-righteousness, combined with the perception of Israel as the victim (and hence having no responsibility for what happens, a party that cannot be held accountable). Disdain toward Arabs also allows Israel to harm Palestinian (and again Lebanese) civilian populations with impunity and no sense of guilt or wrongdoing.

Although Israel has a small but vital peace movement, and dissident voices are heard among intellectuals and in the press, the combination of mystification ("there is no partner for peace"), disdain, vilification, and dehumanization of the Palestinians, a self-perception of Israelis-as-victims, the supremacy of all-encompassing "security" concerns, and a compelling but closed metanarrative means that little, if any, space exists for a public debate that could actually change policy. Because the Israel public has effectively removed itself as a player—except in granting passive support to its political leaders, who pursue a program of territorial expansion and conflict management—a genuine, just, and sustainable peace will not come to the region without massive international pressure. This is starting to happen as the Occupation assumes global proportions and as churches, together with other civil society groups, weigh campaigns of divestment and economic sanctions against Israel—forms of the very nonviolent resistance that the world has been demanding. The Israeli Jewish public, unfortunately, has abrogated its responsibility. Zionism, which began as a movement of Jews to take charge of their lives and to determine their own fate has ironically become a skein of pretexts serving only to prevent Israelis from taking their fate in their own hands. The "deal" with the political parties has turned Israeli government policies into mere pretexts for oppression, for "winning" over another people, for colluding with the American empire.

The problem with Israel is that, for all the reasons given in this paper, it has made itself impervious to normal political processes. Negotiations do not work, because Israeli policy is based on "bad faith." If Israel's actual agenda is territorial expansion, retaining control of the entire country west of the Jordan, and foreclosing any viable Palestinian state, then any negotiations that might threaten that agenda are put off, delayed, or avoided. All Israeli officials and their surrogates—local religious figures, representatives of organized Jewish communities abroad, liberal Zionist peace organizations, intellectuals and journalists defining themselves as "Zionist," "pro-Israel" public figures in any given country and others—become gatekeepers. In effect—deliberately or not—their essential role is not to engage but to deflect engagement, to "build a fence" around the core Israeli agenda so as to appear to be forthcoming but to actually avert any negotiations or pressures that might threaten Israel's unilateral agenda.

It's a win-lose equation. If Ben-Gurion's principle that the Arabs will sue for peace even after we get everything we want is true, then why compromise? True, we could have had peace, security, and normalization years ago, but not a "unified" Jerusalem, Judea, or Samaria. If the price is continued hostility of the Arab and Muslim masses and no integration into the region, well, that's certainly something we can live with. In the meantime, we can rely on our military to handle any challenges to either our Occupation or our hegemony that might arise.

This logic carried us through almost to the end, to Olmert's Convergence Plan that was intended to "end" the Occupation and establish a permanent regime of Israeli dominance. And then Israel hit the wall, a dead-end: the rise of Hamas to power in the Palestinian Authority and the traumatic "non-victory" over Hezbollah. Both those events exposed the fatal flaw of the nonconflict peace policy. The Palestinians are indeed the gatekeepers, and the Arab governments in whom Israel placed all its hopes are in danger of being swept away by a wave of fundamentalism fueled, in large part, by the Occupation and Israel's open alignment with the American empire. Peace, even a minimally stable nonpeace, cannot be achieved without dealing, once and for all, with the Palestinians. The war in Lebanon has left Israel staring into the abyss. The Oslo peace process died six years ago (with the second Intifada, 2000), the Road Map initiative was stillborn, and, in the wake of the war, Olmert has announced that his Convergence Plan, the only political plan the government had, was being shelved for the time being. *Ha'aretz* commentator Aluf Benn spoke for many Israelis when he reflected:

> Cancellation of the convergence plan raises two main questions: What is happening in the territories and what is the point of continuing Olmert's government? Olmert has no answers. The response to calls to dismiss him is the threat of Benjamin Netanyahu at the helm. But what, exactly, is the difference? Both now propose preservation of the status quo in the territories, rehabilitation of the North and grappling with Iran. At this point, what advantage does the head of state have over the head of the opposition?[10]

Without the ability to end or even manage its regional conflicts unilaterally, faced with the limitations of military power, increasingly isolated in a world for whom human rights does matter, yet saddled with a political system that prevents governments from taking political initiative and a public that can only hunker down, Israel finds itself not in a status quo but in a downward spiral of violence leading absolutely nowhere. Even worse, it finds itself strapped to a superpower that itself is discovering the futility of unilateralism in its own Middle East adventures even while encouraging Israel to join in. Still, knowing that governments will not do the right thing without being prodded by the people, the Israeli peace camp welcomes the active intervention of the progressive international civil society. In the end, we can only hope that the Israeli mainstream will join us.

The door to peace is still wide open. The Palestinian, Lebanese, Egyptian, and Syrian governments have said that war raises new possibilities for peace. Even Peretz said as much, but was forced to backtrack when Tzipi Livni, the foreign minister, declared that the "time was not ripe" for talks with Syria. Instead, the Olmert government appointed the chief of the air force to be its "campaign coordinator" in any possible war with Iran, and then named Avigdor Lieberman, the extremist right-winger who is on record as favoring attacks on Iran as well as a nuclear strike on Egypt's Aswan Dam, as deputy prime minister and "minister of strategy."

Israel will simply not walk through that door, period. There is no indication that one of the lessons learned from the Lebanese disaster will be the futility of imposing a military solution on the region. On the contrary, the chorus of protest in Israel in the wake of the war is: Why didn't the government let the army win? Demands for the heads of Olmert, Peretz, and Halutz come from their military failure, not from a failure of their military policy. But instead of demanding a government inquiry as to why Israel lost the war, the sensible *Ha'aretz* columnist Danny Rubinstein suggests a government inquiry on why Israel has not achieved peace with its neighbors over the past sixty years.

The question then is, will the international community, the only force capable of putting an end to the superfluous destabilization of the global system caused by Israel's Occupation, step in and finally impose a settlement agreeable to all the parties? So far, the answer appears to be "no," constrained in large part by America's view that Israel is still a valuable ally in its faltering war on terror. Only when the international community—led probably by Europe rather than by the United States, which appears to be hopeless in this regard—decides that the price is too high and adopts a more assertive policy toward the Occupation will Israel's ability to manipulate end. Civil society's active intervention is crucial. We—Israelis, Palestinians, and internationals—can formulate precisely what the large majority of Israelis and Palestinians crave: a win-win alternative to Israel's self-serving and failed "security" framing based on irreducible human rights. Such a campaign would contribute measurably to yet another critical project: a metacampaign in which progressive forces throughout the world articulate a truly new world order founded on inclusiveness, justice, peace, and reconciliation. If, in the end, Israel sparks such a reframing, if it generates a movement of global inclusiveness and dialogue, then it might, in spite of itself, yet be the "light unto the nations" it has always aspired to be.

## Notes

1. James Bennet, "Palestinian Mob Attacks Pollster over Study on Right of Return," *New York Times*, 14 July, 2003. www.nytimes.com/2003/07/14/international/middleeast/ 14MIDE.htm.
2. Avi Shlaim, *The Iron Wall* (New York: W.W. Norton, 2001), 49.
3. Benny Morris, *Righteous Victims: A History of the Zionist-Arab Conflict* (New York: Random House, 2001).
4. Uri Savir, *The Process* (New York: Vintage, 1999), 47.
5. Based on the assessment in *Jane's Defence Weekly*, May 2, 2006. See, for confirmation, Alon Ben-David, "Israel's Arms Sales Soar to Hit Record in 2006," *Jane's Defence Weekly*, January 10, 2007.
6. Ze'ev Maoz, "Israel's Non-Strategy of Peace," *Tikkun* 21 (5) (September 2006), 49–50.
7. Morris, *Righteous Victims*, 280.
8. Savir, *The Process*, 81, 99, 207–208.
9. Jeff Halper, "Israel and the Middle East Union: A 'Two Stage' Approach to the Conflict," *Tikkun*, 20(1) (January/February 2005), 17–21.
10. Aluf Benn, "U.S. Warns Israel Not to Build Up West Bank Corridor," *Ha'aretz*, August 25, 2006.

# CHAPTER EIGHTEEN

## Genocide Hides behind Expulsion

### ADI OPHIR

### (1-16-2004)

At some point in Ari Shavit's interview with Benny Morris,[1] when the reader might think that Morris has already said the most terrible things, he brings up, in passing, the extermination of the Native Americans. Morris contends that their annihilation was unavoidable. "The great American democracy could not have been achieved without the extermination of the Indians. There are cases in which the general and final good justifies difficult and cruel deeds that are carried out in the course of history." Morris seems to know what the general and final good is: the good of the Americans, of course. He knows that this good justifies partial evil. In other words, under specific conditions and specific circumstances, Morris believes that it is possible to justify genocide. In the case of the Indians, it is the existence of the American nation. In the case of the Palestinians, it is the existence of the Jewish state. For Morris, genocide is a matter of circumstances that can be justified under certain conditions, all according to the perceived threat that the people to be annihilated represent to the people carrying out the genocide, or just to their form of government. The murderers of Rwanda or Serbia, who are standing trial today in international courts for their crimes against humanity, might like to retain Morris as an adviser.

The circumstantial justifications for transfer and for genocide are exactly the same: in some circumstances there's no choice. It is just a question of the circumstances. Sometimes you have to expel. Sometimes expulsion is not enough, and you must kill, exterminate, destroy. If, for instance, you have to expel, and those expelled insist on returning to their homes, there's no choice but to eliminate them. Morris documents this solution in his book on Israel's border wars in the 1950s. A straightforward reading might lead one to think that he is describing the State of Israel's greatest sin: the sin is not that Israel expelled the Palestinians in the course of a bloody war, when the Jews faced a genuine threat, but that they shot to death anyone who tried to return to their homes and would not allow the defeated refugees to return to their deserted villages, accept the new authorities, and be citizens, as they allowed the Palestinians who did not flee. But Morris the careful commentator offers a different interpretation from Morris the historian: there was no choice. Not then and not today. He suggests that we see ourselves as remaining for at least another generation in the cycle of expulsion and killing, ready at any moment to take the harshest measures, when required. At the present stage we have to imprison the Palestinians. Under graver conditions we will have to expel them. If circumstances require, and if the "general, final good" justifies it, extermination will be the final solution. Behind the threat of prison and expulsion lies the threat of extermination. You don't need to read between the lines. He stated it clearly in the interview. *Ha'aretz* printed it.

It would not be surprising if the Palestinians see in him an irredeemable enemy. For the Palestinians, Morris, along with many Israelis who enthusiastically accept the logic of transfer and elimination, presents himself as the enemy against whom there is no choice but to fight to the death. "That's the Israeli mentality," the concerned Palestinian will say, "there's nothing we can do about it. The Israelis are prepared to do anything in order to negate our presence in their surroundings. There is a problem in the depths of Israeliness. The sense of victimhood and persecution takes a central place in the culture of Jewish nationalism. The people standing opposite us are ready to give up the last moral restraints every time that they feel threatened, and they tend to feel threatened whenever they become more aggressive. You can never compromise with people like that. Every compromise is a trap. The Oslo agreements prove it."

And indeed, Morris, with his words, creates the enemy with which one cannot compromise, exactly as the cages of occupation create the suicide terrorist with which one must not, and indeed, cannot any longer, compromise. When Morris speaks of the need for transfer, he is not describing something that already exists, but contributing to its creation. And not only transfer for the Palestinians. Morris suggests that Israelis should live out at least another generation chained to the roof of a cage in which barbarians and incurable serial killers are imprisoned, and on the horizon he hints at an Armageddon: "In the coming twenty years there could be a nuclear war here." Under such conditions there is something not quite sane about the decision to stay here. According to Morris's analysis (that uses the language of pathology only to describe the Palestinians, of course), Israel has become the most dangerous place for the Jewish people. If Zionism is motivated first and foremost by a concern for the national existence of the Jewish people, this analysis must lead sane people to emigrate from Israel and leave the people of the "iron wall" to continue alone on the path to their national collapse.

A war to the death, in which one is ready to shed any moral restraint, is the result of a sense of "no exit," not necessarily a real lack of alternatives. The logic of Morris's words creates a feeling of no exit for both sides. In his research, Morris is generally careful and responsible, even conservative, sticking to details while avoiding generalities. Morris the interviewee is a lousy historian and an awful sociologist. His generalities about "a problem in the depths of Islam," on "the Arab world as it exists today," and on "the clash of civilizations" are not the result of historical research, but a smokescreen designed to rule out any possibility of such research. His statements about Palestinian society as a sick society deny the fact that if there is sickness there, then the Israelis—soldiers, settlers, politicians, and intellectuals such as Morris himself—are the virus. If the Palestinians are serial killers, Israel is the traumatic event that haunts the killer. And this is not because of memories of the 1948 catastrophe (the *Nakba*). It is not the victims of the Nakba who have turned into suicide terrorists, but their grandchildren, people responding to the current form of Israeli control of the territories.

The trauma is what is happening today. On the day that Morris's words were published in *Ha'aretz*, the humanitarian coordinating organization of the UN in Palestine published a strong protest against harm to the civilian population of the old city of Nablus and the destruction of ancient buildings during the course of IDF (Israeli Defense Forces) activities in the city. One day, a historian like Benny Morris will arise to document one by one the crimes committed in the course of operations such as this one. For the time being, however, Morris himself is contributing to their denial, by discussing them in future tense. The cage whose establishment he calls for is already here, at least since April 2002. To a certain extent, transfer is here as well. When Morris talks of expulsion, he is dreaming, so it seems, of the return of the trucks of 1948. But under the conditions of Israeli control in the territories today, transfer is being carried out slowly by the Ministry of the Interior, by the civilian authority, at airports and border crossings, by sophisticated means such as forms, certificates, and denial of certificates, and by less sophisticated means such as the destruction of thousands of homes, and checkpoints, and closures, and sieges, that are making the lives of the Palestinians intolerable and leading many of them to try to emigrate in order to survive. Even if the number of new refugees is small for now, the apparatus that can increase their number overnight is already working.

The most frightening thing in this interview is not the logic of mutual destruction that Morris presents. The most frightening thing is that this logic is creeping into *Ha'aretz* and peeks out from the front page of its respected Friday supplement. The interviewer and editors thought it proper to interview Morris. They appreciate the fact that he has dropped the vocabulary of political correctness and says what many are thinking but do not dare to say. If there is a sick society here, the publication of this interview is at one and the same time a symptom of the illness and that which nourishes it.

## Note

1. Ari Shavit, "Survival of the Fittest: An Interview with Benny Morris," *Ha'aretz*, January 9, 2004.

CHAPTER NINETEEN

# Palestine: The Final Solution and Jose Saramago

## JAMES PETRAS

(4-2-2002)

The images of Israel's military force have been transmitted worldwide. Soldiers shooting the wounded in the head; tanks smashing the walls of houses, offices, Arafat's compound; hundreds of boys and men, their heads hooded, being driven with rifle butts into concentration camps; helicopter gun ships destroying markets; tanks destroying olive, orange, and lemon trees. The streets of Ramallah ravaged. Mosques and schools pock-marked with bullets, children's drawings shredded, crucifixes shattered, walls autographed by the military marauders. Millions of Palestinians surrounded by tanks: cut off from electricity, water, telephones, food; the storm troopers smashing doors and furniture and cooking utensils, whatever makes life possible. Today can anyone claim they didn't know that the Israelis were carrying out genocide against a whole people, crowded in the basements, under the ruins of their homes? The living among the wounded, the dying, deliberately denied medical care, systematic and methodical decisions by the Israel High Command to block all ambulances, to arrest and even shoot drivers and emergency medical workers. We have the dubious privilege of watching and reading as this horror unfolds—a horror perpetrated by the descendants of the Holocaust, who with cant and rancor claim a monopoly on the use of a word that describes the attack on a whole people, with the complicity of most Israelis—save a few courageous souls.

The Israeli public, its media, intellectuals, and journalists were scandalized when the Portuguese Nobel prize–winning author, Jose Saramago, confronted them with the historical truth: "What is happening in Palestine is a crime that we can compare to what occurred in Auschwitz."

The Israeli public, instead of reflecting on their violent deeds, instead turned on Saramago for daring to compare them with the Nazis. In his moral blindness, Amos Oz, the Israeli writer and sometime pacifist—until Israel goes to war—accused Saramago of being an "anti-Semite" and of showing "incredible moral blindness." The profound immorality of a war against an entire people is a crime against humanity. There are no special exemptions. It is precisely those Israeli and Diaspora intellectuals who claim to be "progressive" who have exposed their own national blindness and moral cowardice, cloaking their apologetics for Israeli terror today with the shrouds of the victims of the Holocaust fifty years past.

One only has to read the Israeli press to understand the validity of Saramago's historical analogy. Everyday prominent and respectable leaders, elected by the Jewish electorate, "bestialize" their Palestinian adversaries, all the better to justify their own unrestrained violence. According to the Israeli daily *Maariv*—quoted by Robert Fisk—an Israeli officer advises his troops to study the tactics adopted by the Nazis in the Second World War, "If our job is to seize a densely packed refugee camp or take over the Nablus Casbah...an officer...must...analyze...the lessons of past battles even...to analyze how the German army operated in the Warsaw ghetto." When the Hebrew press accused Saramago of being an anti-Semite, were they willing to extend that calumny to their own military officers and their troops for drawing the same analogies? Will Israeli officers also plead that they were merely "taking orders" in blowing up buildings with women, children, and old people inside?

In the world's forums—from the European Union to the United Nations and throughout the third world—Israel is condemned for acts against humanity. Israeli apologists will discover that calling critics "anti-Semites" no longer intimidates people. World public opinion has seen and read too much. We are realizing that victims can become executioners; that military occupation leads to ethnic cleansing and mass expulsions; that scratches can become gangrene.

Predictably, Washington responds to the powerful Jewish organizations and the ultra-right militarists: it is the only government that endorses Israeli state terror, against the leaders of the Christian and Muslim faith, and contrary to the interests of the major petroleum companies and their Saudi and Kuwaiti allies.

While small groups of Israeli dissidents protest and many reservists refuse to serve in the occupation army, Saramago's commentary on the general Israeli public applies equally to the majority of the pro-Israeli Diaspora: "A sense of impunity characterizes today the Israeli people and its army. They have been converted into rentiers of the Holocaust." In the fashion of all police states, Israel has removed all of Saramago's books from the bookstores and libraries. Equally serious in preparing for genocide, the Israeli state has banned all journalists from the Palestinian ghettoes, except those who rewrite Israeli military press releases.

Like in Nazi Germany, all Palestinian males from sixteen to sixty years are rounded up; many are stripped naked, handcuffed, and interrogated, and many are tortured. Families of Palestinian resistance fighters are held hostage, without water, food, or electricity. Israeli soldiers pillage houses and steal any valuables, destroying furniture. As with the Nazis, hundreds of wounded Palestinians are left to die, as Israeli troops block all ambulances. Hundreds of thousands face dehydration and death through starvation, as all water and food has been cut off. Israeli troops, tanks, and helicopters have smashed into all the major towns and refugee camps: Tulkarm, Al Bireh, Bethlehem, Al Jader, Beit Jala, Qalqilya, Hebron. The discovery of a single resistance fighter results in collective guilt and punishment: fathers, sons, uncles, and neighbors are rounded up and taken to the concentration camps, reconverted football stadiums, and children's playgrounds.

It is evident that Israeli and Jewish outrage at Saramago's equation of Israeli terrorism with Auschwitz struck a sensitive memory: the self-hate of executioners who realize that they are disciples of their persecutors and, at all costs, must deny it. To date, all appeals by Arab moderates for Bush to intervene to end the Israeli slaughter have been futile. Washington has reiterated its support for Sharon, the invasion, and the war against the Palestinians. There is no power in the United States that can counter the money and influence of the Israeli lobby and its powerful Jewish allies. Elsewhere, however, there is hope. Via Campesino, and the supporters of Bove have called for an international boycott of Israeli goods and services. Israel depends heavily on its exports to the European Union. Reductions in oil shipments by the oil-exporting countries, particularly Saudi Arabia, Kuwait, Iraq, Iran, and Libya, would provoke a steep rise in oil prices and a major economic crisis in the United States, Europe, and Japan. This could stiffen the spine of the Europeans and awaken the conscience of the U.S. public. What is absolutely clear is that while Tel Aviv has the leverage of the Israeli lobby in Washington and Bush's support, any number of United Nations resolutions, Geneva Conventions, and European appeals will be completely ignored. In the bunker mentality of Sharon and his paranoid Israeli followers, they are all anti- Semites, followers of the Protocols of Zion, attempting to demoralize the Israelis from realizing the biblical mission of a Greater Israel, one people, one nation, one God: the expulsion of all Palestinians from their Promised Land. World public opinion must not stand passive and repeat the tragedy of the twentieth-century Jewish Holocaust in the twenty-first century. There is still time. But how long can even a heroic people resist without food and water? Ariel Sharon's offer to Arafat—freedom to leave without return—is meant for all the Palestinian people.

CHAPTER TWENTY

# The British in Palestine, 1945–1948:
# A Conveniently Forgotten Holocaust

ROBERT FISK

(9-3-2002)

In the years that followed the Second World War, Lord Beaverbrook's old *Sunday Express* would regale its readers with the secret history of the 1939–1945 conflict: "What Hitler would have done if England was under Nazi occupation"; "How Ike almost cancelled D-Day"; "Churchill's plans for using gas on Nazi invaders." Often—though not always—the stories were true. After war come the facts. It's not so long ago, after all, that we discovered that NATO's mighty 1999 blitz on Serbia's army netted a total of just ten tanks.

But it took Eric Lowe of Hayling Island in Hampshire to remind me of the inversion of history, the way in which historically proven facts, clearly established, come to be questioned decades later or even deleted from the record for reasons of political or moral weakness. Eric runs a magazine called *Palestine Scrapbook*, a journal for the old British soldiers who fought in Palestine—against both Arabs and Jews—until the ignominious collapse of the British mandate in 1948. In Mr. Lowe's magazine, there are personal memories of the bombing of British headquarters at the King David Hotel in Jerusalem—a "terrorist" bombing, of course, except that it was carried out by a man who was later to become the prime minister of Israel, Menachem Begin.

Dennis Shelton of the King's Royal Rifle Corps writes a letter, recalling an Arab attack on a British Army lorry in Gaza. "We opened up on them, the ones who could still run away. We found two [British] army bodies under the wagon, both badly wounded. I went in the ambulance with them to Rafah hospital. I was holding the side of one's head to keep his brains in. I often wondered if indeed they recovered." Mr. Lowe has asked for information about the soldier whom Dennis Shelton tried to save.

But he's probably wasting his time, because the British army's first post–World War II war—the 1945–48 conflict in Palestine—has been "disappeared," sidelined as something that no one wants to remember. According to Mr. Lowe, many of the British campaign medals for Palestine were never issued. Dennis Peck, of the Sherwood Foresters, only realised he'd been awarded one in 1998. Until two years ago, the campaign was never mentioned at the Armistice parade in London. There's not even a definitive figure for the British troops who died—around four hundred were killed or died of wounds. And it took over fifty years for British veterans to get a memorial for the dead: in the end, the veterans had to pay for it from their own pockets.

But in the late 1940s, all Britain was seized by the war in Palestine. When Jewish gunmen hanged two British sergeants, booby-trapping their bodies into the bargain, Britons were outraged. The British, it must be added, had just hanged Jewish militants in Palestine. But now—nothing. Our dead soldiers in Palestine, far from being remembered at the going down of the sun, are largely not remembered at all.

So who are we frightened of here? The Arabs? The Israelis? And isn't this just a small example of the suppression of historical truth that continues over the twentieth century's first holocaust? I raise this question because of a recent and deeply offensive article by Stephen Kinzer of the *New York Times*. Back in 1915, his paper—then an honorable journal of record—broke one of the great and most terrible stories of the First World War: the planned slaughter of 1.5 million Christian Armenians by the Turkish Ottoman government. The paper's headlines, based in many cases on U.S. diplomats in Turkey, alerted the world to this genocide. By September 16, a *New York Times* correspondent had spoken of "a campaign of extermination, involving the murdering of 800,000 to 1,000,000 persons."

It was all true. Save for the Turkish government, a few American academics holding professorships funded by Turkey and the shameful denials of the Israeli government, there is today not a soul who doubts the nature or the extent of this genocide. Even in the 1920s, Winston Churchill himself called it a "holocaust." But not Mr. Kinzer. Over the course of the past few years, he's done everything he can to destroy the integrity of his paper's brilliant, horrifying, exclusive reports of 1915. Constantly recalling Turkey's fraudulent claim that the Armenians died in the civil unrest in Asia Minor at the time, he has referred to the genocide as "ethnic cleansing" and treated the figure of

1.5 million dead as a claim—something he would surely never do in reference to the 6 million Jews later murdered by the Nazis.

Recently, Mr. Kinzer has written about the new Armenian Genocide museum in Washington, commenting artfully that there's "a growing recognition by advocacy groups that museums can be powerful tools to advance political causes." In other words, unlike the Jewish Holocaust museum—and the Jewish Holocaust itself, which would never be used by Israel to silence criticism of its cruel behaviour in the Occupied Territories—there might be something a bit dodgy about the Armenian version. Then comes the killer. "Washington already has one major institution, the United States Holocaust Museum, that documents an effort to destroy an entire people," Mr. Kinzer wrote. "The story it presents is beyond dispute. But the events of 1915 are still a matter of intense debate." Are they hell, Mr. Kinzer.

But why should we be surprised at this classic piece of historical revisionism? Israel's own ambassador to present-day Armenia, Rivka Cohen, has been peddling more or less the same rubbish, refusing to draw any parallels with the Jewish Holocaust and describing the Armenian Holocaust as a mere "tragedy." She is, in fact, following the official Israeli Foreign Office line that "this [Armenian Holocaust] should not be described as genocide." Israel's top Holocaust scholar, Israel Charney, has most courageously campaigned against those who lie about the Armenian genocide—I advise readers to buy his stunning *Encyclopaedia of Genocide*—and he has been joined by many other Jewish scholars. But with Turkey's alliance with Israel, its membership of NATO, its possible EU entry, and its massive arms purchases from the United States, the growing power of its well-paid lobby groups has smothered even their efforts.

Which raises one last question. Armenian academics have been investigating the identity of those young German officers who were training the Ottoman army in 1915 and who in some cases actually witnessed the Armenian Holocaust—whose victims were, in some cases, transported to their deaths in railway cattle-cars. Several of those German soldiers' names, it now transpires, crop up again just over a quarter of a century later—as senior Wehrmacht officers in Russia, helping Hitler to carry out the Jewish Holocaust. Even the dimmest of us might think there was a frightening connection here. But not, I guess, Mr. Kinzer. Nor the modern-day *New York Times*, which is so keen to trash its own historic exclusives for fear of what Turkey—or Israel—might say. Personally, I'd call it all a form of Holocaust denial. And I know what Eric Lowe would call it: cowardice under fire.

# PART 3

## Rule by Law or Defiance

> Unauthorized statements have been made to the effect that the purpose in view is to create a wholly Jewish Palestine....His Majesty's Government regard any such expectation as impracticable and have no such aim in view. Nor have they at any time contemplated...the disappearance or the subordination of the Arabic population, language or culture in Palestine. They would draw attention to the fact that the terms of the (Balfour) Declaration referred to do not contemplate that Palestine as a whole should be converted into a Jewish National Home, but that such a Home should be founded IN PALESTINE....His Majesty's Government therefore now declare unequivocally that it is not part of their policy that Palestine should become a Jewish State.
>
> (Command Paper 1922, from the Avalon Project at Yale Law School, 1996–2000), www.avalon.law.yale.edu/20th_century/brwh1039.asp.

The above statement was approved by the Council of the League of Nations, thus establishing the legal charge for the British Mandate government. Together with the Catling papers introduced in the Introduction of this book, they graphically demonstrate how the Zionist-controlled forces within the Jewish community defied the legally established authorities in Palestine. And as the chapters in this book testify, this defiance continues to the present day.

If justice becomes the beacon that guides the UN toward peace, it would have to begin at Resolution 181, the partition of Palestine. Assumptions were made at that point, assumptions that had both positive and negative effects. A moral determination was made that the Jews deserved a homeland as a consequence of the horrific slaughter that had decimated their people. The world accepted a moral responsibility to right that atrocity; in so doing they, perhaps unwittingly, assumed that they could grant to the Jews a portion of another people's land. That assumption, however, was not shared by the natives of that area. Yet the reality remains that the division and its assumptions became the basis for the existence of an Israeli and a Palestinian state.

Justice demands that Israel and the United Nations address the enormous inequities that exist in Palestine. There is no justice if the division of the land remains 86 percent to 14 percent when both populations are of approximately equal size, especially if the right of return is acted upon according to international law. There is no justice if Israel remains the controlling power over a faux state that cannot manage its own affairs and control its own destiny. There is no justice if Israel does not compensate those from whom they have stolen land and return to Palestine the natural resources it has commandeered. There is no justice if a reconfiguration of the land is not achieved so that both peoples can move freely from one sector of their country to another. There is no justice if the separation wall continues to imprison the Palestinians with its constant reminder that Israelis defied international law to impose their own and made visible the unacceptable attitude that one people has a right to psychologically and physically isolate others from communication with their neighbors or the world, a collective punishment that denies the very humanity of the people. There is no justice if the status quo remains the day-to-day reality of the Palestinians, because that way is a slow, torturous route to sickness, psychological torture, deprivation, starvation, and death; it is the Israeli government's heinous action of a slow genocide acted out on the world stage as the European Union, the Asian nations, and America look on indifferently. There is no justice if the United States blocks the UN Security Council from enforcing the means to bring about justice in Palestine, an action that may require the UN to stand against the United States or lose its credibility as an international body that protects the weak as well as the strong. And, conversely, there is no justice if the Palestinians do not accept the people of Israel to live in peace and security, in separate states or in one, so that all may thrive and enjoy the fruits of their labor.

# CHAPTER TWENTY-ONE

# The Russell Tribunal on Palestine

STEPHEN LENDMAN

(5-16-2009)

After two years of "underground" work, the Russell Tribunal was launched in 2009 with a "successful press conference" and announcement:

> The Russell Tribunal on Palestine seeks to reaffirm the primacy of international law as the (way to settle) the Israeli-Palestinian conflict. Its work will focus on "the enunciation of law by authoritative bodies. The International Court of Justice (ICJ), in its opinion on the Separation Wall in Occupied Palestine, addressed relevant "International Humanitarian Law and International Human Rights Law," as well as dozens of international resolutions concerning Palestine.[1]

This tribunal will "address the failure of application of law even though it has been so clearly identified." It begins where the ICJ stopped: "highlighting the responsibilities arising from the enunciation of law, including those of the international community, which cannot continue to shirk its obligations."

The Russell Tribunal is part of the larger B. Russell Tribunal, named after the noted philosopher, mathematician, and antiwar/anti-imperialism activist Bertrand Russell (1872– 1970). Established in 1967 to investigate Vietnam war crimes, it is a hearing committee, most recently on the Iraq war and Bush administration imperialism. Its work continues as "the only game in town for the anti-war movement in America, Britain and Europe" to unite nonviolently for peace on the world's various hot spots, now for Occupied Palestine, to expose decades of injustice against a defenseless civilian population. National committees will be formed globally, including expert ones composed of jurists, lawyers, human rights and international law experts, weapons experts, and others "to work on the evidence against Israel and third parties" to be presented in Tribunal sessions. Two are planned, "the earliest...by the end of this year."

Frank Barat of the Organizing Committee urges activists to spread the news and offer support for this vital project. After Israel's unconscionable Gaza attack, it's never been more vulnerable given mass world public outrage. It is long past time to hold Israel accountable for its decades of crimes of war and against humanity, flaunting international humanitarian law, waging aggressive wars, continuing an illegal occupation, expropriating Palestinian land, and committing slow-motion genocide, so far with impunity. No longer can this be tolerated. The Russell Tribunal on Palestine is dedicated toward that end.

The tribunal's Declaration on Iraq applies to Palestine. Substituting Israel for America and Palestine for Iraq, it reads as follows:

The (Israeli) occupation of (Palestine) is illegal and cannot be made legal. All that has derived from (it) is illegal and illegitimate and cannot gain legitimacy. The facts are incontrovertible. What are the consequences?"

"Peace, stability and democracy in (Palestine) are impossible under occupation. Foreign occupation is opposed by nature to the interests of the occupied people, as proven by:

- the forced Diaspora,
- many others internally displaced or in refugee camps for decades,
- harsh military subjugation,
- a regimented matrix of control,
- the genocidal Gaza siege,
- state-sponsored mass incarceration, violence, and torture,
- the flaunting of international law and dozens of UN resolutions,
- targeted assassinations,
- the many tens of thousands of Palestinians killed, injured, or otherwise grievously harmed,
- massive land theft and home demolitions,
- the lack of judicial redress,
- denying all rights to non-Jews, and
- a decades-long reign of terror against defenseless Palestinian civilians.

Western propaganda tries to justify the unjustifiable, vilify ordinary people, call the legitimate government "terrorist," rationalize savage attacks as self-defense, reject the rights of the occupied, and deny their self-determination. "In resist(ing) the occupation by all means (including armed struggle), (the Palestinian people act) in accordance with international law." The Commission on Human Rights has routinely reaffirmed it. So have numerous General Assembly resolutions. The March 1987 Geneva Declaration on Terrorism states: "Terrorism originates from the statist system of structural violence and domination that denies the right of self-determination to peoples...that inflicts a gross and consistent pattern of violations of fundamental human rights...or that perpetuates military aggression and overt or covert intervention directed against the territorial integrity or political independence of other states," such as Palestine.

The UN General Assembly has "repeatedly recognized" the rights of "peoples who are fighting against colonial domination and alien occupation and against racist regimes in the exercise of their right of self-determination (to) have the right to use force to accomplish their objectives within the framework of international humanitarian law."

It also recognizes the legitimacy of self-determination seeking national liberation movements and their right to strive for and receive appropriate support for their struggle. Further, under the UN Charter's Article 51, "Individual or collective self-defense (shall not be "impair(ed) to respond against) an armed attack."

In other words, armed force is a legitimate form of self-defense as distinguished from "acts of international terrorism," especially by one state against another or any group, organization, or individual. Israel refuses to accept this. It continues an illegal occupation, calls armed resistance "terrorism," and imposes its will oppressively and illegally.

World leaders "continue to justify the negation of popular sovereignty under the rubric of (fighting terrorism), criminalizing not only resistance but also humanitarian assistance to a besieged (and beleaguered) people. Under international law, (Palestinian freedom-fighters) constitute a national liberation movement. Recognition of (them) is consequently a right, (an obligation, and) not an option." World leaders have a duty to hold Israel accountable under the law and no longer support its crimes.

Palestine "cannot recover lasting stability, unity and territorial integrity until its sovereignty is (recognized, affirmed,) guaranteed," and enforced by the world international community.

"If (world leaders) and (Israel want) peace, stability and democracy in (Palestine), they should accept that only the (Palestinian) resistance—armed, civil and political—can achieve these by securing the interests of (their) people. (Their) first demand…is the unconditional withdrawal of (Israeli forces) illegally occupying" their land.

Palestinians are the only legitimate force to secure their own security and rights under international law. "All laws, contracts (and other occupation-related) agreements…are unequivocally null and void. According to international law and the will of the (Palestinian) people, total sovereignty" over Palestine, its resources, culture, and all else (past, present, and future) rests in (their own) hands. Further, international law demands that full "compensation…be paid" to compensate for what Israel plundered and destroyed. Palestinians want self-determination and "long-term peace" and security. They have every right to expect it. "We appeal to all peace loving people in the world to work to support" their struggle. Regional "peace, democracy, progress" and justice depend on it. The Russell Tribunal on Palestine is committed to work toward this end. Nothing short of it is acceptable.

## Note

1. B. Russell Press Conference, March 4, 2009. www.russelltribunalonpalestine.over-blog. org/pages/Press_Conference_Brussels.

# CHAPTER TWENTY-TWO

## The Necessity of Cultural Boycott

### ILAN PAPPE

### (6-23-2009)

If there is anything new in the never-ending sad story of Palestine, it is the clear shift in public opinion in the UK. I remember coming to these isles in 1980 when supporting the Palestinian cause was confined to the Left and in it to a very particular section and ideological stream. The post-Holocaust trauma and guilt complex, military and economic interests, and the charade of Israel as the only democracy in the Middle East all played a role in providing immunity for the State of Israel. Very few were moved, so it seems, by a state that had dispossessed half of Palestine's native population, demolished half of their villages and towns, discriminated against the minority among them who lived within its borders through an apartheid system and divided into enclaves two and a half million of them in a harsh and oppressive military occupation.

Almost thirty years later, it seems that all these filters and cataracts have been removed. The magnitude of the ethnic cleansing of 1948 is well known, the suffering of the people in the Occupied Territories recorded and described— even by the U.S. president —as unbearable and inhuman. In a similar way, the destruction and depopulation of the greater Jerusalem area is noted daily, and the racist nature of the policies toward the Palestinians in Israel are frequently rebuked and condemned.

The reality today in 2009 is described by the UN as "a human catastrophe." The conscious and conscientious sections of British society know very well who caused and who produced this catastrophe. This is not related any more to elusive circumstances, or to the "conflict"—it is seen clearly as the outcome of Israeli policies throughout the years. When Archbishop Desmond Tutu was asked for his reaction to what he saw in the Occupied Territories, he noted sadly that it was worse than apartheid. He should know.

As in the case of South Africa, these decent people, either as individuals or as members of organizations, voice their outrage against the continued oppression, colonization, ethnic cleansing and starvation in Palestine. They are looking for ways of showing their protest, and some even hope to convince their government to change its old policy of indifference and inaction in the face of the continued destruction of Palestine and the Palestinians. Many among them are Jews, as these atrocities are done in their name according to the logic of the Zionist ideology, and quite a few among them are veterans of previous civil struggles in this country for similar causes all over the world. They are not confined any more to one political party, and they come from all walks of life.

So far the British government is not moved. It was also passive when the anti-apartheid movement in this country demanded of it to impose sanctions on South Africa. It took several decades for that activism from below to reach the political top. It takes longer in the case of Palestine: guilt about the Holocaust, distorted historical narratives, and contemporary misrepresentation of Israel as a democracy seeking peace and the Palestinians as eternal Islamic terrorists blocked the flow of the popular impulse. But it is beginning to find its way and presence, despite the continued accusation of any such demand as being anti-Semitic and the demonization of Islam and Arabs. The third sector, that important link between civilians and government agencies, has shown us the way. One trade union after the other, one professional group after the other, have all sent recently a clear message: enough is enough. It is done in the name of decency, human morality and basic civil commitment not to remain idle in the face of atrocities of the kind Israel has and still is committing against the Palestinian people.

In the last eight years, the Israeli criminal policy escalated, and the Palestinian activists were seeking new means to confront it. They have tried it all, armed struggle, guerrilla warfare, terrorism and diplomacy: nothing worked. And yet they are not giving up and now they are proposing a nonviolent strategy—that of boycott, sanctions, and divestment. With these means they wish to persuade Western governments to save not only them, but ironically also the Jews in Israel from imminent catastrophe and bloodshed. This strategy bred the call for cultural boycott of Israel. This demand is voiced by every part of the Palestinian existence: by the civil society under occupation and by Palestinians in Israel. It is supported by the Palestinian refugees and is led by members of the Palestinian exile communities. It came in the right moment and gave individuals and organizations in the UK a way to express their disgust at the Israeli policies and at the same time an avenue for participating in the overall pressure on the government to change its policy of providing immunity for the impunity on the ground.

It is bewildering that this shift of public opinion has had no impact so far on policy; but again we are reminded of the tortuous way the campaign against apartheid had to go before it became a policy. It is also worth remembering that two brave women in Dublin, toiling on the cashiers in a local supermarket, were the ones who began a huge movement of change by refusing to sell South African goods. Twenty-nine years later, Britain joined others in imposing sanctions on apartheid. So while governments hesitate for cynical reasons, out of fear of being accused of anti–Semitism or maybe because of Islamophobic inhibitions, citizens and activists do their utmost, symbolically and physically, to inform, protest, and demand. They have a more organized campaign, that of the cultural boycott, or they can join their unions in the coordinated policy of pressure. They can also use their name or fame for indicating to us all that decent people in this world cannot support what Israel does and what it stands for. They do not know whether their action will make an immediate change or they would be so lucky as to see change in their lifetime. But in their own personal book of who they are and what they did in life and in the harsh eye of historical assessment they would be counted in with all those who did not remain indifferent when inhumanity raged under the guise of democracy in their own countries or elsewhere.

On the other hand, citizens in this country, especially famous ones, who continue to broadcast, quite often out of ignorance or out of more sinister reasons, the fable of Israel as a cultured Western society or as the "only democracy in the Middle East" are not only wrong factually; they provide immunity for one of the greatest atrocities in our time. Some of them demand we should leave culture out of our political actions. This approach to Israeli culture and academia as separate entities from the army, the occupation, and the destruction is morally corrupt and logically defunct. Eventually, one day the outrage from below, including in Israel itself, will produce a new policy— the present U.S. administration is already showing early signs of it. History did not look kindly at those filmmakers who collaborated with U.S. Senator Joseph McCarthy in the 1950s or endorsed apartheid. It would adopt a similar attitude to those who are silent about Palestine now.

A good case in point unfolded last month in Edinburgh. Filmmaker Ken Loach led a campaign against the official and financial connections the city's film festival had with the Israeli embassy. Such a stance was meant to send a message that this embassy represents not only the filmmakers of Israel but also its generals who massacred the people of Gaza, its tormentors who torture Palestinians in jails, its judges who sent ten thousand Palestinians—half of them children—without trial to prison, its racist mayors who want to expel Arabs from their cities, its architects who built walls and fences to enclave people and prevent them from reaching their fields, schools, cinemas and offices and its politicians who strategize yet again how to complete the ethnic cleansing of Palestine they began in 1948. Ken Loach felt that only a call for boycotting the festival as a whole would bring its directors into a moral sense and perspective. He was right; it did, because the case is so clear-cut and the action so simple and pure.

It is not surprising that a counter voice was heard. This is an ongoing struggle and would not be won easily. As I write these words, we commemorate the forty-second year of the Israeli occupation—the longest, and one of the cruellest in modern times. But time has also produced the lucidity needed for such decisions. This is why Ken's action was immediately effective; next time even this would not be necessary. One of his critics tried to point to the fact that people in Israel like Ken's films, so this was a kind of ingratitude. I can assure this critic that those of us in Israel who watch Ken's movies are also those who salute him for his bravery, and unlike this critic, we do not think of this an act similar to a call for Israel's destruction, but rather the only way of saving Jews and Arabs living there. But it is difficult anyway to take such criticism seriously when it is accompanied by description of the Palestinians as a terrorist entity and Israel as a democracy like Britain. Most of us in the UK have moved far away from this propagandist silliness and are ready for change. We are now waiting for the government of these isles to follow suit.

# CHAPTER TWENTY-THREE

## European Collusion in Israel's Slow Genocide

### OMAR BARGHOUTI

### (1-21-2008)

The European Union (EU), Israel's largest trade partner in the world, is watching as Israel tightens its barbaric siege on Gaza, collectively punishing 1.5 million Palestinian civilians, condemning them to devastation, and visiting imminent death upon hundreds of kidney dialysis and heart patients, prematurely born babies, and all others dependent on electric power for their very survival.

By freezing fuel and electric power supplies to Gaza, Israel, the occupying power, is essentially guaranteeing that "clean" water—only by name, as Gaza's water is perhaps the most polluted in the whole region after decades of Israeli theft and abuse—will not be pumped out and properly distributed to homes and institutions; hospitals will not be able to function adequately, leading to the eventual death of many, particularly the most vulnerable; whatever factories that are still working despite the siege will now be forced to close, pushing the already extremely high unemployment rate even higher; sewage treatment will come to a halt, further polluting Gaza's precious little water supply; academic institutions and schools will not be able to provide their usual services; and the lives of all civilians will be severely disrupted, if not irreversibly damaged. And Europe is apathetically watching.

Princeton academic Richard Falk considered Israel's siege a "prelude to genocide," even before this latest crime of altogether cutting off energy supplies. Now, Israel's crimes in Gaza can accurately be categorized as acts of genocide, albeit slow. According to Article II of the 1948 United Nations Convention on the Prevention and Punishment of the Crime of Genocide, the term is defined as:

> [A]ny of the following acts committed with intent to destroy, in whole or in part, a national, ethnical, racial or religious group, as such: (a) Killing members of the group; (b) Causing serious bodily or mental harm to members of the group; (c) Deliberately inflicting on the group conditions of life calculated to bring about its physical destruction in whole or in part.

Clearly, Israel's hermetic siege of Gaza, designed to kill, cause serious bodily and mental harm, and deliberately inflict conditions of life calculated to bring about partial and gradual physical destruction qualifies as an *act* of genocide, if not all-out genocide yet. And the EU is suspiciously silent.

But why accuse Europe in particular of collusion in this crime when almost the entire international community is not lifting a finger, and the UN's obsequious secretary-general, Ban Ki-moon, who surpassed all his predecessors in obedience to the U.S. government, is pathetically paying only lip service? In addition, what of the U.S. government itself, Israel's most generous sponsor that is directly implicated in the current siege, especially after President George W. Bush, on his recent visit, gave a hardly subtle green light to Israeli prime minister Ehud Olmert to ravage Gaza? Why not blame the Palestinians' quiet Arab brethren, particularly Egypt—the only country that can immediately break the siege by reopening the Rafah crossing and supplying through it the necessary fuel, electric power, and emergency supplies? And finally, why not blame the Ramallah-based Palestinian Authority (PA), whose subservient and visionless leader openly boasted in a press conference its "complete agreement" with Bush on all matters of substance?

After Israel, the United States is, without a doubt, the guiltiest party in the current crime. Under the influence of a fundamentalist, militaristic, neoconservative ideology that has taken over its helms of power and an omnipotent Zionist lobby that is unparalleled in its sway, the United States is in a category by itself. It goes without saying that the PA, the UN, and also Arab and international governments maintaining business as usual with Israel should all be held accountable for acquiescing, whether directly or indirectly, to Israel's crimes against humanity in Gaza. It is also true that each one of the above bears the legal and moral responsibility to intervene and apply whatever necessary pressure to stop the crime before thousands perish.

But the EU commands a unique position in all this. Not only is it silent and apathetic about Israeli crimes, but also most European countries welcome

Israel and Israeli institutions with unprecedented warmth, generosity, and deference in all fields—economic, cultural, academic, athletic, and so on. For instance, Israel was invited as the guest of honor to a major book fair in Turin, Italy. Israeli government-funded films are featuring in film festivals all over the continent. Israeli products, from avocados and oranges to hi-tech security systems, are flooding European markets like never before. Israeli academic institutions are enjoying a special, very lucrative, association agreement with the relevant organs in the EU. Israeli dance groups, singing bands, and orchestras are invited to European tours and festivals as if Israel were not only a normal, but in effect a most favored, member of the so-called civilized world. Official Europe's once lackluster embrace of Israel has turned into an intense, open, and enigmatic love affair.

If Europe thinks it can thus repent for its Holocaust against its own Jewish population, it is in fact shamefully and consciously facilitating the perpetration of fresh acts of genocide against the people of Palestine. But Palestinians, it appears, do not count for much, as they are viewed not only by Israel, but also by its good old "white" sponsors and allies as lesser, or relative, humans. The continent that invented modern genocide and was responsible for massacring in the last two centuries more human beings, mostly "relative humans," than all other continents put together is covering up crimes that are reminiscent in quality, though certainly not in quantity, of its own heinous crimes against humanity.

In no other international affair, perhaps, can the European establishment be accused of being as detached from and as indifferent to its own public opinion. While calls for boycotting Israel as an apartheid state are slowly but consistently spreading among European civil society organizations and trade unions, drawing disturbing parallels with the boycott of South African apartheid, European governments are finding it difficult to distinguish themselves from the overtly complicit U.S. position vis-à-vis Israel. Even European clichés of condemnation and "expressing deep concern" have become rarer than ever nowadays. Moreover, Israel's relentless and defiant violation of Europe's own human rights laws and conditions are ignored whenever anyone questions whether Israel should continue to benefit from its magnanimous association agreement with the EU despite its military occupation, colonization, and horrific record of human rights abuse against its Palestinian victims. If this is not complicity, what is?

Morality aside, sinking Gaza into a sea of darkness, poverty, death, and despair cannot bode well for Europe. By actively propping up an environment conducive to the rise of fanaticism and desperate violence near its borders, Europe is foolishly inviting havoc to its doorstep. Instead of heeding—or at least seriously considering—calls for boycott, divestment, and sanctions against apartheid Israel, adopted by virtually the entire spectrum of Palestinian civil society, it may soon have to reckon with uncontainable forces of irrational and indiscriminate violence and its resulting chaos.

It seems that European elites are currently determined never to oppose Israel, no matter what crimes it commits. It is as if the bellowing—and increasingly hypocritical—slogan upheld by Jewish survivors of European genocide, "Never Again!" is now being espoused by European elites with one difference: the two letters, "s" and "t," are added at the end.

# CHAPTER TWENTY-FOUR

# The Israeli Agenda and the Scorecard of the Zionist Power Configuration for 2008

## JAMES PETRAS

## (2-24-2008)

The Israeli agenda openly defended, publically practiced, and aggressively pursued by the Zionist power configuration (ZPC) has greatly influenced the US presidential elections and the likely future course of Washington's Middle East policy.

The strategy of the Jewish state is the complete Zionization of Palestine; the takeover of land, water, offshore gas (estimated to be worth 4 billion dollars) and other economic resources; and the total dispossession of the Palestinian people. Tel Aviv's tactics have included daily military assaults, the erection of giant walls ghettoizing entire Palestinian towns, the construction of military outposts, and the institution of controls that undermine commerce and production to force bankruptcy, poverty, severe deprivation, and population flight. The second priority of the Israeli colonial state is to bolster the Jewish state's political and military supremacy in the Middle East, using preposterous arguments of "survival" and "existential threats." The key postulate of Israeli Middle East policy is to destroy or intimidate the principal adversaries of its Zionization of Palestine and its expansionist Middle East policy. In pursuit of that policy, it invaded southern Lebanon to destroy Hezbollah, bombing neighborhoods and critical infrastructure in Beirut and other cities, and it also bombed Syria as a provocation. Earlier, the Israeli

state played a major role in directing the ZPC in formulating U.S. war policy
toward destroying Iraq as a viable nation.

Recently, Israel—through the ZPC in the United States—has engaged in a
comprehensive, intense, and highly charged political, diplomatic, economic,
and military campaign to isolate and ultimately destroy the Islamic Republic
of Iran as a political counterweight to its ambitions in the Middle East.[1] The
principal propaganda tool of the ZPC and its Israeli patrons is to claim that Iran
represents a "military threat" to Israel, Iraq, the Gulf oil producers, and the
United States. This outlandish charge is repeatedly made by ZPC ideologues.
According to the 2008 edition of the International Institute of Strategic Studies
Military Balance, Iran's total defense spending for 2006 was nearly 55 percent
less than Israel's despite having ten times the population of the Jewish state
and facing hundreds of U.S.-supported terrorist incursions across its borders.
Per capita, Israeli military expenditures were seventeen times more than Iran's
($1,737 per Israeli, not counting U.S. direct military assistance versus $110 for
each Iranian citizen).[2] It is widely acknowledged that Israel has over 200 nuclear
weapons capable of striking Iranian population centers, while Iran has none.
Israel receives over 3 billion U.S. dollars a year in direct U.S. military aid,
including the most advanced offensive military technology, while Iran receives
no foreign military aid and has little defensive technology. According to U.S.
Budgetary Hearings, from 2009 to 2018, Israel will receive a 30-billion-dollar
package of direct foreign military financing from the United States, while Iran
will receive nothing from any foreign state.

Contrary to Israeli and ZPC propaganda, the Gulf states, Iraq, and many
U.S. military commanders do not consider Iran a military threat, but rather
a factor in stabilizing the volatile situation. The Gulf states invited Iran to
their annual meetings; Iraqi government leaders meet with Iranian officials
on trade and security, and Saudi Arabia is following a similar course by inviting Iranian leaders to Mecca for the hajj.

After the destruction of the secular republic of Iraq, the job of the ZPC
has been to push for greater U.S. military aggression against Israel's perceived
adversary, Iran, through massive falsification of the actual correlation of military forces between Israel and Iran.

## Israeli and ZPC Intervention in
## the US Presidential Elections and Economic Policy

The second task of the ZPC in pursuit of Israel's agenda is to ensure no
major political candidate debates or questions Israeli genocidal policies toward
the Palestinians or Israeli military ambitions in the Middle East. In the U.S.

presidential election of 2008, the ZPC's role is to ensure that all major candidates endorse, support, and promote the Israeli political agenda, despite its genocidal policies and repudiation of international law.[3] The ZPC has imposed on all presidential candidates Israel's bellicose posture toward Iran and its explicit policy of liquidating Hamas political leaders. According to the Israeli minister of housing and construction, Zeev Boim, "All members of Hamas political leadership are involved in terrorist acts against Israel so they must be liquidated."[4]

The third task of the ZPC is to use their strategic positions in the White House, Treasury, Pentagon, and State Department to undermine Iran's economy, politically isolate it, and provoke internal and external confrontations.

## Israel 2008: The Theory and Practice of Genocide

Israel has totally shredded any and all verbal commitments made at the Bush-organized Annapolis Middle East Conference in November 2007. The Jewish state is building 1,000 new housing units in "Palestinian" East Jerusalem. It allows one hundred new settler posts to occupy Palestinian land. It has attacked and killed Palestinian civilians, police, and supporters of its "negotiating partner" Abbas throughout the West Bank. Israel retains its 300 checkpoints throughout the West Bank, undermining travel, transport, trade, and medical treatment. Jewish colonial settlements expand, further encroaching on Palestinian land, under the flimsy pretext that the peace process only precludes whatever the Jewish officials designate as "new settlements," in effect isolating and reducing Palestinian East Jerusalem into a walled enclave.

Israeli leaders have intensified their military assaults on Gaza, killing nearly 800 and wounding over 1,000 Palestinians since the democratically elected Hamas government took effective control over Gaza in 2007.[5] Worse still, they have imposed the genocidal strategy of starving 1.4 million residents of Gaza into submission, practicing the internationally outlawed practice of collective punishment against civilians in order to incite them into overthrowing their elected government. Israeli officials have publicly embraced and defended their totalitarian policies of cutting off electricity generation in the Gaza Strip, thus drastically reducing or eliminating the supply of safe water, halting all sewage treatment and electricity for hospitals, refrigerators, food and vaccine storage, and home, school, and business lighting. The Israeli Supreme Court has approved this policy of mass, brutal collective punishment of over 1.4 million civilians.[6] They have imposed a tight blockade on food and medical supplies, resulting in what the United Nations officials and international human rights groups have called a humanitarian disaster of unprecedented magnitude, with widespread disease and famine becoming a reality. The Israeli army blocks even the movement of sick and critically injured children. The Israeli judicial system, led by its Supreme Court judges, has ruled in favor of the power cuts, bombing of generators and water treatment plants, and blockage of food, providing an unprecedented "legal" framework for genocide. The Conference of Presidents of Major American Jewish Organizations (CPMAJO) has publicly defended Israeli genocidal policies, and the ZPC has been successful in securing the support of both major U.S. political parties and presidential candidates for Israeli collective punishment against Palestinian civilians.

## Deliberate State Genocide in the Service of Colonial Aggrandizement

Israeli policymakers claim that their totalitarian tactics are a "response to rocket attacks" by Palestinian "terrorists." In fact, there are no attacks from the West Bank, not a single rocket attack throughout the past two years. Even more significant, Israel has repeatedly rejected Hamas' offer to sign a joint comprehensive long-term cease-fire involving an end to rocket fire in exchange for an end to Israeli military air and tank assaults. All Israeli leaders have categorically rejected Hamas's cease-fire offers and have refused to even negotiate with or recognize the duly elected Hamas leadership. In complete violation of international law, the Jewish state has affirmed its policy of political extraterritorial assassinations of democratically elected political leaders irrespective of rocket or other attacks as part of its strategy of practicing international state terrorism against the Palestinian people.

In summary, genocide and state terror at the service of ethnic dispossession and racial-ethnic colonial settlements is the openly stated, judicially sanctioned practice of the Israeli state. There is no basis for speaking of a Jewish, Zionist, or Israeli "conspiracy" against the Palestinians. State terror is practiced openly and publicly defended by the Israeli Supreme Court, while international law is publicly dismissed as irrelevant to the extent that it infringes on the freedom of action, expansion, and "security" of Jewish territorial ambitions, military superiority in the Middle East, and Israeli influence over U.S. Middle East policy.

As Israeli policymakers embrace totalitarian policies, engaging and justifying the international assassination of adversaries and the collective punishment of over 1.4 million civilians in Gaza, their political, academic, and journalistic apologists rely on unadulterated vituperation and paranoid screeds against Israel's critics in the United States. The now-deceased super-Zionist

Congressperson Tom Lantos (D-CA) accused ex-President Carter of being filled with "venom" for comparing the oppression of the Palestinians to South African apartheid. Zionist zealot Eugene Kontorovich, professor of law (sic) at Northwestern University, claims that the Geneva Conventions do not apply to Israel's violent seizure and settlement of Palestinian lands.[7] Alex Safian "refutes" Professors Walt and Mearsheimer's classic study of the Israel lobby in the United States as "a fraud." The Israeli ambassador to Canada, Alan Baker, refers to Israel's privileging of Jews over Palestinians in the Occupied Territories as the "poisonous myth of Israel's Apartheid."[8]

The violent vituperative language follows the deep frustration that Zionist leaders feel in failing to stem the growing rejection of Israel's totalitarian politics. Their belief that no one should ever attack Israel's colonial and racist policies leads them to blind rage, blacklisting, censorship, and vicious character assassinations. Israel's expansionist and militarist policies, in violation of international law, are accompanied by a powerful tendency among mainstream Zionist leaders to reject international law, vilifying the United Nations and insulting the International Court of Justice.

Pro-Israel Western leaders adopt Israel's paranoid style of politics and translate it into the American political discourse. Zionist zealot and head of U.S. Homeland Security Michael Chertoff engages in widespread internal espionage of U.S. citizens in violation of constitutional protections. Zionist fanatic and U.S. attorney general Michael Mulkasy refused to investigate the illegal but widely acknowledged practice of torturing suspects in U.S. custody, including water torture (waterboarding), considering this internationally outlawed torture "acceptable under certain conditions." The most egregious example of Israel's political and intellectual degeneration is found in the logic of its chain of enemies. Israeli military targeting starts with attacking the Palestinian armed resistance; then it extends to attacking their family members, neighbors, their homes, schools, workshops, offices, and fields. It implicates civilians, ambulances, and food distribution outlets. It proceeds to target the entire community, a whole people, with round-ups of all males less than forty-five years of age. Paranoia leads to verbal assaults of overseas European and U.S. critics of Israeli crimes against humanity. Israeli death squads cross borders, assassinate political leaders, and train terrorists in Iraq, Iran, Colombia, and elsewhere to weaken countries, regimes, and groups who politically support the Palestinian struggle for independence and sovereignty. Accompanying the Israeli policy of permanent global war and paranoia are the entire leadership of the ZPC in the United States. The ZPC's introduction of the Israeli paranoid style of politics in our country becomes one of the biggest threats to American freedom and our desire to avoid Israeli entrapment in another brutal war in the Middle East.

## The Zionist Power Configuration: 2008

The ZPC is made up of all the major Jewish organizations, pro-Israel plu-
tocrats, media barons, and government officials who are Israel Firsters. In
the face of the unprecedented humanitarian catastrophe imposed by Israel's
food and energy blockade of Gaza, and its thorough repudiation of the terms
of the Annapolis peace negotiation, the Zionist power configuration had its
work cut out for it in selling the Israeli genocidal agenda as a defensive, jus-
tifiable policy of a peace-loving democracy. The second task of the ZPC was
to overcome the 2007 U.S. National Intelligence Estimate (NIE) on Iran,
which refuted Israeli and White House propaganda, painting Iran as a nuclear
threat. The Israeli state propaganda machine went on an all-out assault of the
NIE, claiming to have superior knowledge of hidden Iranian research programs without providing a shred of reliable evidence. Once the Israeli state
defined its position to the NIE, the entire leadership of the Conference of the
Presidents of Major American Jewish Organizations (CPMAJO), all the major
Zionist-controlled propaganda centers ("think tanks"), and an army of Israel-
First academics (self-styled "intelligence experts") and ideologues deluged the
print and electronic mass media with attacks on the NIE report, echoing
and citing the rhetoric and claims of the Israeli state. The White House and
Congress (with few exceptions) followed the line of the ZPC, downplaying
and distorting the NIE report, escalating ZPC bellicose rhetoric and pressure
for sanctions on Iran at the UN Security Council and among the EU and
NATO countries. The success of the ZPC in sustaining U.S. confrontational
policies against Iran, and forcefully selling the Israeli policy to the U.S. political elite—even against the findings and report of all the U.S. intelligence
agencies—is a measure of the decisive power of the ZPC over U.S. Middle
East policy. Never, in the entire history of the United States, has a small and
economically insignificant foreign power wielded so much influence over
Washington in a strategic region, through its overseas representatives, over
and against the advice of America's entire intelligence establishment.

The key to Zionist power is its ability to leverage and multiply its influence
through non-Zionist contacts in Congress, the media, pension fund manag-
ers, state and municipal officials, and a host of trade union, academic, and
other notables and civic organizations. Strategically placed Zionists focused
on the single issue of Israel bringing to bear the economic and organizational
resources of their 1 million affiliates, supporters, and media publicists in targeting policymakers in all relevant fields. The targeted individuals and organizations representing many millions of American gentiles and non-Zionist
Jews usually capitulate to the pressure or payoffs, or are persuaded to follow
the lead of the aggressive Zionist zealots. The propaganda value of having

non-Zionists with a mass organizational base carrying out Israeli policies is immense. Leveraging the "others" allows the pro-Israel liberal ideologues to obfuscate, downplay, and dilute the real power of Israel and the ZPC in the making of U.S. Middle East policy. As a consequence, we find what I call "mish-mash" analyses, which argue that "the Zionist pro-Israel lobby (*sic*) is only one of many groups and interests influencing U.S. Middle East policy." In other words, Zionist-leveraged politicians are given a degree of autonomy and attributed a set of interests, which effectively hides Zionist initiatives, pressures, and tactical leverage. In 2008, Zionist direct and leveraged power is manifested in several decisively important areas of U.S. politics, especially in foreign policy.

## The ZPC and the Presidential Elections

All of the major U.S. presidential candidates have slavishly followed the most extreme pro-Israel positions promoted by the presidents of the Major American Jewish Organizations. John McCain, the Republican frontrunner in the 2008 presidential elections, declares his unconditional support for Israel's territorial expansion, settlements, and genocidal policy toward Gaza. According to the Jewish weekly *The Forward* (February 13, 2008), "On Israel, McCain has been uncharacteristically conventional. He offers unqualified support, expressed in years of public statements." The same article emphasizes how in 2006 McCain capitulated to Zionist pressure in a matter of days by recanting his position on Israel returning to its 1967 borders: "I've never held the position that Israel should return to the 1967 lines and that is not my position today."[9] On February 7, 2008, McCain defined U.S.-Iranian policy on strictly Zionist terms: "Those (Democratic) senators won't recognize and seriously address the threat posed by an Iran with nuclear ambitions to our ally Israel in the region."[10] In 2007, McCain happily echoed Israeli demands to bomb Iran with the vulgar and sinister new refrain to an old Beach Boys rock song, "Bomb, Bomb, Bomb, Bomb-Bomb Iran."

Hillary Clinton and Barack Obama have supported every major position and demand of the ZPC: both have pledged unconditional support for Israel; they have backed Israel's genocidal policies against Gaza, the expansion of settlements, and the total takeover of Jerusalem. Hillary Clinton urges recognizing Jerusalem as Israel's capital, contrary to the United Nations, the European Union, and even the Bush administration's position. Zionist ideologues are among the top foreign policy and Middle East advisers of all three top contenders for their party's presidential nomination. The public record reads Zionist decisive influence over the next U.S. president's Middle East policy. The only possible deviation is Obama's statement that he is willing to negotiate with the Iranian government, a policy that the Bush regime, in part, already practices at a lesser official level via meetings in Iraq. For his minor deviation from the Zionist war rhetoric toward Iran, Obama was chastised by Malcolm Hoenlein, the head of the CPMAJO.[11] To compensate for talking too much about "change," which worries paranoid Jewish leaders like Hoenlein, Obama went out of his way to blame the civilians living in Gaza for the Israeli campaign to starve them into surrender, and called on them to revolt against their democratically-elected Hamas government. The ZPC is the only major national political-social apparatus that engages in a comprehensive, persistent, and intensive campaign to direct U.S. foreign policy into a full-scale (diplomatic, military, and economic) confrontation with Iran.

## Silencing Potential Critics of the ZPC

Almost every major centrist, leftist, or progressive journal, weekly magazine, radio, and website has refused to discuss the singular influence of the ZPC over the U.S. presidential candidates' Middle East policy—a further indication of the reach and influence of the ZPC. The best indication that the ZPC is not "just another lobby" as Mearsheimer and Walt claim, or simply another bellicose neoconservative current of opinion, is found in their slavish adherence to the Israeli state's policies, even when they blatantly defy and repudiate the right-wing policies of President Bush. At Annapolis (November 2007) President Bush called on Israel to cease building new settlements in order to further peace negotiations. Exactly three months later, Israel announced plans to build over 1,000 (1,250) new Jews-only homes in Palestinian East Jerusalem.[12] The *Daily Alert* propaganda sheet of the Conference of Presidents of Major American Jewish Organizations (CPMAJO) immediately endorsed the Israeli position and set in motion its major lobbyists, op-ed ideologues, and media "experts" to justify Israel's crass repudiation of its agreement with President Bush. Rather than confront this flagrant, highly public, unilateral, and shameful Israeli repudiation of its agreement with the White House, President Bush's secretary of state, Condoleezza Rice, and defense secretary Robert Gates all played "'Mickey the Dunce." The White House press secretary, Dana Perino, claimed she had not seen the report about Israel's plans to build new apartments in East Jerusalem, though it was "news" in all the mass electronic and print media. In fear of the ZPC, Perino responded as if the entire affair was simply a problem for the Palestinians: "But obviously, there is no doubt that an announcement of that sort (building 1,125 new Jews-only segregated apartments) would make the Palestinians concerned."[13]

## Zionist Power: Treasury Department

Within the government, the principal architect and key operative of the U.S. worldwide campaign to strangle the Iranian economy is a top Treasury Department official, Stuart Levey, a zealous Zionist and key agent of the ZPC in the executive branch. Levey has successfully browbeaten the reticent, persuaded the gullible, and teamed up with cothinkers who control state, municipal, and private pension funds to withdraw investments from any enterprise that deals with Iran. Levey is a major architect of the Treasury's economic sanctions policy, which Washington has promoted in the United Nations Security Council. Levey's policies have succeeded in blocking Iranian private bank transactions. They have received the support of the White House and the National Security Council despite the National Intelligence Estimates (NIE) report, which found that Iran was not engaged in a nuclear weapons program. Mohamed El Baradei and the International Atomic Energy Agency have confirmed the position of the NIE.[14] Unlike Levey, the NIE and the International Atomic Energy Agency (IAEA) are agencies that are not influenced by the Zionist power configuration.

Nevertheless, the Israeli demands (pushed by the ZPC) for further sanctions based on unfounded claims of continued nuclear arms programs trumps the NIE and IAEA intelligence findings. The White House, France, England, and Germany demand new and harsher sanctions against Iran. Never in the history of Israeli influence over U.S. Middle East policy has the pro-Israel power configuration so much influence as it has today: the U.S. government (president to Congress to presidential hopefuls) repudiates its own intelligence agencies in favor of the "intelligence" claims of a foreign power. Never has the U.S. Treasury Department been so influenced by Israel-Firsters such as Stuart Levey, Daniel Glaser, and their colleagues in putting the interests of Israel above and beyond the interests of the major U.S. and European oil companies.

At every American Israel Public Affairs Committee (AIPAC) meeting since 2004, in every publication of the Presidents of Major American Jewish Organizations over the past five years, in each and every state and citywide conference of Jewish community councils, every effort has been made to promote U.S. military action or economic sanctions against Iran. In fact, the ZPC escalated its campaign against Iran after the NIE was published and intensified its campaign in favor of Israel's fabricated "intelligence claims."[15] The dual power position of Israel-Firsters in key policy positions and civil society defines their influence over U.S. Middle East policy.

## The International Dimension

The U.S. ZPC has been immensely aided in securing its bellicose anti-Iranian agenda by the appointments of prominent Zionists to key foreign policy positions in England and France. David Milliband, the British foreign minister, has close family ties with Jewish settlers from Britain colonizing the occupied West Bank. During a visit to Israel, he spent several days with Israeli officials and an evening with his relatives while totally ignoring the issue of the 1.4 million Palestinians in Gaza suffering from Israel's genocidal blockade. Milliband has been a fierce defender of keeping the "military option on the table," heightening economic sanctions against Iran, and is an unconditional supporter of Israel's brutal policy of preventing the shipment of food and fuel from reaching the suffering people of the Gaza strip.

Bernard Kouchner, the French foreign minister, is a lifelong zealous Zionist who, upon taking office, pronounced himself in favor of a military attack on Iran "if negotiations fail." As the new foreign minister, Kouchner went to U.S.-occupied Iraq and praised the occupation and puppet "government," despite the over 1 million civilian deaths and 4 million destitute refugees that have resulted from the invasion and occupation. Kouchner (appointed by the French president Nicolas Sarkozy under pressure from the Zionists), like President Bush, gave strong backing to any Israeli "military pre-emptive action" (offensive military assault), though a strong negative reaction from the French public forced him to tone down his overt support of Israeli military actions.

With such powerful political allies and cothinkers in the American, French, and British governments and the controlling role of the ZPC over U.S. policymakers in the United Nations, it comes as no surprise that Israel received no reprimand for its daily murders and abductions of civilians and Palestinian officials in Gaza and the West Bank. Zionist power prevents the UN from even applying its own basic international principles to prosecute crimes against humanity, including torture and collective punishment. Since its founding in the late nineteenth century and its spread to the United States, especially after World War II, organized Zionism has never been so influential in so many spheres of government and had so much control over U.S. Middle East policy as it possesses today. Most major pro-Israel Jewish leaders in moments of candor have publicly acknowledged that they are at the pinnacle of influence, to the effect that "we have never had an administration as favorable to Israel as under President Bush." Certainly this is an understatement that speaks to an underlying truth: never has the United States engaged in a very costly Middle Eastern war to benefit a foreign power; never has the United States deliberately prevented big oil companies from signing billion-dollar oil contracts by imposing economic sanctions on Iran in order to weaken a regional opponent of Israel.

## The Show Must Go On

Not only does the ZPC directly influence U.S. policy against Palestine, Iraq, and Iran, but it has also extended its campaign against "third parties": countries such as China that have economic relations with Sudan (a Muslim nation with an independent foreign policy that supports Palestinian rights). To an overwhelming degree, the propaganda campaign behind the so-called Darfur genocide campaign is the Israeli state and its political apparatus in the United States, namely the ZPC. Most of the media celebrities, led by prominent Zionist Hollywood director Steven Spielberg, have engaged in an exercise of selective moral indignation by supporting Israel while ignoring Israel's starvation blockade of Gaza, and of supporting the U.S. occupation of Afghanistan and Iraq while attacking China for its "immoral" oil contracts with the Sudan. The CPMAJO has focused on the Darfur "genocide" because by doing so it favors the brutal separatists in southern Sudan, armed and advised by Israel, as a means of depriving pro-Palestinian Sudan of a large oil rich region in the south of the country. The Darfur campaign deliberately and systematically excludes any mention of the Israeli Supreme Court's approval of Israel's food and fuel blockade and deliberate prevention of the movement of medical personnel in Gaza and the West Bank, its approval of Israel's practice of torture ("forceful interrogations"), and armed assaults on the vital infrastructure and civilian population centers of Gaza.

Hollywood's Darfur sideshow is a sham propaganda effort at selective humanitarian concern, which does not deviate a millimeter from the official line promoted by the Israeli state and publicized in the United States by the *Daily Alert*, the principle bulletin of the ZPC.

## ZPC Scorecard for 2008

From January to the middle of February 2008, Israeli had killed, wounded, and arrested nearly 1,000 Palestinians, mostly but not exclusively from Gaza. Over half of those killed, arrested, and wounded were unarmed civilians; the rest included Hamas and PLO security officials, militia members, and anti-colonial resistance fighters. Of the 700 primitive rockets and shells launched from Gaza, not a single Israeli Jew was killed, and fewer than a dozen suffered serious bodily harm. Only a contract farm laborer from Ecuador died on the Israeli side from the rockets.

In a speech to Jewish-American leaders in mid-February, Prime Minister Olmert spelled out the gist of Israel's totalitarian strategy. According to the BBC News, Mr. Olmert said, "Israel had *a free hand* to respond and attack anyone who has *any kind of responsibility.* This applied to everyone, *first and foremost Hamas*," (my emphasis).[16] The entire leadership of the major Jewish organizations wholeheartedly approved the use of unrestrained and unlimited violence (a "free hand") against the entire Palestinian population ("any kind of responsibility"), which would include individuals who transport, feed, educate, shelter, vote for, or interact with Hamas, as well as their family members, friends, neighbors 99 percent of the residents of Gaza. Giving priority to targeting "first and foremost Hamas" includes targeting several hundred thousand voters who elected Hamas in free and democratic elections.

The ZPC has succeeded in securing near-unanimous U.S. congressional support for Israel's mass arrests and daily assaults on Gaza, even when a few mass media outlets published photos of Israeli colonial soldiers parading eighty arbitrarily arrested Palestinian civilians bound and blindfolded to notorious Israeli interrogation centers for unlimited detention with no legal guarantees against physical and psychological torture.[17]

The ZPC has swamped the U.S. mass media with praise of Israel's cross-border assassinations, such as the political murder of Hezbollah leader Imad Mughniyeh in Damascus, Syria.[18] Reproducing articles from the Israeli press (*Jerusalem Post, Ha'aretz*) and Zionist think tanks and weeklies (Washington Institute for Near East Policy, *New York Jewish Week*, *YNET* News, CAMERA, *New York Sun*, and Middle East Strategy at Harvard), the *Daily Alert* has provided legitimacy to international assassinations by official state-directed death squads, thereby extending the violence and counterviolence throughout the world. This is a fact recognized by the U.S. FBI and Israeli officials. Heads of the Israeli international secret police, the Mossad, openly acknowledge the role of Israeli assassinations in provoking terrorist reprisals by sending a worldwide alert to Jews to avoid Islamic and Arab countries as well as locations where "there is a high concentration of Israelis."[19]

The Israeli practice of staging international assassinations of opposition leaders in major cities will not only invite retaliation against Israelis and Jews but will also endanger sites in the United States and EU for tolerating these acts of state-sponsored terror. In other words, Israeli terror invites terrorist counterattacks such as the one on September 11, 2001. Israel, by provoking a new round in the Palestinian "war through global terror," and the US and EU, by embracing an Israeli car bomb assassination in Damascus, endanger Western lives everywhere. The CPMAJO, its publicists, and op-ed ideologues in the mass media are making the entire Western world vulnerable to terrorist attacks. By supporting Israeli terror and increasing the chance of Muslim reprisals, the ZPC strengthens the repressive structure of a growing police state in the United States. The "professional" killing by Israeli operatives of a major figure in Damascus, Syria, raises the question of the role of Israeli operatives in the as-yet-unsolved series of car bomb assassinations in Lebanon given Israel's desire to maintain a state of internal tension in that country. The brilliant and precocious Ivy League academic apologists of each and every act of official Israeli state-sponsored international terror apparently dissociate these acts of assassination from likely reprisals in the United States and the consequent further destruction of our remaining precarious democratic freedoms. Could it be that Zionist American intellectuals welcome more U.S. police state agencies and laws in order to prosecute a rising number of Americans who are critical of Zionist influence over the American political process? They might do well to recall that police state structures and laws could be used against them in the future. Except for a small, courageous, and isolated band of Anglo-American-Canadian Jewish intellectuals and academics, all the mainline Jewish organizations raised not a single question, let alone criticism, regarding Israel's role in instigating international terror.

From the beginning of 2008, the ZPC has intensified its campaign to strangle the Iranian economy through U.S.-promoted sanctions in the UN. They raised the ante in demonizing Iran as a military-nuclear threat to Israel, the United States, and the Gulf States. Almost a third of every issue of the *Daily Alert* (from January 1 to February 20, 2008) is devoted to reproducing propaganda pieces from Israeli officials claiming that the Iranians are a nuclear threat and are advancing toward nuclear war. They repeat Israeli propaganda about an "existential threat to the survival of Israel." The CPMAJO never mentions that Israel has a current Middle East monopoly of over 200 nuclear weapons and missiles. Since most leading U.S. Zionists believe that they will not have another president as servile to Israeli interests as President Bush (a doubtful proposition), they are pushing hard to find a pretext for a U.S. attack or an Israeli strike backed by Washington before Bush leaves office. While the White House has raised its bellicose rhetoric and aggressively pursued new sanctions, Washington and its backers in the ZPC have failed to isolate Iran. In late 2007 and into 2008, Iran met with top Iraqi politicians in Baghdad and Teheran, reached agreements with U.S. military officials to stabilize Iraq, and addressed the Gulf Cooperation Council at their annual meeting in Doha, while the Saudi monarch invited the Iranian president Ahmadinejad to fulfill the Haj pilgrimage in Mecca in December 2007.[20] In other words, the ZPC's militarist anti-Iran strategy has succeeded in isolating the United States from its conservative Gulf allies, split U.S. civilians and military policymakers, and cost major U.S. and EU oil companies over 20 billion dollars in lost Iranian oil contracts. While the ZPC, via its influence in the mass media and contributions to the leading presidential candidates, has shaped elite opinion in defense of Israeli genocide in Gaza and Israel's war policy toward Iran, it has failed to "turn" the great majority of the American public opposed to Middle East wars from favoring the prompt withdrawal of U.S. troops from Iraq and condemning the officially acknowledged use of torture in detainee interrogations.

### Cracks in the Zionist Monolith

There are even some cracks in the ZPC monolithic control of public debate on the Israeli colonization of Palestine and the disastrous role of the pro-Israel power configuration in formulating U.S. domestic security and war policy. Despite the *Daily Alert's* reproduction of at least a dozen vitriolic, histrionic, ad hominem attacks on Professors Mearsheimer and Walt and their book on the Israel lobby and on former president Jimmy Carter's book on the Israeli apartheid policy against Palestinians, the issues they raise have circulated widely and continue to influence millions of Americans. Jewish critics, both secular and religious, Zionist and anti-Zionist (especially the younger generations), are publicly challenging the pretense of the mainline Jewish organizations' claim to speak for the Jewish community with regard to Israel and U.S. Middle East policies.

Canadians for Justice and Peace in the Middle East, a primarily anti-Zionist Jewish organization, has joined with the province of Ontario's biggest public sector trade union in denouncing Israeli colonial policy in Palestine and challenging Zionist dominance of the Jewish community and influence over the Canadian trade union movement.

Major Protestant denominations in the United States, including the Presbyterians and Methodists, are supporting divestment of U.S. companies aiding Israel's brutal colonial rule in the West Bank and Gaza. In the first week of February, the student government at the London School of Economics voted by an overwhelming majority in favor of divestment campaign against companies supporting Israeli occupation. A growing number of universities organized well-attended teach-ins throughout North America, protesting Israel's apartheid regime and policy, despite vitriolic attacks from prominent Jewish administrators and Zionist academics. Top U.S. military commanders, active and retired, have taken initiatives that directly contravene the ZPC dictates on Iran by praising its cooperation in stabilizing Iraq and playing a critical supporting role in overthrowing the Taliban in Afghanistan.

The major intelligence agencies in the U.S. report on Iran's absence of a nuclear weapon development program, contradicting the propaganda line of the administration. This has struck a powerful blow against the ZPC warmongers and their Israel-First agents in the Treasury Department (Levey, Glaser), the National Security Council (Elliott Abrams), the White House (Joshua Bolton), State Department (Wolfowitz), and Pentagon (Shumsky). We are engaged in a life-and-death struggle against war, terror, and genocide against imperial and Zionist barbarism. As the ZPC pushes for a military confrontation with Iran before Bush leaves office; as the ZPC backs Israel's policy of economic blockades to starve the people of Gaza, assassinate its leaders and shred all public order in Gaza; as the ZPC backs Israeli state-sponsored extraterritorial murders (likely to provoke new terror retaliatory attacks in the United States and EU and the end of democratic freedoms in America); and as the ZPC actively supports the shredding of constitutional and judicial liberties of American citizens and residents and the expansion of a repressive security state, we should recognize the following: in the final instance, in fighting the ZPC, we should be aware of powerful enemies in high places, acting against the interests of our country.

But we should recognize we also have enormous support among the American people and even tactical allies among some officials in the military and intelligence community. We have a new generation of active, dissident, Christian, secular, and Jewish critics of Israel and the ZPC, as well as billions of supporters among Muslims worldwide, among secular Arabs, and among the majority of citizens in Europe, Latin America, Asia, and Africa. Above all, we are defending our own, hard-won democratic freedoms, our own families' and communities' security from Israeli-provoked terrorist attacks and, even more important, our right to develop policies in the interest of the American people, free from the dictates of Israel and its agents.

## Notes

1. "Israel: Iran Building Nuclear Arms," *Al Jazeera,* February 12, 2008.
2. International Institute of Strategy Studies Military Balance, 2006. www.iliss.org/publications/military-balance. Tables: Defence Expenditures.
3. Gideon Levy, "The Lights Have Been Turned Off," *Ha'aretz,* February 4, 2008.
4. Zeev Boim, Israeli Army Radio—Galei Tzahal, February 9, 2008 (cited in *Ha'aretz*).www.youtube,com/watch?v=dPPuLvZUgPo.
5. "IDF to Step Up Gaza Assassinations," *Ha'aretz,* February 13, 2008.
6. *Ha'aretz,* February 2, 2008.
7. *Daily Alert,* February 15, 2008. www.dailyalert.org/archive/2008–02/2008–02-15.html.

8. *National Post,* February15, 2008. See also Jonathan Kay, "Full Comment Exclusive,"
     *National Post,* May, 6, 2008.
 9. *The Forward,* February 13, 2008.
10. Shmuel Rosner, "McCain Finds a Tool with Which to Woo Conservatives: Israel," *Ha'aretz,*
     February 10, 2008.
11. *Ha'aretz,* January 18, 2008.
12. *BBC News,* February 12, 2008.
13. *Santa Barbara News,* February 12, 2008.
14. *Associated Press,* February 23, 2008.
15. *Daily Alert,* November 2007 and February 2008. www.dailyalert.org/archive/2008–11
     /2008–11–14.html.
16. *BBC News,* February 18, 2008.
17. Ibid.
18. *Daily Alert,* February 15, 2008.
19. Ibid.
20. *Al Jazeera,* February 16, 2008. See also www.wmdinsights.com/123/123_ME2_FearingUS
     Military.htm.

CHAPTER TWENTY-FIVE

# Genocide in Gaza

## ILAN PAPPE

### (2-20-2007)

Not long ago, I claimed that Israel is conducting genocidal policies in the Gaza Strip. I hesitated a lot before using this very charged term and yet decided to adopt it. Indeed, the responses I received, including from some leading human rights activists, indicated a certain unease over the usage of such a term. I was inclined to rethink the term for a while, but came back to employing it today with even stronger conviction: it is the only appropriate way to describe what the Israeli army is doing in the Gaza Strip.

On December 28, 2006, the Israeli human rights organization B'Tselem published its annual report about the Israeli atrocities in the occupied territories. This last year (2006) Israeli forces killed 660 citizens. The number of Palestinians killed by Israel last year tripled in comparison to those killed in the previous year (around 200). According to B'Tselem, the Israelis killed 141 children in the last year (2006). Most of the dead are from the Gaza Strip, where the Israeli forces demolished 300 houses and slew entire families. This means that since the year 2000, Israeli forces killed almost 4000 Palestinians, half of them children; more than 20,000 were wounded.

B'Tselem is a conservative organization, and the numbers may be higher. But the point is not just about the escalating intentional killing, it is about the trend and the strategy. As 2007 commences, Israeli policymakers are facing two very different realities in the West Bank and the Gaza Strip. In the former, they are closer than ever to finishing the construction of their eastern border. Their internal ideological debate is over, and their master plan for annexing half of the West Bank is being implemented at an ever-growing speed. The last phase was delayed because of the promises made by Israel, under the Road Map, not to build new settlements. Israel found two ways of circumventing this alleged prohibition. First, it defined a third of the West Bank as Greater Jerusalem, which allowed it to build within this new annexed area towns and community centers. Second, it expanded old settlements to such proportions that there was no need to build new ones. This trend was given an additional push in 2006 (hundreds of caravans were installed to mark the border of the expansions, the planning schemes for the new towns and neighborhoods were finalized, and the apartheid bypass roads and highway system completed). In all, the settlements, the army bases, the roads, and the wall will allow Israel to annex almost half of the West Bank by 2010. Within these territories there will be a considerable number of Palestinians, against whom the Israeli authorities will continue to implement slow and creeping transfer policies—too boring a subject for the Western media to bother with and too elusive for human rights organizations to make a general point about them. There is no rush; as far as the Israelis are concerned, they have the upper hand there: the daily abusive and dehumanizing mixed mechanisms of army and bureaucracy are as effective as ever in contributing their own share to the dispossession process.

The strategic thinking of Ariel Sharon that this policy is far better than the one offered by the blunt "transferists" or ethnic cleansers, such as Avigdor Liberman, is accepted by everyone in the government, from Labor to Kadima. The petit crimes of state terrorism are also effective as they enable liberal Zionists around the world to softly condemn Israel and yet categorize any genuine criticism of Israel's criminal policies as anti-Semitism.

On the other hand, there is no clear Israeli strategy as yet for the Gaza Strip; but there is a daily experiment with one. Gaza, in the eyes of the Israelis, is a very different geopolitical entity from that of the West Bank. Hamas controls Gaza, while Abu Mazen seems to run the fragmented West Bank with Israeli and American blessings. There is no chunk of land in Gaza that Israel covets, and there is no hinterland, like Jordan, to which the Palestinians of Gaza can be expelled. Ethnic cleansing is ineffective here.

The earlier strategy in Gaza was to ghettoize the Palestinians there, but this is not working. The ghettoized community continues to express its will for life by firing primitive missiles into Israel. Ghettoizing or quarantining unwanted communities, even if they were regarded as subhuman or danger-ous, never worked in history as a solution. The Jews know it best from their own history. The next stages against such communities in the past were even more horrific and barbaric. It is difficult to tell what the future holds for the Gaza population, ghettoized, quarantined, unwanted, and demonized. Will it be a repeat of the ominous historical examples, or is a better fate still possible?

Creating the prison and throwing the key to the sea, as UN special reporter John Dugard has put it, was an option the Palestinians in Gaza reacted against with force as early as September 2005. They were determined to show at the very least that they were still part of the West Bank and Palestine. In that month, they launched the first significant, in number and not quality, barrage of missiles into the Western Negev. The shelling was a response to an Israeli campaign of mass arrests of Hamas and Islamic Jihad activists in the Tul Karem area. The Israelis responded with Operation "First Rain."

It is worth dwelling for a moment on the nature of that operation. It was inspired by the punitive measures inflicted first by colonialist powers, and then by dictatorships, against rebellious, imprisoned, or banished communities. A frightening show of the oppressor's power to intimidate preceded all kind of collective and brutal punishments, ending with a large number of dead and wounded among the victims. In Operation "First Rain," supersonic flights were flown over Gaza to terrorize the entire population, succeeded by the heavy bombardment of vast areas from the sea, sky, and land. The logic, the Israeli army explained, was to create pressure so as to weaken the Gaza community's support for the rocket launchers. As was expected, by the Israelis as well, the operation only increased the support for the rocket launchers and gave impetus to their next attempt.

The real purpose of that particular operation was experimental. The Israeli generals wished to know how such operations would be received at home, in the region, and in the world. And it seems that instantly the answer was "very well"; namely, no one took an interest in the scores of dead and hundreds of wounded Palestinians left behind after Operation "First Rain" subsided.

And hence, since "First Rain" and until June 2006, all the following operations were similarly modeled. The difference was in their escalation: more firepower, more causalities, and more collateral damage, and, as to be expected, more Qassam missiles in response. Accompanying measures in 2006 were more sinister means of ensuring the full imprisonment of the people of Gaza through boycott and blockade, with which the EU is still shamefully collaborating.

The capture of Gilad Shalit in June 2006 was irrelevant in the general scheme of things, but nonetheless provided an opportunity for the Israelis to escalate even more the components of the tactical and allegedly punitive missions. After all, there was still no strategy that followed the tactical decision of Ariel Sharon to take out 8,000 settlers whose presence complicated "punitive" missions and whose eviction made him almost a candidate for the

Nobel Peace Prize. Since then, the "punitive" actions continue and become themselves a strategy.

The Israeli army loves drama and therefore also escalated the language. "First Rain" was replaced by Operation "Summer Rains," a general name that was given to the "punitive" operations since June 2006 (in a country where there is no rain in the summer, the only precipitation that one can expect are showers of F-16 bombs and artillery shells hitting people of Gaza). "Summer Rains" brought a novel component: the land invasion into parts of the Gaza Strip. This enabled the army to kill citizens even more effectively and to present it as a result of heavy fighting within dense populated areas, an inevitable result of the circumstances and not of Israeli policies. With the close of summer came Operation "Autumn Clouds," which was even more efficient: on November 1, 2006, in less than 48 hours, the Israelis killed 70 civilians; by the end of that month, with additional mini operations accompanying it, almost 200 were killed, half of them children and women. As one can see from the dates, some of the activity was parallel to the Israeli attacks on Lebanon, making it easier to complete the operations without much external attention, let alone criticism.

From "First Rain" to "Autumn Clouds," one can see escalation in every parameter. The first is the disappearance of the distinction between civilian and noncivilian targets: the senseless killing has turned the population at large to the main target for the army's operation. The second one is the escalation in the means: employment of every possible killing machine the Israeli army possesses. Thirdly, the escalation is conspicuous in the number of casualties: with each operation, and each future operation, a much larger number of people are likely to be killed and wounded. Finally, and most importantly, the operations become a strategy—the way Israel intends to solve the problem of the Gaza Strip.

A creeping transfer in the West Bank and a measured genocidal policy in the Gaza Strip are the two strategies Israel employs today. From an electoral point of view, the one in Gaza is problematic as it does not reap any tangible results; the West Bank under Abu Mazen is yielding to Israeli pressure, and there is no significant force that arrests the Israeli strategy of annexation and dispossession. But Gaza continues to fire back. On the one hand, this would enable the Israeli army to initiate more massive genocidal operations in the future. On the other hand, there is a great danger that, as happened in 1948, the army would demand a more drastic and systematic "punitive" and collateral action against the besieged people of the Gaza Strip.

Ironically, the Israeli killing machine has rested lately. Even relatively large number of Qassam missiles, including one or two quite deadly ones, did not stir the army to action. Though the army's spokesmen say it shows "restraint," it never did in the past and is not likely to do so in the future. The army rests, as its generals are content with the internal killing that rages on in Gaza and does the job for them. They watch with satisfaction the emerging civil war in Gaza, which Israel foments and encourages. From Israel's point of view, it does not really matter how Gaza would eventually be demographically downsized, be it by internal or Israeli slaying. The responsibility of ending the internal fighting lies of course with the Palestinian groups themselves, but American and Israeli interference, continued imprisonment, and the starvation and strangulation of Gaza are all factors that make such an internal peace process very difficult. But it will take place soon, and then, with the first early sign that it has subsided, the Israeli "Summer Rains" will fall down again on the people of Gaza, wreaking havoc and death.

And one should never tire of stating the inevitable political conclusions from this dismal reality of the year we left behind and in the face of the one that awaits us. There is still no other way of stopping Israel besides boycott, divestment, and sanctions. We should all support these measures clearly, openly, and unconditionally, regardless of what the gurus of our world tell us about the efficiency or raison d'être of such actions. The UN will not intervene in Gaza as it does in Africa; the Nobel peace laureates will not enlist to Gaza's defense as they do for causes in Southeast Asia. The numbers of people killed there are not staggering as far as other calamities are concerned, and it is not a new story—it is dangerously old and troubling. The only soft point of this killing machine is its oxygen lines to "Western" civilization and public opinion. It is still possible to puncture them and make it at least more difficult for the Israelis to implement their future strategy of eliminating the Palestinian people either by cleansing them in the West Bank or genociding them in the Gaza Strip.

# CHAPTER TWENTY-SIX

## Genocide among Us

### CURTIS F. J. DOEBBLER

### (1-28-2007)

This week, the international community is commemorating one genocide: the holocaust, in which millions of Jews, political dissenters, Roma, and just about anyone who protested Nazi politics were brutally killed. This is an important and tragic event to remember, but even as the international community commemorates this tragic event, it is forgetting other genocides and even participating in contemporary genocide.

Perhaps instead of concentrating on our past mistakes, more attention should be paid to the mistakes we are making today. Evidently, some of the survivors of genocide in the holocaust have failed to learn the lessons of their past. And even presidents of some of the most powerful countries in the world appear to be willing to undertake acts of genocide if it serves their political aims. Recounting the tradition of genocide, its legal prohibition, and its application to contemporary events is a contribution to the commemoration of the holocaust that is more fitting than any wreaths or kind words about the victims we failed to save then.

## Genocidal Traditions

The history of genocide is a complex one. The man who coined the term in the mid-twentieth century, Raphael Lemkin, saw genocide as "a coordinated plan aimed at destruction of the essential foundations of the life...so that these groups wither and die like plants that have suffered a blight...accomplished by the forced disintegration of political and social institutions, of the culture of the people, of their language, their national feelings and their religion...[or]...by wiping out all bases of personal security, liberty, health and dignity." Lemkin added that "[w]hen these means fail the machine gun can always be utilized as a last resort."[1]

Since the term was coined, it has grown to become both a larger-than-life term for applying to all acts of mass killing or extermination by some people. If one views genocide in this broad manner, it would apply to any mass killing or mass act of inhumane treatment against a group of people who should not be discriminated against. When he created the term to apply to these acts of extermination, for example, Lemkin was concerned for the massacre of Armenians as the Ottoman empire was coming to an end. This broad term, however, would equally apply to the massacre of almost the entire native Indian populations in Mexico and in Central and South America by Spanish conquerors. It would also apply to the slaughters conducted by slave-trading western European and North American governments in Africa as they sought to exploit people whom they viewed as uncivilized.

A broad definition of genocide would also apply to perhaps the most successful act of mass murder and extermination of a people in relatively modern history: the slaughter of millions of Native Americans to create the United States of America. The United States slaughtered millions of these indigenous people using a combination of brute force and lies. In cowardly acts of deception, the United States even signed sacred peace treaties with the Native Americans and then violated these treaties—sometimes by merely slaughtering the Native Americans or more often by placing them in conditions that were calculated to ensure that all or most of them died.

The broad definition of genocide has been alleged to apply to the modern-day treatment meted out to their indigenous citizens by some North American and European governments. It is alleged to apply to the treatment of Kurds in Iraq, Turkey, and Iran. The United States pressed for the prosecution of the former Iraqi president on charges of genocide, but we may never know whether he was guilty of this crime because the United States silenced him by summarily executing him after an unfair trial conducted after its illegal invasion of his country, acts that themselves constitute other very serious international crimes as defined by international law. The American obsession with murdering Sunnis and Ba'ath party members in Iraq, the Taliban in Afghanistan, and supporters of the elected Hamas government in Palestine might all constitute genocide if one takes a broad view of genocide.

## The Legal Prohibition of Genocide

Stirred by the inhumanity of the mass killing and extermination of people, the international community adopted a legal definition of genocide about the same time as it created the United Nations. It was too late to apply this treaty to the World War II holocaust, however, because the Nüremberg trials were already under way. Nevertheless, in 1948, the Convention on the Prohibition and Punishment of Genocide was adopted.[2] Article II of this widely ratified treaty defines genocide as both specific categories of acts and a specific intention. The prohibited acts include killing, inhumane treatment, deliberately inflicting conditions of life calculated to destroy a group of people in whole or in part, preventing births through specific measures, and transferring children from one group of people to another by force.

The intention required to constitute genocide when these acts are committed by a person is the "intent to destroy, in whole or in part, a national, ethnical, racial or religious group."[3] This legal definition has been adopted by the ad hoc international criminal tribunals for the former Yugoslavia and Rwanda and in the treaty creating the International Criminal Court. This definition has been applied by the two ad hoc international criminal tribunals.

The International Criminal Tribunal for Rwanda was the first court to ever convict a person of genocide. This happened in the cases of Mr. Jean-Paul Akayesu, a former mayor of the city of Taba in Rwanda, and Mr. Jean Kambanda, the former prime minister of Rwanda. Akayesu had encouraged others to kill or rape Tutsi Rwandan women and intended to participate in such acts. In this case, the tribunal made it clear that genocide could take place even by acts that "may fall short of causing death." The tribunal also pointed out that intention could be presumed by acts that had a clear goal of destroying all or part of a group. Kambanda had pleaded guilty, apparently accepting that his mere participation in cabinet meetings where the massacre of Tutsi Rwandans was discussed was sufficient grounds for a charge of genocide. The court made clear that intention could be extrapolated from the actions of the accused. The Rwanda Tribunal also convicted Mr. Alfred Musema of both the crime against humanity of extermination and the crime of genocide. The tribunal found that Musema had both personally taken part in attacks against Tutsi Rwandans and had helped others kill Tutsi Rwandans by transporting them and telling them to kill others. His intention was shown by the mere fact that his deeds contributed to the larger policy of killing Tutsi Rwandans.[4]

In 2005, the International Criminal Tribunal for the Former Yugoslavia found Mr. Vidoje Blagojevic guilty of complicity in genocide because he had killed and tortured numerous Bosnian Muslims.[5] There have also been domestic convictions for genocide. In 2003, a Rwandan court convicted about one hundred people for participation in genocide. And in 2006, after a twelve-year trial, an Ethiopian military court found the country's former ruler Lt. Col. Mengistu Haile Mariam guilty of genocide in absentia.

Some of these cases of genocide were committed in a very short period of time, others over years. Some of these cases involved direct killings, others involved placing people in conditions of life that would destroy them as a group. For example, genocide can be committed when a group is deliberately deprived of the resources needed to survive, such as drinking water, food, clothing, shelter, and medical services. When genocide has been considered such a terrible act and has been relatively well-defined, can it still be happening?

## Palestine: A Case of Contemporary Genocide

No single example better exemplifies the international community's failure to stop genocide than the case of Israel's ongoing genocide of Palestinians. This contemporary genocide has existed since and as long as the international crime of genocide has been defined. The Palestinians owned approximately 94 percent of Palestine prior to the creation of Israel in 1947. United Nations General Assembly Resolution 181(II) of 1947, however, gave Israel 54 percent of the land of Palestine. By the end of the 1948 war, this had climbed to about 80 percent, approximately where it stands today.

Since 1967, Israel has confiscated an estimated 60 percent of the West Bank and an estimated 33 percent of the Gaza Strip; Israel has also confiscated an estimated 33 percent of the Palestinian land in Jerusalem for public, semipublic, and private use in order to create Israeli military zones, settlements, industrial areas, and elaborate "bypass" roads and quarries, as well as to hold "state land" for exclusive Israeli use. While Israel withdrew its settlements in Gaza, it often reoccupies territory in Gaza and maintains about 200 settlements in the West Bank.   Israel's intention in undertaking these acts appears clear. In fact, Israel's intention was illustrated long ago by its government officials, starting with the first prime minister of Israel, Golda Meir, who infamously told the *Sunday Times* on June 16, 1969, that "[t]here were no such thing as Palestinians." Then, in an attempt to justify her earlier statement, Meir told the *New York Times* on January 14, 1976, that she meant to say that "[t]here is no Palestine people. There are Palestinian refugees." Both quotes provide at least prima facie evidence of stated intentions to destroy the Palestinian people by pretending that they just don't exist. By following the Israeli intention as evidenced in Meir's statements through forty years of acts of illegal and oppressive occupation, it is not too difficult to see that Israel believes that if Palestinians do not exist then they can be exterminated without violating any law. To see this is Israel's view, one just has to recount how this state has maintained nearly forty years of occupation with inhumane results. Israel has intentionally and directly killed thousands of Palestinians since the 1960s. The regular reports about how many Palestinians have been killed by Israel aggression have been ongoing for forty years. Israel has deliberately inflicted conditions of life on Palestinians calculated to destroy them at least in part. One only has to read the reports of human rights NGOs or of the United Nations human rights bodies to understand how Israel has intentionally caused serious bodily or mental harm to thousands of Palestinians through widespread beatings, torture, rape, arbitrary detention, and other acts, including the deliberate deprivation of resources needed for the group's physical survival. The recent withholding of the vital customs taxes that Israel collected for, and then stole from, the Palestinians is an example of the latter. The frequent denial of access to medical services, including emergency resources—clean water, food, clothing, and shelter—are also duly recorded by numerous sources.

Israel has also destroyed Palestinian civilian infrastructure, confiscated land, depleted water supplies, uprooted trees and vegetation, and dumped toxic waste and other pollutants on Palestinian land. A 2000 UN report documents how "children born to Arab parents in Jerusalem...often cannot be registered and issued birth certificates if their parents do not have the necessary residency status." It then estimates that "there are approximately ten thousand unregistered children in Jerusalem [alone] who will not be entitled to receive an identity card when they reach the age of 16" and that this "lack of residency status also deprives them of health and social insurance and the right to enroll in municipal schools."[6]

Both directly and indirectly, these acts constitute acts of genocide and, by their continuation for such a long period of time, are evidence of genocidal intention. There are also numerous lesser acts that Israel has undertaken to destroy the people of Palestine. The Spanish newspaper *El País*, for example, reported in 2002 on the Israeli destruction of Palestinian records in Ramallah as a "scientific and systematic destruction of all the archives and databases of the public administration."[7]

Israel has prevented the births of Palestinian children by arbitrarily arresting and thereby separating for long periods of time Palestinian spouses, and Israel has prevented Palestinian children who are born from recognizing their adherence to the Palestinian people by repeatedly refusing to allow the registration of Palestinian births.

Moreover, Israel had demolished hundreds of Palestinian homes throughout Palestine as collective punishments of families and in intentional military actions. Since 1987, these violent demolitions have made more than an estimated 20,000 Palestinians homeless, including almost 10,000 children.

Israel has built a wall and numerous barriers that separate not only husbands and wives, but even children from their families. It has accomplished a similar de facto separation of children from their families by arbitrary arrest of thousands of Palestinian men and women. And Israel has imposed by direct force or by fear of violence, duress, detention, psychological oppression, or other methods of coercion the fleeing of whole families, and indirect forcible transfer of children from Palestine. And it should be remembered that many of these acts have been undertaken in violation of a long list of UN resolutions from both the Security Council and the General Assembly. Moreover, some of the acts mentioned above have already been recognized to be illegal by decisions of the International Court of Justice.

It should also be remembered that genocide can be committed by acts that do not kill or cause the death of members of a group. Indirect or direct commission of the acts mentioned above when committed as part of a policy to destroy a group's existence is genocide. And participation in genocide includes incitement, conspiracy, direct and public incitement, attempts to commit genocide, and complicity in genocide.

Most important, we should remember that these acts of genocide by Israel against Palestinians are being carried out today, in clear view. Ironically, this last week of January (2007), the world remembers one genocide, while another continues with the compliancy and collaboration of the international community. Shouldn't we ask ourselves when will we ever learn from history?

## Notes

1. Raphael Lemkin, *Axis Rule in Occupied Europe* (Washington D.C.: Carnegie Endowment for International Peace, 1944), 79–95.
2. United Nations Convention on Genocide, December 9, 1948, New York.
3. Ibid.
4. International Criminal Tribunal for Rwanda, www.unhcr.org/refworld/publiation/ictr/html.
5. International Criminal Tribunal for Yugoslavia, www.icty.org/sections/Aboutthecity.
6. Economic and Social Council, "Questions of the Violation of Human Rights in the Occupied Arab Territories Including Palestine," March 15, 2000. www.unispal.un.org/unispal.nsf.
7. *El Pais*, reporting on the 2002 destruct9559ion of Palestinian records in Ramallah, www.star.com.jo/index.php?Itemid=57&id=.

# CHAPTER TWENTY-SEVEN

## Bleaching the Atrocities of Genocide

KIM PETERSEN

(6-7-2007)

A team of public health researchers have called for the expunging of the term "ethnic cleansing" from official use, declaring that it "bleaches the atrocities of genocide and its continuing use undermines the prevention of genocide."[1] In their paper, published in the *European Journal of Public Health* (EJPH), the researchers Rony Blum, Shira Sagi, and Elihu D. Richter in Jerusalem, and Gregory H. Stanton in Fredericksburg, VA, write that the term "ethnic cleansing" emerged politically with Slobodan Milosevic to describe what he deemed the Kosovar Albanians' violence against Serbs. Blum et al. lament the creeping prominence "ethnic cleansing" has since gained, especially in diplomatic and legal language, noting that it has even entered the lexicon of the United Nations. The problem is that, unlike "genocide," "ethnic cleansing" has no legally recognized status and no legal obligations.

The researchers draw a historical link between genocide and such phrases as *Judenrein* (used by Nazis to refer to an area without Jews; *rein* means "pure, clean" in German). "The genocides of the past century have shown the propagation of an in-group exterminatory exclusivity based upon myths of hygiene or purity, and dehumanization of the other group, are warning signs of imminent genocide."[2] To which I would append, "or a genocide in perpetration." Some experts point to a vagueness over what "ethnic cleansing" is. Andrew Bell-Fialkoff, the author of *Ethnic Cleansing*, wrote that "ethnic cleansing"

> defies easy definition. At one end it is virtually indistinguishable from forced emigration and population exchange while at the other it merges with deportation and genocide. At the most general level, however, ethnic cleansing can be understood as the expulsion of an "undesirable" population from a given territory due to religious or ethnic discrimination, political, strategic or ideological considerations, or a combination of these.[3]

The definitional murkiness plays into the hands of "genociders." Blum et al. argue, "The role of 'reverse jargon' in reversing ordinary social ethics has been crucial to the genocidal agenda of the perpetrators and to sustaining in-group self-esteem. The term 'ethnic cleansing' 'normalizes' the delusion that massacres are measures to promote 'hygiene.'"[4] The researchers identify avoidance of the term "genocide" as a pretext for inaction. They speculate that earlier labeling as "genocide" may have saved tens of thousands of lives in Bosnia, Kosovo, Rwanda, and Darfur.[5]

Herein lies a criticism of Blum et al.'s study While the etymology of the term "ethnic cleansing" and its misuse demand attention and action, the examples provided in Blum et al.'s paper are suggestive of an agenda. The regions where they determined genocide to have occurred (Bosnia, Kosovo, Rwanda, and Darfur) are those that concur with the expressed view of the U. S. government. Aside from Rwanda, the occurrence of genocide is disputed. The International Court of Justice determined that Serbia committed no genocide in Bosnia.[6] Veteran journalist John Pilger referred to Kosovo as "the site of a genocide that never was"[7]; this was backed by a UN court.[8] Darfur is the scene of African Muslim fighting African Muslim. Neither the UN nor EU finds what happened in Darfur to be genocide.[9] Neither do the CIA or MI6, who deal openly with Sudanese government officials.[10] Missing from Blum et al.'s study are, for instance, the genocides in the Democratic Republic of the Congo (DRC), Iraq, and Palestine.

## Genocide in the DRC

Genocide has been wreaked in the Congo since before the days of the genocidal Belgian monarch Leopold. In Leopold's day it was elephant tusks and rubber that spurred European greed.[11] The plunder of the DRC's resources still attracts Western corporations. The people of the DRC still suffer.[12]

Dr. Les Roberts's epidemiological studies into Iraqi civilian mortalities stirred up some minor controversy in the corporate media before being directed to the Memory Hole. Previously, he had less controversially led survey teams in the DRC that concluded:

- 1.7 million excess deaths or more have occurred over the past twenty-two months as a result of the fighting in the eastern DRC. This equates to 77,000 deaths per month, and the International Rescue Committee (IRC) believes this is a conservative estimate.
- Young children are missing from the demographic profile. Some 34 percent of the excess deaths are children under five and, depending on the location, 30 to 40 percent are children under two years of age. In addition to the violent deaths of children in battles zones, it is presumed that excessive infant mortality rates and high maternal death rates have contributed to this troubling discovery.[13]
- Violent deaths and "nonviolent" deaths are inseparable.
- Violence against civilians is indiscriminate. Women and children constituted 47 percent of the violent deaths reported.[14]

Several writers report a figure of 4 million Congolese killed. One writer pointed the finger at Western corporations' lust for the DRC's "black gold" of coltan, used to make tantalum capacitors for cell phones and other high-tech electronics, as driving the genocide. Foreign traders sell the coltan to just three companies: The United States' Cabot Inc., Germany's HC Starc, and China's Nigncxia. Only these firms are capable of refining coltan into the desired tantalum powder. The tantalum powder is sold to Nokia, Motorola, Compaq, Sony and other manufacturers.[15] News of the millions killed in the DRC, however, has been largely propagandized or marginalized in the corporate media.

## Genocide in Iraq

This use of racist epithets characterizes the language of U.S. occupation soldiers to describe Iraqis. U.S. soldier Joshua Key wrote:

Iraqis, I was taught to believe, were not civilians; they were not even people. We had our own terms for them. Our commanders called them ragheads, so we did the same. We called them habibs. We called them sand niggers. We called them hajjis; it wasn't until I was sent to war that a man in Iraq explained to me that hajji was a complimentary term for a Muslim who had made the pilgrimage to Mecca. In training, all I knew was that a hajji was someone to be despised.[16]

Former staff sergeant Jimmy Massey, a twelve-year veteran of the Marines, described the U.S.-initiated violence in Iraq:

As far as I'm concerned, the real war did not begin until they saw us murdering innocent civilians. I mean, they were witnessing their loved ones being murdered by US Marines. It's kind of hard to tell someone that they are being liberated when they just saw their child shot or lost their husband or grandmother.

Massey unequivocally identified what was happening in Iraq. "We are committing genocide in Iraq," he bluntly declared, "and that is the intention."[17] That the U.S.-UK invasion-occupation is genocide in perpetuation is attested to by excess mortality data published in the esteemed medical journal the *Lancet.* The researchers carried out a national cross-sectional cluster sample survey of mortality in Iraq, randomly selecting fifty clusters from sixteen governorates between May and July in 2006. They concluded a probability that 655,000 excess mortalities had occurred since the invasion in March 2003. The researchers also stated that the mortalities were increasing year by year.[18]

One academic extrapolated and updated the *Lancet* data, arriving at a figure of a million excess civilian mortalities among Iraqis. This does not include the genocidal UN-U.S. sanctions prior to 2003 that killed another million or more Iraqis.[19]

### Genocide in Palestine

Zionists' dehumanization of Palestinians is well documented. Various Israeli prime ministers have called Palestinians, among other slights, crocodiles, cockroaches, beasts on two legs, and nonexistent. As Noam Chomsky has said, "Contempt for the Arab population is deeply rooted in Zionist thought."[20] In March, I reviewed expatriate Israeli historian Ilan Pappe's recent book that forthrightly affirmed that Zionists had carried out an ethnic cleansing of Palestine. Gary Zatzman and I took exception with Pappe's fudging on the question of genocide. Pappe writes,

> Massacres accompany the operations [of ethnic cleansing], but where they occur they are *not part of a genocidal plan*: they are a key tactic to accelerate the flight of the population earmarked for expulsion ( 2) [italics added]. . . . *Ethnic cleansing is **not** genocide*, but it does carry with it atrocious acts of mass killing and butchery" (197) [emphasis added].

Pappe is generous with the definition of "ethnic cleansing" (e.g., "part of the essence of ethnic cleansing is the eradication, by all means available, of a region's history") but parsimonious with the definition of "genocide." Pappe considers 1948 a "clear-cut case, according to informed and scholarly definitions, of ethnic cleansing." Simply put, "genocide" is the killing of a group, and "ethnic cleansing" is the removal of a group. But "genocide" is not so simple. Article 2 (a, b, c, & d) of the Convention on the Prevention and

Punishment of the Crime of Genocide seems to apply well to the case of 1948 and also to events occurring today.[21]

## Linguistic Cleansing

The EJPH paper calls for linguistic accuracy so that agents of flagrant criminal actions will bear full culpability and responsibility. Blum et al. compellingly make the case for discarding the term "ethnic cleansing" and calling genocide what it is. Given the horror and massive moral repulsion of genocide, linguistic cleansing is required. I had previously used "ethnic cleansing" in the denotation of "forced mass expulsions," unaware of its sinister etymology. However, mere linguistic accuracy *per se* is insufficient.[22]

While linguistic accuracy is important, of greater importance is the recognition and identification of the perpetrators of genocide. Blum et al. focused on countries outside their backyards and overlooked genocides perpetrated by their own countries. This is not only intellectually dishonest, but it detracts from the morality that implicitly underlies their position in the EJPH paper.

## Stopping Genocide

Juan Mendez, a UN special adviser on the prevention of genocide, said, "We need to talk about early warning and early action in ways that can help prevent genocide without waiting until the last minute."[23] Already the legal apparatus exists to deal with the perpetrators of genocide once it has been identified. But the former UN secretary-general Kofi Annan lamented countries' continued reluctance to honor their obligations under international law.

"We continue to lack the needed political will, as well as a common vision of our responsibility in the face of massive violations of human rights and humanitarian catastrophes occasioned by conflict." Despite massacres of "near genocide proportions" in the DRC, Liberia, and elsewhere, "our response to them has been hesitant and tardy."[24] What is needed is an independent international institution fully empowered to investigate and identify genocide wherever it may occur in the world and to make public its findings. The ghastly crimes of genocide must not be left to the inexpertise of ad hoc bureaucracy.

Countries must not shirk from prosecuting genocidal crimes. They must speak out unhesitatingly, with linguistic clarity, and act with forthright remediation. Elementary morality demands, though, that we confront, criticize, act against, atone, and repent of our own great crimes first before we can criticize, with any iota of moral integrity, the great crimes of others. After all, linguistic honesty is more easily practiced when one has a clear conscience.

218      *Kim Petersen*

## Notes

1. Rony Blum, Gregory H. Stanton, Shira Sagi, and Elihu D. Richter, "'Ethnic Cleansing' Bleaches the Atrocities of Genocide," *European Journal of Public Health Advance Access* 18 (2) (2008): 204–209.
2. Ibid, 1.
3. Andrew Bell-Fialkoff, "A Brief History of Ethnic Cleansing," *Foreign Affairs*, Summer 1993. www.foreignaffairs.com/articles/48961/andrew-bell-fialkoff/a-brief-history-of-ethnic-cleansing.
4. Blum et al., 2.
5. Ibid., 4.
6. "ICJ: Serbia Not Guilty of Bosnia Genocide but Broke Law by Not Preventing Srebrenica," *JURIST*, February 26, 2007.
7. John Pilger, "John Pilger Reminds Us of Kosovo," *New Statesman*, December 13, 2004.
8. "Kosovo Assault 'Was Not Genocide,'" *BBC News*, September 7, 2001.
9. Rupert Cornwell, "Darfur Killings Not Genocide, Says UN Group," *Independent*, January 31, 2005. Rory Carroll, "Sudan Massacres Are Not Genocide, Says EU," *Guardian*, August 10, 2004.
10. Jonathan Steele, "Darfur Wasn't Genocide and Sudan Is Not a Terrorist State," *Guardian*, October 7, 2005. Steele held that there is "not genocide or classic ethnic cleansing" in Darfur; rather, it "was, and is, the outgrowth of a struggle between farmers and nomads."
11. Adam Hochschild, *King Leopold's Ghost: A Story of Greed, Terror and Heroism in Colonial Africa* (Boston: Houghton Mifflin, 1999).
12. Kim Petersen, "Canadian Predation in Africa," *Dissident Voice,* June 5, 2003.
13. Congo Crisis Special Report. "Mortality Study, Eastern D.R. Congo (April–May 2000)," International Rescue Committee, 2000. www.theirc.org/mortality-study-eastern-dr-congo-april-may-2000.
14. Sprocket, "High-Tech Genocide," *Lughnasadh* (July–August 2005). Available at www.*Earth First!Journal*.org/author.php?author=sprocket. Press Release, "Security Council Condemns Illegal Exploitation or the Democratic Republic of Congo's Natural Resources," UN Security Council, March 5, 2001.
15. Ibid.
16. Nilanjana S. Roy, "Jarheads, Ragheads and Deserters," *BS Online*, May 22, 2007.
17. Jeff Riedel, "We're Committing Genocide in Iraq," *World Socialist Web Site*, November 11, 2004.
18. Gilbert Burnham, Riyadh Lafta, Shannon Doocy, and Les Roberts, "Mortality after the 2003 Invasion of Iraq: A Cross-Sectional Cluster Sample Survey," *Lancet* 368 (October 2006): 1421–1428.
19. Gideon Polya, "US Iraqi Holocaust And One Million Excess Deaths," *Countercurrents*, February 7, 2007.
20. Noam Chomsky, *Fateful Triangle: The United States, Israel & The Palestinians* (Cambridge, MA: South End Press, 1999).
21. Ilan Pappe, *The Ethnic Cleansing of Palestine* (Oxford: Oneworld Publications, 2006).
22. Kim Petersen, "Nakba: The Israeli Holocaust Denial," *Dissident Voice*, March 18, 2007.
23. In Mary Kimani, "Protecting Civilians from Genocide," *Africa Renewal* 20, no. 2 (July 2006): 4.
24. Ibid.

# CHAPTER TWENTY-EIGHT

## Looking from the Side, from Belsen to Gaza

### JOHN PILGER

### (1-18-2007)

A genocide is engulfing the people of Gaza while a silence engulfs its bystanders. "Some 1.4 million people, mostly children, are piled up in one of the most densely populated regions of the world, with no freedom of movement, no place to run and no space to hide," wrote the senior UN relief official, Jan Egeland, and Jan Eliasson, then Swedish foreign minister, in *Le Figaro*. They described people "living in a cage," cut off by land, sea and air, with no reliable power and little water and tortured by hunger and disease and incessant attacks by Israeli troops and planes.

Egeland and Eliasson wrote this four months ago (September 28, 2006) as an attempt to break the silence in Europe, whose obedient alliance with the United States and Israel has sought to reverse the democratic result that brought Hamas to power in last year's Palestinian elections. The horror in Gaza has since been compounded; a family of eighteen has died beneath a 500-pound American/Israeli bomb; unarmed women have been mown down at point-blank range. Dr. David Halpin, one of the few Britons to break silence on what he calls "this medieval siege," reported the killing of fifty-seven children by artillery, rockets, and small arms and has shown evidence that civilians are Israel's true targets, as in Lebanon last summer. A friend in Gaza, Dr. Mona El-Farra, e-mailed: "I see the effects of the relentless sonic booms [a collective punishment by the Israeli air force] and artillery on my thirteen year old daughter. At night, she shivers with fear. Then both of us end up crouching on the floor. I try to make her feel safe, but when the bombs sound I flinch and scream."

When I was last in Gaza, Dr. Khalid Dahlan, a psychiatrist, showed me the results of a remarkable survey. "The statistic I personally find unbearable," he said, "is that 99.4 per cent of the children we studied suffer trauma. Once you look at the rates of exposure to trauma you see why: 99.2 percent of their homes were bombarded; 97.5 percent were exposed to tear gas; 96.6 percent witnessed shootings; 95.8 percent witnessed bombardment and funerals; almost a quarter saw family members injured or killed." Dr. Dahlan invited me to sit in on one of his clinics. There were thirty children, all of them traumatized. He gave each pencil and paper and asked them to draw. They drew pictures of grotesque acts of terror and of women with tears streaming down their faces.

The excuse for the latest Israeli terror was the Palestinian resistance's capture in June 25, 2006, of an Israeli soldier, a member of an illegal occupation. This was news. Israel's kidnapping a few days earlier of two Palestinians—two of thousands taken over the years—was not news. A historian and two foreign journalists have reported the truth about Gaza. All three are Israelis. They are frequently called traitors. The historian Ilan Pappe has documented that "the genocidal policy [in Gaza] is not formulated in a vacuum" but part of Zionism's deliberate, historic ethnic cleansing. Gideon Levy and Amira Hass are reporters on the Israeli newspaper *Ha'aretz*. In November 2006, Levy described how the people of Gaza were beginning to starve to death: "There are thousands of wounded, disabled and shell-shocked people unable to receive any treatment...the shadows of human beings roam the ruin...they only know the [Israeli army] will return and what this will mean for them: more imprisonment in their homes for weeks, more death and destruction in monstrous proportions."

Amira Hass, who has lived in Gaza, describes it as a prison that shames her people. She recalls how her mother, Hannah, was being marched from a cattle-train to the Nazi concentration camp at Bergen-Belsen on a summer's day in 1944. "[She] saw these German women looking at the prisoners, just looking," she wrote. "This image became very formative in my upbringing, this despicable 'looking from the side.'"

"Looking from the side" is what those of us who are cowed into silence by the threat of being called anti-Semitic do. Looking from the side is what too many Western Jews do, while those Jews who honor the humane traditions of Judaism and say, "Not in our name!" are abused as "self-despising." Looking from the side is what almost the entire U.S. Congress does, in thrall to or intimidated by a vicious Zionist "lobby." Looking from the side is what "even-handed" journalists do as they excuse the lawlessness that is the source of Israeli atrocities and suppress the historic shifts in the Palestinian resistance, such as the implicit recognition of Israel by Hamas.

The people of Gaza cry out for better.

CHAPTER TWENTY-NINE

# Hope Destroyed, Justice Denied: The Rape of Palestine

## WILLIAM A. COOK

## (1-7/8-2006)

"The Estate of Zion is pitiful because of sin and iniquity."
"The Lord hath accomplished his fury; he hath poured out his fierce anger, and hath kindled a fire in Zion, and it hath devoured the foundations thereof."

*(Lamentations of Jeremiah* 4:11)

The Prophet Jeremiah (626–586 b.c.) lamented the pitiful state of Zion as it "shed the blood of the just in the midst of her," and as the "sons of Zion" "wandered as blind men in the streets, they (have) polluted themselves with blood, so that men could not touch their garments" (Lam. 4: 13–14). And he prophesied that Zion would become "a terror to thyself, and to all thy friends." As we witness Ariel Sharon slide ineluctably into that great dark night, the words of Jeremiah come back to haunt Israel. This man, like no other in recent Israeli politics, has left his indelible mark on Palestine, carved like a searing branding iron on the landscape, the mark created by his Wall of Fear, which marks the Israel he strove to create out of stolen Palestinian land even as he herded 3 million people into walled corrals like cattle. This man, who wielded euphemistic words to kill truth as skillfully as he thrust his sword to kill the innocent, created a new party, the National Responsibility Party, to retain power that he might finish his job of cleansing Israel of Palestinians. Who better to create a still-born party of such a name than the man who severed the national spirit of the Jews by wielding a sword that cut in two the very fabric of Jewish morality.

Let's view this man as he stumbles off the political stage in Israel, when but a week ago he hoped to grasp the olive branch of the Labor Party to swing back into power. As America's mainstream press prepares to eulogize this man for his many accomplishments following the lead of *USA TODAY*— "Ariel Sharon first came to prominence as an army officer in the 1950s. After leaving the military he entered politics, forging the hard line Likud Party. In 1982, Sharon was forced to step down as the party's defense minister, but re-emerged as prime minister in 2001"—they will pen other nondescript passages that overlook the truth of what the man did.

In 1982, Sharon was forced to leave his post because he oversaw and permitted the slaughter of Palestinian civilians in the refugee camps of Sabra and Shatila, an event, together with his mass killings in the Jenin refugee camp in the West Bank some twenty years later, for which he faces prosecution for war crimes in Belgium. These details the American people are not to know, nor are they to know that the UNSC passed Resolution 521 condemning those massacres. So as Sharon awaits the inevitable, let us view him against a moral mirror that will reflect his most grievous crimes. Let's view what Sharon's IDF (Israeli Defense Forces) has done and continues to do in light of a resolution adopted by the UN unanimously and without abstentions, a document that Israel signed at a later date, the UN Convention against Genocide.

In 1944, the term "genocide" appeared in Raphael Lemkin's *Axis Rule in Occupied Europe*. This passage by Frank Chalk and Kurt Jonassohn summarizes Lemkin's understanding:

> Under Lemkin's definition, genocide was the coordinated and planned annihilation of a national, religious, or racial group by a variety of actions aimed at undermining the foundations essential to the survival of the group as a group. Lemkin conceived of genocide as "a composite of different acts of persecution or destruction." His definition included attacks on political and social institutions, culture, language, national feelings, religion, and the economic existence of the group. Even non-lethal acts that undermined the liberty, dignity, and personal security of members of a group constituted genocide if they contributed to weakening the viability of the group. Under Lemkin's definition, acts of ethnocide—a term coined by the French after the war to cover the destruction of a culture without the killing of its bearers—also qualified for genocide.[1]

It was Lemkin's work that paved the way for the United Nations Convention against Genocide in 1948. Lemkin's "composite of different acts of persecution or destruction" includes attacks on a people's political institutions, its culture, its national feelings, its religion, and its economic existence. It also includes nonlethal acts that undermine the liberty, dignity, and personal security of members of the group, as such acts weaken the viability of the group. It would appear that many of the actions perpetrated by Sharon and his government and carried out by the IDF fit Lemkin's definition.[2] Let's consider the wording of the convention as we review Sharon's tenure in office.

These are the criteria that determine genocide under the UN Convention:

Article II:
"In the present Convention, genocide means any of the following acts committed with intent to destroy, in whole or in part, a national, ethnical, racial, or religious group, as such:

  a. Killing members of the group;
  b. Causing serious bodily or mental harm to members of the group;
  c. Deliberately inflicting on the group conditions of life calculated to bring about its physical destruction in whole or in part;
  d. Imposing measures intended to prevent births within the group;
  e. Forcibly transferring children of the group to another group."

Article III:
"The following acts shall be punishable:

  a. Genocide;
  b. Conspiracy to commit genocide;
  c. Direct and public incitement to commit genocide;
  d. Attempt to commit genocide;
  e. Complicity in genocide."

Let's focus on "a" and "b" only from Article II, leaving "c" for another article since space is at a premium. But let's note in passing that the acts described in the UN Convention are not restricted to a nation-state and its people, but also apply to groups, groups such as the Palestinians, who have no recognized state but do represent "an ethnical, racial, and religious group." The UN, while recognizing Israel as a state for Jews in 1947, also recognized a state for the indigenous population of Palestine, though that group failed to acquiesce to the UNGA Resolution at that time. The UN has consistently maintained recognition for Palestine since 1947 through approximately 169 resolutions that identify the Palestinian group as aggrieved by the Israelis. Thus, it is appropriate that we consider the acts the Sharon government has perpetrated on the Palestinians to determine whether in fact they constitute a breach of the UN Convention on the Prevention of the Crime of Genocide.

## Killing Members of the Group

Following Ariel Sharon's blatant desecration of the Al Aqsa Mosque with his entourage of 1,000 IDF soldiers, the start of the current intifada in 2000, an act intended to force the Palestinians to anger and rioting, the most recent count of Israeli-inflicted death on Palestinians stands at 4,140 (Palestine Center for Human Rights [PCHR] reports a higher number of Palestinianskilled, 4,871), 852 of these children, 117 caused by IDF forces denying access to medical care, and another 31 still-born births resulting from IDF checkpoints denying the mothers access to hospitals.[3] By contrast, during this same time period, 1,113 Israelis were killed. The Palestinian Red Crescent Society (PRCS) counts 29,198 injuries, with 3,530 of these permanently disabled (PRCS website, October 23, 2005). In short, Israeli soldiers kill in excess of 1,000 Palestinians each year and permanently maim a similar number. Let us note that the Hague Court has determined that the killing of 7,000 Muslim men and boys in Srebrenica in 1995 by General Radislav Krsyic constituted genocide, rejecting his argument that the numbers were too insignificant to be called genocide.

Since these killings result not only from rifle fire but from tanks, bombs, missiles, and F-16 fighter jets, and since approximately 1,300 were women and children or those killed by prevention of access to medical care, they constitute crimes against Article 33 of the Geneva Convention relative to the Protection of Civilian Persons in Time of War, an article that states explicitly, "No protected person may be punished for an offense he or she has not personally committed. Collective penalties and likewise all measures of intimidation or of terrorism are prohibited...Reprisals against protected persons and their property are prohibited." This means that IDF force that can produce death and/or injury to noncombatants must not be used, nor can collective punishment be inflicted, yet that is the modus operandi of the IDF in its acts against Palestinians.

Perhaps a recent (October 10, 2005) and all-too-familiar vignette might make the above statistics come alive. "Three Palestinian teenagers were shot by Israeli troops patrolling the southern section of Israel's border with Gaza."[4] The bodies were discovered by medics next to the security fence near the Kissufim crossing; none were armed, though they carried bags with food and clothing. An Israeli army spokesman said that troops had opened fire toward three "suspicious figures" crawling close to the Palestinian side of the fence. No attempt had been made to intercept the youngsters or to determine where they were going. Such acts of indifferent brutality are contrary to the laws that govern occupation armies even as they proclaim the intent of the IDF to wantonly kill Palestinians.

Furthermore, since almost all of the above killings occurred on Palestinian land, occupied by the invading Israeli military, they constitute breaches of international law that requires occupying forces to behave in a manner that respects and protects the rights and individuality of the population suffering the occupation (See 75 U.N.T.S. 287 [1949] and Protocol I 1125 U.N.T.S. 3 [1979]). In addition, the United Nations Security Council Resolution 1544 (2004) "cites Israel's obligations as an 'occupying power' under international law and references the Territories 'occupied' since 1967."[5]

As we moved through month after month of 2005, Sharon's forces have continued their illegal "targeted killing" of Hamas militants, a shorthand way of saying Israel has disbanded the basis of law in the West to reintroduce the law of the ancient barbarian states that granted license to the tribal chief or absolute authority to the local tyrant to determine guilt without arrest, without issuance of a charge, without counsel, without a plea, and without a court, resulting in illegal assassination that goes unnoticed and unpunished in Israel and the United States, the self-extolled bulwarks of democracy in the world. What hypocrisy. Thus have we come full circle in the Mid-East as a new barbarian horde inflicts its merciless power on the innocent as well as the condemned—for it inevitably happens, as it did this week (January 1, 2006), that innocent bystanders suffer the same fate as the objects of extrajudicial execution. The IDF record, as reported by the PCHR as of January 2004, shows 309 civilians killed as a result of 157 executions. Rule without law, an action approved by the U.S. government and supported by the American tax dollar. Yet no one objects.

The above evidence of Sharon's brutality constitutes what is countable in the way of deaths attributable to the illegal actions of the IDF. But there are other consequences to this occupation that are lost to the nonobservant eye. Were it not for the international community, the strangulation imposed on the Palestinians would result in many more deaths by malnutrition and starvation. Since close to three-quarters of the Palestinian population is unemployed, the population depends on outside sources for survival. This cloaks the real savagery of the Israeli occupation, since the international community maintains a level of food and medical supplies that keep many who would have died without such aid alive. This also removes the expense of this aid from the government of Sharon that should, under international law, have to carry the cost of the occupation. There is a terrible irony in this, since Americans pay for the settlers to live on stolen Palestinian land while Sharon saves his government's money to further the theft of more and more land.

## Causing Serious Bodily or Mental Harm to
## Members of the Group

Where does one begin to describe the bodily or mental harm inflicted on the Palestinians by the Israeli Offensive Forces (IOF) and its pit bulls, the squatters? Since we are focusing here on the efforts of Sharon to ethnically cleanse the Palestinians from their land, we will say nothing of early voices such as Ben-Gurion's that claimed, "We will abolish the partition of the country, and we will expand to the whole land of Israel," a statement guaranteed to create mental anguish in the population. More importantly, such disregard of the UN's Partition Plan would, of necessity, result in bodily harm, and itemize a few of the thousands of acts that constitute genocide under the definition as stated in the UN Convention, acts done while Sharon governed and continues to govern the country.

Let's begin with the October 2004 Human Rights Watch report, "Razing Rafah" (6), that observes IOF activity in Gaza: "IDF positions fire with large caliber machine guns and tanks at civilian areas [shooting which] appears to be largely indiscriminate and in some cases unprovoked." The report continues, "Violence against Palestinians has by no means been confined to the soldiers of the IDF. Settlers, too, have weighed in with their own abuses, actions that have increased sharply since 2000. These include blocking roads in order to disrupt the lives of Palestinians, shooting solar panels on roofs of buildings, torching cars, smashing windowpanes and windshields, destroying crops, uprooting trees and generally abusing the population." According to the Israel B'Tselem human rights organization, "The intent was often to force Palestinians to leave their homes and farmland, and thereby enable the settlers to gain control of them." These are dispassionate words, merely descriptions of acts that, if witnessed, would cause revulsion.

Consider this account reported by B'Tselem:

> Raja'a Taysir Muhammad Abu 'Ayesha, age seventeen, a high school student and resident of Hebron in the West Bank. She describes the experience of growing up under Israeli occupation. "I have no social life. Our house is like a cage. It is completely fenced in, including the entrance. My grandfather set it up that way in 1996 to protect us, after settlers broke all of our windows. Our house looks like an island surrounded by a sea of soldiers, settlers and a violent atmosphere. The settlers have also attacked my school. Almost every day, the settlers' children block the path for me and my sister, Fida'a, age fourteen. They throw stones, water

and leftover food at us. The settlers throw stones and leftover food at the house while we are inside, and sometimes at night while we are sleeping. My brothers and I wake up frightened, worried, and scared there is not one family member that hasn't been attacked by settlers.'"

I've walked the streets of Hebron, hunched my shoulders instinctively as I moved beneath the chicken wire strung above to catch the stones and garbage thrown at the Palestinians who must pass through this gauntlet to get to the market, and felt the humiliation that falls like a wet, heavy blanket over the soul beneath the taunting slurs cast from above.

This is intentional, calculated, heinous psychological torture—genocidal "mental harm," as described in the UN Convention.

"The decline in the well-being and quality of life of Palestinian children," reports Human Rights Watch, "[in the occupied territories] over the past two years has been rapid and profound. According to CARE, 17.5% of children in Gaza are malnourished." Thirteen percent of children between the ages of six months and five years "have moderate to severe acute malnutrition." Nearly half of Palestinians live below the poverty line. Hospitals are in dire need of basic supplies including water and electricity. Almost 90 percent of the Rafah population depends on food aid. And while malnutrition and poverty imposed by the Israeli oppressors seems hideous enough, it pales in comparison to the reality facing the children as they grow up in the occupation. Dr. Shamir Quota, the director of research for the Gaza Community Mental Health Programs, makes this observation: "Ninety percent of children two years old or more have experienced many, many times the [Israeli] army breaking into the home, beating relatives, destroying things. Many have been beaten themselves, had bones broken, were shot, tear gassed, or had things happen to siblings and neighbors."[6]

Contemplate that statistic: 90 percent of two-year-olds growing up have witnessed soldiers bursting through the door of their home, rifles pointed at their mother or father, pushed against walls, beaten perhaps, shouted at certainly, cursed we might assume, and left in fear knowing another raid is imminent. What torture is here? This is intentional, calculated, psychological torture, genocidal "mental harm," as described in the UN Convention.

But there's more. I left Palestine shortly after the "disengagement" from Gaza, a word that masks the reality of that "peace" move by Sharon. There is no disengagement: Sharon's government owns the sky above Gaza; it owns the fence around Gaza; it owns access and exit from Gaza; it owns sea passage and use of the sea that borders Gaza; and it owns the missiles that it hurls from F-16s into the cities and refugee camps inside Gaza indifferent to the innocent incinerated by its savagery. The only real disengagement that Sharon authorized in Gaza is disengagement from responsibility under the Geneva Conventions for occupying powers to provide adequately and humanely for the people so occupied. That means Israel does not have to pay for the care of the people who are locked into their prison in this most heinous apartheid on the face of the planet.

Consider how this mental torture is inflicted. Three months ago (October 2005), Israeli warplanes dropped thousands of leaflets on Gaza directed to the residents of the Strip. This is the text:

- The terrorist actions originating from your areas are forcing the Israel Defense Forces to respond harshly to those who are subjecting the citizens of the State of Israel to danger.
- We call on the Palestinian Authority to shoulder its responsibility to prevent these criminal acts.
- We warn you of the danger of remaining in the areas which are being used to launch terrorist actions and we advise you to leave your homes.
- We are not responsible for the consequences if you ignore our warning.[7]

Article 33 of the Geneva Conventions states, "No protected person may be punished for an offence he or she has not personally committed. Collective penalties and likewise all measures of intimidation or of terrorism are prohibited." This action by the Israeli forces is calculated to instill fear. It attempts to coerce the residents to leave their homes. But where can they go? The Israelis control the exits from Gaza; they alone determine who can go and who can come. The people are left to find safety in the maze of alleys that constitutes the cities and the refugee camps; left in fear that the missiles can fall anywhere; left in the conflicted horror of their minds and emotions that long for the security of their children uncertain that they may be carrying them to an unknown death flung from the sky. This is intentional psychological fear imposed by a government and against every moral sense that rests on the recognition that innocent humans cannot be collectively punished when they are in no position to prevent the demands made upon them.

Move now to the West Bank. Chris McGreal reported on October 20, 2005, that the Israeli military "blocked Palestinians from driving on the main artery through the West Bank in a first step towards what Israeli human rights groups say is total 'road apartheid' being enforced throughout the occupied territory." He further explains that the military has been authorized to bar all Palestinians from roads used by Israelis in the West Bank, the result being that Palestinians are being forced to use secondary roads, "many little more than dirt tracks or roads which have yet to be built."[8] Anyone who has taken these "secondary" roads understands that they are generally scraped gravel passages between buildings or tracks carved into the hilly landscape lacking finished surfaces or protective guardrails. They wander over the mogul hills designed originally for farmers to access distant fields, not for today's traffic and ready access to cities and towns. This insidious action creates a silent anger that seeps inside the soul and festers there, a tormenting anger against those who would inflict such wanton harm collectively on a group simply because they are Palestinian. This blatant racism is not lost on the children who must endure both the humiliation and the swelling hatred that arises visibly in the adults who curse the conditions imposed by the occupiers.

The West Bank, we must remember, belongs to the Palestinians. The Israeli roads are built on confiscated land. The action approved by Sharon prevents the indigenous people from using their own land or roads built on their land; it prevents not only personal and community interaction, it prevents commercial activity as well. It is nothing more than a calculated attempt to destroy the viability of a people to provide for themselves, an attempt to cause deep and continuing mental harm, actions contrary to the UN Genocide Convention.

Again in October 2005, Israeli troops invaded the town of Bil'in, going house to house to arrest peaceful demonstrators who had participated in public pacifist actions against the erection of the Sharon Wall of Fear. The IOF distributed leaflets in Arabic warning people not to take part in direct action against the wall—this in a purported democratic country. Never forget that this wall is being built on Palestinian land against their expressed desires. "For the last ten months, Bil'in has launched an ongoing non-violent campaign against the annexation barrier supported by hundreds of Israeli and international activists. It has been met with brutally violent Israeli repression. Israel designed the current route of the barrier to annex sixty percent of Bil'in's agricultural land to Israel, and expand the settlement of Modi'in Elite."[9]

None of this activity, the peaceful demonstrations or the brutality of the Israeli forces, has been reported in America's mainstream press or shown on the major channels. Why? Why haven't Dobbs, Brown, Cooper, and Olberman let the cameras roll so that Americans can witness the use of their tax dollars that support the racism that is at the heart of Sharon's bestial behavior against the Palestinians? Let them compare the treatment our government provides for the 35.9 percent that live in poverty in New Orleans and the suburban life style we provide for Jewish immigrants to a foreign state, the state of Israel. Why?

The Israeli historian Ilan Pappe wrote of the Jews currently residing in Israel who lived through 1948 that they know what happened; it is not a distant memory: they know and have experienced the attempted genocide, but they "succeed in erasing it totally from their own memory while struggling rigorously against anyone trying to present the other, unpleasant, story of 1948." These same individuals witness Sharon's new set of atrocities and do nothing. Perhaps they, too, like most Americans, can do nothing to change their government's actions, can do nothing to force their representatives to investigate the genocide they support with American tax dollars, and can do nothing to make those who accept torture as an American practice flinch at genocide.

If the above is not enough to stamp indelibly in a compassionate mind the intolerable actions perpetrated on the Palestinian people by Sharon's militaristic government, then I advise the doubters to travel to Palestine, to witness firsthand what bodily and mental harm means in fact to those who must endure it day after day. A true accounting is long overdue of these barbaric acts done on behalf of Jews and Americans, acts that demean and destroy the morality inherent in Judaism and Christianity.

It's time for the United Nations to stand against America's bought regime that fosters this genocide; to call upon the peoples' representatives to acknowledge the atrocities they have permitted and continue to permit; to assert the relevance of the UN as the voice of humanity by prohibiting this administration to veto the resolution that accepted the judicial ruling of the International Court of Justice condemning Sharon's Wall of Fear as not just illegal but inhumane; and, finally, to take control of the conflict in Palestine by stating plainly, forcefully, and with absolute determination the need for Israel to remove its people from Palestinian land, to accept the internationally recognized right of the Palestinian people to return to their homes (in accordance with Article 12.4 of the International Covenant on Civil and Political Rights), and to tear down the icon that now characterizes Judaism around the world, a wall that incarcerates a people, isolating them from the community of nations—a new ghetto wall erected on behalf of the one people in the world who have experience with this kind of racism and know the mental suffering and bodily harm it imposes on generation upon generation, singed on the soul like the tattoos that marked the imprisoned Jew in Europe.

Jews in the thousands around the world decry Sharon's attempt to ethnically cleanse the Palestinians from their homeland by acts that cause bodily harm and mental anguish. "Traditional Jews are much troubled by the increasing frequency of references to Jewry and their supposed connection to Israel in political and media rhetoric such as was heard at the recent political conventions. Focusing on this issue only serves to inflame anti-Semitism, an historically essential component to the advancement of Zionism, while endangering traditional Jews who are wrongly and unfairly blamed for the deplorable actions of the secular state of Israel."[10] Indeed, many Jews living in Israel actively work on behalf of Palestinians, rebuilding demolished homes, teaching the truth of the Nakba, participating in peaceful demonstrations with Palestinians, as at Bil'in, working in the Israeli courts to seek some sort of justice for those wrongfully detained or imprisoned, working hand in hand with Palestinian organizations to bring about reconciliation, and serving as witnesses to the acts of Sharon's government through B'Tselem Human Rights Watch. Sharon has created an anti-Semitic state by destroying the very foundation of Judaism as it survived over the centuries, a foundation built on tolerance for all peoples and their beliefs, a tolerance that gave them license to retain and practice their own.

The existence of the state of Israel attests to the world's recognition that lack of such tolerance will not be accepted, that when another state imprisons and attempts to destroy another people, the world will not stand by, but act to protect those subject to such racial outrage. That is the purpose of the UN Genocide Convention. When a demagogue like Sharon takes control of the state, when his policies erode, nay destroy hope in a people, when he denies justice to that people, when he lets his hordes humiliate, abuse, and kill a people disregarding international law and all the conventions the people of the world have designed to care for each other, and when a president of the United States condones and supports those acts, then it is the responsibility of the Jewish people and the American people who have supported this racist government to renounce allegiance to that government and call upon the international body to investigate the actions taken by Sharon as he attempts to commit genocide against the Palestinians. Should this ravishment of the Palestinians go unattended, this rape of Palestine, then the words of Jeremiah will ring again across the hills and valleys of Palestine, the land where the ancient prophets admonished the Jews of old, where Christ called upon the people to love one another, to, indeed, love thy enemy, and the Prophet's words will once again warn of impending doom, "Behold, I will make thee a terror to thyself, and to all thy friends."

## Notes

1. Frank Chalk and Kurt Jonassohn, *The History and Sociology of Genocide* (New Haven, CT: Yale University Press, 1990), 8–9.
2. Raphael Lemkin, *Axis Rule in Occupied Europe* (Washington D.C.: Carnegie Endowment for International Peace, 1944), 79–95.
3. Palestine Center for Human Rights, No. 38, September 21–27, 2006. www.pchrgaza.org. See also The Palestine Central Bureau of Statistics (PCBS), Palestine Ministry of Higher Education, Applied Research Institute Jerusalem.
4. "Chronological Review of Events," *Monthly Media Monitoring Review.* October 2005. www.unispal.un.org.

5. PLO Negotiations Affairs Department, October 2004. www.nad-plo.org/listing.php?
   view=palisrael_wall_press.
6. "Trauma, Grief, and PTSD in Palestinian Children Victims of War in Gaza" (updated
   study, 2009), www.gamhp.net.
7. *Al Watan*, October 1, 2005. www.alwatan.com.kw.
8. Chris McGreal, "Israel Accused of Road Apartheid in West Bank," *Guardian*, October 20,
   2005.
9. ISM, "Israeli Military Raids Bil'in Arrests Eleven Non Violent Activists Monday,"
   *Occupation* Magazine, October 24, 2005. www.kbush.co.il/show-file.asp?num-9467.
10. Torah True Jews, "Traditional Jews Apalled (*sic*) by Connection to Israel," Rense.com,
    October 20, 2004. www.rense.com/general58/zzin.htm.

CHAPTER THIRTY

# Relative Humanity:
## The Essential Obstacle to a One-State Solution

OMAR BARGHOUTI

(12-13/14-2003)

"Conquest may be fraught with evil or with good for mankind, according to the comparative worth of the conquering and conquered peoples."

(Theodore Roosevelt, *The Winning of the West*)[1]

## Introduction

Good riddance! The two-state solution for the Palestinian-Israeli conflict is finally dead. But someone has to issue an official death certificate before the rotting corpse is given a proper burial and we can all move on and explore the more just, moral, and therefore enduring alternative for peaceful coexistence between Jews and Arabs in Mandate Palestine: the one-state solution.

Blinded by the arrogance of power and the ephemeral comfort of impunity, Israel, against its strategic Zionist interests, failed to control its insatiable appetite for expansion and went ahead with devouring the very last bit of land that was supposed to form the material foundation for an independent Palestinian state. Since the eruption of the second Palestinian intifada, Israel has entered a new critical phase where its military repression against the Palestinians in the occupied West Bank and Gaza has reached new lows, and its flouting of UN resolutions new heights, where its incessant land grab has led it to erect a wall around Palestinian population centers, separating Palestinians from their lands—thus dispossessing them yet again—and where moral corruption and racial discrimination have more lucidly eroded the internal coherence of Israeli society as well as its marketed image as a "democracy." As a result, Israel's standing in world public opinion has nosedived, bringing it closer to the status of a pariah state.

This phase has all the emblematic properties of what may be considered the final chapter of the Zionist project. We are witnessing the rapid demise of Zionism, and nothing can be done to save it, for Zionism is intent on killing itself. I, for one, support a symbolic euthanasia for Zionism. The two-state solution, besides having passed its expiry date, was never a moral solution to start with. In the best-case scenario, if UN Resolution 242 were meticulously implemented, it would have addressed most of the legitimate rights of less than a third of the Palestinian people over less than a fifth of their ancestral land. More than two-thirds of the Palestinians—refugees as well as the Palestinian citizens of Israel—have been dubiously and shortsightedly robbed of their identity as Palestinians. Such exclusion can only guarantee the perpetuation of conflict.

But who is offering the "best-case" scenario to start with? No one, as a matter of fact. The best offer so far falls significantly short of even Resolution 242—not to mention the basic principles of morality. After decades of trying to convince the Palestinians to give up their rights to the properties they had lost during the *Nakba* (the 1948 catastrophe of dispossession and exile) in return for a sovereign, fully independent state on all the lands that were occupied in 1967, including East Jerusalem, Israel has shown that it really never had any intention to return all those illegally acquired lands. From Camp David II to Taba to Geneva, the most "generous" Israeli offer was always well below the minimal requirements of successive UN resolutions and the basic tenets of justice.[2] Admitting that justice is not fully served by his government's offer at Camp David, for instance, the former Israeli foreign minister Shlomo Ben-Ami gave the Palestinians a choice between "justice or peace."[3] Peace decoupled from justice, though, is not only morally reprehensible but pragmatically unwise as well. It may survive for a while, but only after it has been stripped of its essence, becoming a mere stabilization of an oppressive order, or what I call the master-slave peace, where the slave has no power or will to resist and therefore submits to the dictates of the master, passively, obediently, without a semblance of human dignity. As Jean-Jacques Rousseau once wrote:

> The strongest man is never strong enough to be master all the time, unless he transforms force into right and obedience into duty.... Force

is a physical power; I do not see how its effects could produce morality. To yield to force is an act of necessity, not of will; it is at best an act of prudence. In what sense can it be a moral duty?[4]

Well, the Palestinians' "prudence" is running out. The yielding of their official leadership to force merely led to more colonization and promises for yet more to come.

## Relative Humanity and the Conflict

From the onset, the two main pretences given by the Zionists to justify their colonization of Palestine were:

1. Palestine was a land without a people, an uncivilized wasteland;
2. The Jews had a divine right to "redeem" Palestine, in accordance with a promise from no less an authority than God, and because, according to the Bible, the Israelites built their kingdoms all over the Land of Canaan a couple of thousand years ago, giving them historical rights to the place. Thus, any dispossession of the natives of Palestine, if they existed, was an acceptable collateral damage to the implementation of God's will.

If this sounds too close to Bush's jargon, it is mere coincidence. By now, both the political and the religious arguments have been shown to be no more than unfounded myths, thanks in no small part to the diligent work of Israeli historians and archaeologists.[5]

Doing away with both political fabrication and biblical mythology, Joseph Weitz, the head of the Jewish Agency's Colonization Department in 1940, explained the truth about how this "redemption" was to be carried out:

Between ourselves it must be clear that there is no room for both peoples together in this country. We shall not achieve our goal if the Arabs are in this small country. There is no other way than to transfer the Arabs from here to neighboring countries—all of them. Not one village, not one tribe should be left.[6]

At the very core of the rationalization of such an expulsion lies an entrenched colonial belief in the irrelevance, or comparative worthlessness, of the rights,

needs, and aspirations of the native Palestinians. For instance, the author of
the Balfour Declaration wrote:

> The four Great Powers are committed to Zionism. And Zionism,
> be it right or wrong, good or bad, is rooted in age-long traditions,
> in present needs, in future hopes, of far profounder import than the
> desires and prejudices of the 700,000 Arabs who now inhabit that
> ancient land.[7]

It is a classic case of what I call relative humanization. I define relative
humanity as the belief, and relative humanization as the practice based on
that belief, that certain human beings, to the extent that they share a common
religious, ethnic, cultural, or other similarly substantial identity attribute,
lack one or more of the necessary attributes of being human, and are therefore human only in the relative sense, not absolutely, and not unequivocally.
Accordingly, such relative humans are entitled to only a subset of the otherwise inalienable rights that are due to "full" humans.

Perceiving the Palestinians as relative humans can explain why Israel—
supported by the United States and in many cases by Europe too—has gotten
away with a taking-for-granted attitude toward the Palestinians that assumes
that they cannot, indeed ought not, have needs, aspirations, or rights equal to
those of Israeli Jews. This factor has played a fundamental role in inhibiting
the evolution of a unitary state solution, as will be shown below.

Besides relative humanization, there are many impediments on the way
to the morally superior solution of a single state. Given the current level of
violence, mutual distrust, and hate between the two sides, for example, how
can such a solution ever come true? Besides, with the power gap between
Israel and the Palestinians being so immense, why would Israeli Jews accept
this unitary state, where, by definition, Jews will be a minority? Is Israeli con-
sent really necessary as a first step, or can it be eventually achieved through
a combination of intensive pressure and lack of viable alternatives, just as in
the South African case (where boycotts by external organizations and states
forced the end of apartheid)?

These concerns are indeed valid and crucial to address, but rather than delv-
ing into each one of them, I shall limit myself to showing how the alternatives
to the one-state solution are less likely to solve the conflict, partially because
the principle of equal human worth, which is the fundamental ingredient in
any lasting and just peace, is conspicuously ignored, breached, or repressed in
each of them. This in itself may not logically prove that the one-state solution
is the only way out of the current abyss, but it should at least show that it
certainly deserves serious consideration as a real alternative.

## Paths to Ending the Conflict

At this time, and given the impossibility of achieving a negotiated two-state solution that can give Palestinians their minimal inalienable rights, there are three logical paths that can be pursued:

1. Maintaining the status quo, keeping some form of the two-state solution alive, if only on paper;
2. "Finishing the job," or reaching the logical end of Zionism, by implementing full ethnic cleansing of the Palestinians out of the entire Mandate Palestine. Since genocide of the scale committed to rid America or Australia of their respective natives is not politically viable nowadays, ethnic cleansing is the closest approximation;
3. Launch new visionary and practical processes that will lead to the establishment of a unitary democratic state between the Jordan and the Mediterranean.

Let us explore each of these three options:

### Maintaining the Status Quo

Above everything else, the status quo is characterized by three attributes: denial of the Palestinian refugees' rights, military occupation and repression in the West Bank and Gaza, and Zionist apartheid in Israel proper.

### a. Denial of Palestinian Refugees' Rights

Far from admitting its guilt in creating the world's oldest and largest refugee problem, and despite overwhelming incriminating evidence, Israel has systematically evaded any responsibility. The most peculiar dimension in the popular Israeli discourse about the "birth" of the state is the almost wall-to-wall denial of wrongdoing. Israelis by and large regard as their "independence" the ruthless destruction of Palestinian society and the dispossession of the Palestinian people. Even committed leftists often grieve over the loss of Israel's "moral superiority" after occupying the West Bank and Gaza in 1967, as if prior to that Israel were as civil, legitimate, and law-abiding as Finland! In a classic self-fulfilling prophecy, Israel has always yearned to be a normal state to the extent that it actually started believing that it was.[8] It is as if most of those Israelis who actively participated or bore witness to the Nakba were collectively infected by some chronic selective amnesia.

This denial has its roots in the Holocaust and in the unique circumstances created as a result of it, which allowed Israel to argue that, unlike any other state, it was obliged to deny Palestinian refugees their unequivocal right to return to their homes and lands. Preserving the Jewish character of the state, the argument went, was the only way to maintain a safe haven for the world Jewry, the "super-victims" who are unsafe among the gentiles, and that of course was of much more import than the mere rights of the Palestinians. Even if we ignore the compelling comparison between the safety of Jews in Israel versus in France, Morocco, Spain, the United States, or, for that matter, Germany, we cannot overlook the fact that no other country on earth today can ever get away with a similarly overt, racist attitude about its right to ethnic purity.

Besides being morally indefensible, Israel's denial of the right of return also betrays a level of moral inconsistency that is in many ways unique. The Israeli law of return for Jews, for instance, is based on the principle that since they were expelled from Palestine over 2,000 years ago, they have a right to return to it. So by denying the rights of Palestinian refugees, whose fifty-five-year-old exile is a much younger injustice, to say the least, Israel is essentially saying that Palestinians cannot have the same right because they are just not equally human.

Here are some more examples of this moral inconsistency:

- Thousands of Israelis whose grandparents were German citizens have successfully applied for their right to return to Germany, to gain German citizenship, and to receive full compensation for pillaged property. The result was that the Jewish population of Germany jumped from 27,000 in the early 1990s to over 100,000 last year.[9]
- Belgium has also passed a law "enabling properties that belonged to Jewish families to be returned to their owners." It also agreed to pay the local Jewish community 55 million euros in restitution for stolen property that "cannot be returned" and for "unclaimed insurance policies belonging to Holocaust victims."[10]

But the quintessence of moral hypocrisy is betrayed by the following example reported in *Ha'aretz*:

More than five centuries after their ancestors were expelled from Spain, Jews of Spanish origin...called on the Spanish government and parliament to grant them Spanish nationality...Spain should pass a law "to recognize that the descendants of the expelled Jews belong to Spain and to rehabilitate them," said Nessim Gaon, president of the World

Sephardic Federation...Some Sephardic Jews have even preserved the keys to their forefathers' houses in Spain.[11]

Supporting the right of return of Palestinian refugees to their homes is, in my view, the litmus test of morality for anyone suggesting a just and enduring solution to the Palestinian-Israeli conflict. However, many, including Bill Clinton and the entire spectrum of the official Left in Israel, have flunked the test. "Left" and "Right" are relative terms everywhere, but in Israel the distinction can be totally blurred at times. On the issues of ethnic purity, demography, and chauvinism, Israeli politicians and intellectuals on the Left, even those self-proclaimed as "the left,"[12] have made the Far Right parties of Europe sound as humane as Mother Teresa. The crucial difference, however, is that in the case of Israel, the immorality is aggravated by the fact that, unlike the Spanish Jews, who were foreign immigrants to Europe, the displaced peoples are in fact the natives of the land.

Despite the above, one must not deny that the right of return of Palestinian refugees contradicts the requirements of a negotiated two-state solution. Israel simply will never accept it, making it the Achilles' heel of any negotiated two-state solution, as the record has amply shown. It has nothing to do with the merits or skills of the Palestinian negotiators, as lacking as they may have been, but rather with a staggering imbalance of power that allows an ethnocentric and colonial state to safeguard its exclusivist nature by dictating conditions on a pathetically weaker interlocutor. This is precisely why the right of return cannot really be achieved, except in a one-state solution. That would allow the Palestinian weakness to be turned into strength, if they decide to adopt a nonviolent path to establishing a secular democratic state, thereby gaining crucial international backing and transforming the conflict into a nondichotomous struggle for freedom, democracy, equality, and unmitigated justice. Again, South Africa's model has to be tapped into for inspiration in this regard.

### b. Military Occupation: War Crimes,[13] Large and Small

Following a visit to the completely fenced in Gaza Strip, Oona King, a Jewish member of the British parliament, commented on the irony that Israeli Jews face today: "In escaping the ashes of the Holocaust, they have incarcerated another people in a hell similar in its nature—though not its extent—to the Warsaw ghetto."[14] Any human being with a conscience who has recently visited the Occupied Territories cannot but agree with King. Faced with the Palestinians' seemingly inextinguishable aspiration for justice and emancipation, Israel has resumed for the last three years (2000–2003) a campaign of wanton destruction, indiscriminate atrocities, and medieval-like sieges with the clear intention of collectively punishing the Palestinians, potentially forcing them to abandon their lands en masse. The rest are mere details, painful and tormenting as they may be.

### c. Israel's Apartheid Wall,[15] Palestinian Human Rights vs. Israeli Animal and Plant Rights

Although Israel is now trying to present the separation wall as a security barrier to "fend off suicide bombers," the truth is that the current path of the wall is anything but new.[16] It was recommended to Ariel Sharon by the infamous "prophet of the Arab demographic threat," the Israeli demographer Amon Sofer, who insists that the implemented map was all his. And unlike the slick Israeli politicians, Sofer unabashedly confesses that the wall's path was drawn with one specific goal in mind: maximizing the land to be annexed to Israel, while minimizing the number of "Arabs" that would have to come along. But Sofer may be taking too much credit for himself. Ron Nahman, the mayor of the West Bank settlement of Ariel, has revealed to the Israeli daily *Yedioth Ahronoth* that " the map of the fence, the sketch of which you see here, is the same map I saw during every visit [Ariel Sharon] made here since 1978. He told me he has been think-ing about it since 1973." There weren't many "suicide bombings" going around then!

Four years ago (1998), well before the intifada started, Ariel Sharon himself, it turned out, had evocatively called the wall project the "Bantustan plan," according to *Ha'aretz*. Despite the wall's grave transgression against Palestinian livelihood, environment, and political rights, a "near-total consensus"[17] exists amongst Israeli Jews in supporting it. Several official and nongovernmental bodies in Israel, however, are concerned about the adverse effects the wall might have on animals and plants. The Israeli environment minister Yehudit Naot protested against the construction of the wall, saying,

> The separation fence severs the continuity of open areas and is harmful to the landscape, the flora and fauna, the ecological corridors and the drainage of the creeks. The protective system will irreversibly affect the land resource and create enclaves of communities [of animals, of course] that are cut off from their surroundings. I certainly don't want to stop or delay the building of the fence, because it is essential and will save lives. On the other hand, I am disturbed by the environmental damage involved.[18]

Her ministry and the National Parks Protection Authority mounted diligent rescue efforts to save an affected reserve of irises by moving it to an alternative reserve. They've also created tiny passages for animals and enabled the continuation of the water flow in the creeks. Still, the spokesperson for the parks authority was not satisfied. He complained:

> The animals don't know that there is now a border. They are used to a certain living space, and what we are concerned about is that their genetic diversity will be affected because different population groups will not be able to mate and reproduce. Isolating the populations on two sides of a fence definitely creates a genetic problem.[19]

Even Thomas Friedman, has predicted—quite accurately, in my view—in the *New York Times*[20] that the wall will eventually "kill" the two-state solution, thereby becoming "the mother of all unintended consequences."

### d. Smaller Crimes of the Occupation
Not all the crimes of the Israeli military occupation are as overbearing as the wall. I shall address below only four examples of smaller, yet rampant, war crimes:

i. Birth and Death at an Israeli Military Checkpoint: Rula, a Palestinian woman, was in the last stages of labor. Her husband, Daoud, could not convince the soldiers at a typical military checkpoint to let them through to meet the ambulance that was held up by the same soldiers on the other side. After a long wait, Rula could no longer hold it. She started screaming in pain, to the total apathy of the soldiers. Daoud described the traumatic experience to *Ha'aretz*'s exceptionally conscientious reporter Gideon Levy, saying:

> Next to the barbed wire there was a rock...My wife started to crawl toward the rock and she lay down on it. And I'm still talking with the soldiers. Only one of them paid any attention, the rest didn't even look. She tried to hide behind the rock. She didn't feel comfortable having them see her in her condition. She started to yell and yell. The soldiers said,"Pull her in our direction, don't let her get too far away." And she was yelling more and more. It didn't move him. Suddenly, she shouted, "I gave birth, Daoud! I gave birth!" I started repeating what she said so the soldiers would hear in Hebrew and Arabic. They heard. Rula later shouted "The girl died! The girl died!" Daoud, distraught and fearing

for his wife's own life, was forced to cut the umbilical cord with a rock. Later, the doctor who examined the little corpse at the hospital revealed that the baby girl had died "from a serious blunt force injury received when she shot out of the birth canal."[21]

Commenting on the similar death of another Palestinian newborn at another Israeli checkpoint, a spokeswoman for the Israeli Physicians for Human Rights said:

> We don't know how many have died like this because many people don't even bother to set out for hospital, knowing the soldiers will stop them.... These people offer no threat to Israel. Those who do, like the suicide bombers, of course never go through roadblocks, which exist only to control, subjugate and humiliate ordinary people. It is like a routine terrorism.[22]

ii. Hunting Children for Sport: The veteran American journalist Chris Hedges exposed in *Harper's Magazine* how Israeli troops in Gaza systematically curse and provoke Palestinian children playing in the dunes of southern Gaza. Then, when the boys finally get irritated enough and start throwing stones, the soldiers premeditatedly respond with live ammunition from rifles fitted with silencers. Later, writes Hedges, "in the hospital, I will see the destruction: the stomachs ripped out, the gaping holes in limbs and torsos." He then concludes, "Children have been shot in other conflicts I have covered...but I have never before watched soldiers entice children like mice into a trap and murder them for sport."[23]

iii. Patients & the Siege: Reporting on a particularly appalling incident, Gideon Levy writes in *Ha'aretz*:

> The soldiers made Bassam Jarar, a double amputee with kidney disease, and Mohammed Asasa, who is blind in both eyes, get out of the ambulance. Both men had come from dialysis treatment. About half an hour passed, and then blood started to drip from the tube that is permanently inserted in Jarar's lower abdomen.
> "I told the soldier on the tank that I was bleeding. He told me to sit there and that they'd take me to a doctor. We sat there in the sun for almost an hour." The bleeding increased. After about an hour, two soldiers came and lifted up Jarar and placed him on the floor of their jeep. "I told them that I couldn't travel in a jeep. They said that's all there was and that they were going to take me to a doctor. The guy drove like a

maniac and I was bouncing up and down and my whole body hurt. I told them that it hurt. They said, 'Don't be afraid, you're not going to die.' There were four soldiers in the jeep and I was on the floor. He wouldn't slow down. And the soldiers were laughing and not looking at me at all."[24]

iv. Sexual Assault: In another crime, two Israeli Border Police officers coerced a Palestinian shepherd to wear on his back the saddle of his donkey and walk back and forth before them; and then, at gunpoint, one of the two forced him to have sex with his donkey for half an hour, as documented by B'Tselem.[25]

Based on this culture of relative humanization of "the other," Nathan Lewin, a potential candidate for a federal judgeship in Washington and former president of the International Association of Jewish Lawyers and Jurists, writes:

If executing some suicide-bomber families saves the lives of even an equal number of potential civilian victims, the exchange is, I believe, ethically permissible . . . It is a policy born of necessity—the need to find a true deterrent when capital punishment is demonstrably ineffective.[26]

Diplomacy aside, "civilian" here stands for "Jewish" only, of course. Harvard Law professor Alan Dershowitz has likewise advised Israel to entirely level any Palestinian village that harbors a suicide bomber.[27] Little wonder, then, that someone as morally consistent as Shulamit Aloni, a former member of the Knesset, finds it necessary to say, "We do not have gas chambers and crematoria, but there is no one fixed method for genocide."[28]

*e. Do Israelis Know?*

In my view, the British journalist Jonathan Cook hit it right on when he wrote:

[Israelis] know exactly what happens: their Zionist training simply blinds them to its significance. As long as the enemy is Arab, as long as the catch-all excuse of security can be invoked, and as long as they believe anti-Semitism lurks everywhere, then the Israeli public can sleep easy as another [Palestinian] child is shot riding his bike, another family's house is bulldozed, another woman miscarries at a checkpoint . . . It seems that a people raised to believe that anything can be done in its name—as long as it serves the interests of Jews and their state—has no need of ignorance. It can commit atrocities with eyes wide open.[29]

And this is not new. The Zionist thinker Ahad Ha'am described the anti-Arab attitude of the Jewish settlers that came to Palestine to escape repression in Europe, long before Israel was created, as follows:

> Serfs they were in the lands of the Diaspora, and suddenly they find themselves in freedom [in Palestine]; and this change has awakened in them an inclination to despotism. They treat the Arabs with hostility and cruelty, deprive them of their rights, offend them without cause, and even boast of these deeds; and nobody among us opposes this despicable and dangerous inclination.[30]

But if that's the case, then two possible explanations—not necessarily mutually exclusive –may be put forth to explain the Israelis' acceptance of, and sometimes fervent support for, this systematic violation of basic human rights:

1. Widespread belief that their demographic war against the Palestinians could be won by implementing the suggestion of Cabinet Minister Benny Elon, who called for intensifying the siege and repression in order to "make their life so bitter that they will transfer themselves willingly."[31]
2. Secular or not, the root of the entrenched Israeli perception of the Palestinians as less human is nourished by a racist colonial tradition and rising Jewish fundamentalism. I'll expand a bit on this last point. It is commonplace to read about Islamic fundamentalism and its militancy, anachronism, and intrinsic hate of "the other." Jewish fundamentalism, on the contrary, is a taboo issue that virtually never gets mentioned at all in the West for reasons that are beyond the scope of this essay. But, since Jewish fundamentalism is increasingly gaining ground in Israel, making the state, as the veteran British journalist David Hirst describes it, "not only extremist by temperament, racist in practice, [but also] increasingly fundamentalist in the ideology that drives it."[32] For example, referring to Jewish Law, or *Halacha*, Rabbi Ginsburg, the leader of a powerful Hassidic sect, defended the 1994 massacre of Muslim worshippers in a mosque in Hebron, saying:

> Legally, if a Jew does kill a non-Jew, he's not called a murderer. He didn't transgress the Sixth Commandment... There is something infinitely more holy and unique about Jewish life than non-Jewish life.[33]

Rabbi Shaul Israeli, one of the highest rabbinic authorities of the National Religious Party and of religious Zionism in general, justified the 1953 Qibya massacre, perpetrated by an Israeli army unit led by Ariel Sharon, by also citing Jewish law. He wrote:

> We have established that there exists a special term of "war of revenge" and this is a war against those who hate the Jews and [there are] special laws applying to such war... In such a war there is absolutely no obligation to take precautions during warlike acts in order that non-combatants would not be hurt, because during a war both the righteous and wicked are killed... the war of revenge is based on the example of the war against the Midianites in which small children were also executed, and we might wonder about this, for how they had sinned? But we have already found in the sayings of our Sages, of blessed memory, that little children have to die because of the sin of their parents.[34]

### f. Israel's System of Racial Discrimination: Intelligent, Nuanced but Still Apartheid

American academic Edward Herman writes:

> If Jews in France were required to carry identification cards designating them Jews (even though French citizens), could not acquire land or buy or rent homes in most of the country, were not eligible for service in the armed forces, and French law banned any political party or legislation calling for equal rights for Jews, would France be widely praised in the United States as a "symbol of human decency" (New York Times) and paragon of democracy? Would there be a huge protest if France, in consequence of such laws and practices, was declared by a UN majority to be a racist state?[35]

Advocating comprehensive and unequivocal equality between Arabs and Jews in Israel has become tantamount to sedition, if not treason. An Israeli High Court justice has recently stated on record that "it is necessary to prevent a Jew or Arab who calls for equality of rights for Arabs from sitting in the Knesset or being elected to it."[36]

A recent survey by the Israel Democracy Institute (IDI) reveals that 53 percent of Israeli Jews oppose full equal rights for the Palestinian citizens of Israel, and a staggering 57 percent believe they should be "encouraged to emigrate." One main finding was that when Israeli Jews say "we" or "us" they hardly ever include the Palestinian citizens of the state.[37]

In land ownership rights, the inequality is categorical. "It is forbidden to sell apartments in the Land of Israel to Gentiles," said Israel's chief rabbi in 1986, commenting on an attempt by a Palestinian to buy an apartment owned by the Jewish National Fund in East Jerusalem.[38] In other vital areas of life, including marriage laws, urban development, and education, Israel has perfected a comprehensive apparatus of racial discrimination against its Palestinian citizens that is unparalleled anywhere today.

From all the above-described dimensions of the military occupation, the status quo is untenable, if not because of Palestinian resistance, then because of rising international condemnation.

### Finishing the Job

#### Ethnic Cleansing: Israel's Final Solution to the
#### Palestinian Demographic Threat

Israeli politicians, intellectuals, and mass media outlets often passionately debate how best to face the country's demographic "war" with the Palestinians. Few Israelis dissent from the belief that such a war exists or ought to exist. The popular call to subordinate democracy to demography,[39] however, has entailed the adoption of population-control mechanisms to keep the number of Palestinians in check.

In a stark example of such mechanisms, the Israel Council for Demography was reconvened last year (2002) to "encourage the Jewish women of Israel— and only them—to increase their child bearing; a project which, if we judge from the activity of the previous council, will also attempt to stop abortions," as reported in *Ha'aretz*. This prestigious body, which comprises top Israeli gynecologists, public figures, lawyers, scientists, and physicians, mainly focuses on how to increase the ratio of Jews to Palestinians in Israel, by employing "methods to increase the Jewish fertility rate and prevent abortions."[40]

Besides demographic engineering, this all-out "war" on Palestinian population growth has always involved enticing non-Arabs, Jewish or not, from around the world—preferably, but not necessarily, the white part of it—to come to Israel, and eventually be "Israelized."[41] Israeli scholar Boaz Evron writes:

> Fear of the "demographic threat" has haunted Zionism from the very beginning. In its name Ethiopians were turned into Jews over the objections of rabbis. In its name hundreds of thousands of Slavs came here wearing the Law of Return as a fig leaf. In its name emissaries have gone out across the world seeking out more and more Jews.[42]

With the support of the Israeli government, for example, one Zionist organization, Amatzia,[43] has organized the adoption of foreign children by Jewish families that have fertility problems, insisting only on the condition of converting all the children to Judaism upon arrival in Israel. Romania, Russia, Guatemala, Ukraine, and the Philippines were the main sources of children; but now, after they've "dried up," India has become the source of choice, mainly for the relative ease of acquiring the "goods" there. Amatzia's director, Shulamit Wallfish, has sought children from the northern parts of India in particular, "where the children's skin is lighter, which would better suit Israeli families," according to her.

More concerned about the imminent rise of an Arab majority between the Jordan and the Mediterranean than with the oft-invoked and sanctified notion of "Jewish purity," Ariel Sharon has indeed called on religious leaders to smooth the progress of the immigration and absorption of non-Arabs, even if they weren't Jewish, in order to provide Israel with "a buffer to the burgeoning Arab population," reports the *Guardian*. The Israeli government's view is that "while the first generation of each wave of immigration may have difficulty embracing Israel and Jewishness, their sons and daughters frequently become enthusiastic Zionists. In the present climate, they are also often very rightwing."[44]

Albeit vastly popular, such a policy is not endorsed across the board. Eli Yishai, the leader of the largest Sephardic Jewish party Shas, for example, who is particularly alarmed at the influx of gentiles, hysterically forewarns:

> By the end of the year 2010 the state of Israel will lose its Jewish identity. A secular state will bring…hundreds of thousands of goyim who will build hundreds of churches and will open more stores that sell pork. In every city we will see Christmas trees.[45]

The Israeli Far Right minister, Effi Eitam, prescribes yet another alternative: "If you don't give the Arabs the right to vote, the demographic problem solves itself."[46] One conscientious Israeli who is revolted by all this language of demographic control is Dr. Amnon Raz-Krakotzkin of Ben-Gurion University. He writes: "It's frightening when Jews talk about demography."[47] Also dissenting from the mainstream Israeli view, Boaz Evron argues that

> when we give up defining our national essence by religious criteria, and forcing conversion on people who are good Israeli citizens, and give up the effectively illegal preferences afforded to Jews, it will suddenly become apparent there is no need to worry about the "demographic threat."[48]

But, by far, the all-time favorite mechanism has always been ethnic cleansing. Incessantly practiced, forever popular, but persistently denied by the Zionists, ethnic cleansing has in the last few years been resurrected from the gutters of Zionism to occupy its very throne. The famous Israeli historian Benny Morris has recently argued that completely emptying Palestine of its indigenous Arab inhabitants in 1948 might have led to peace in the Middle East.[49] In response, Baruch Kimmerling, a professor at Hebrew University, wrote: "Let me extend Benny Morris's logic...If the Nazi programme for the final solution of the Jewish problem had been complete, for sure there would be peace today in Palestine."[50] Then why doesn't Israel act upon its desire now, one may ask? Professor Ilan Pappe of Haifa University has a convincing answer:

> The constraints on Israeli behaviour are not moral or ethical, but techni-
> cal. How much can be done without turning Israel into a pariah state?
> Without inciting European sanctions, or making life too difficult for
> the Americans?[51]

Offering a diametrically opposed explanation, Martin Van Creveld, Israel's most prominent military historian, who supports ethnic cleansing, arrogantly shrugs off any concern about world opinion, issuing the following formidable warning:

> We possess several hundred atomic warheads and rockets and can
> launch them at targets in all directions, perhaps even at Rome.
> Most European capitals are targets for our air force...Let me quote
> General Moshe Dayan: "Israel must be like a mad dog, too dangerous
> to bother."...Our armed forces are not the thirtieth strongest in the
> world, but rather the second or third. We have the capability to take
> the world down with us. And I can assure you that that will happen,
> before Israel goes under.[52]

That should amply explain why Europeans have lately ranked Israel first among the countries that are considered a threat to world peace.[53]

Yet a third explanation, which concurs with Pappe's, is that Israel currently enjoys the best of both worlds: it is implementing—on the ground—an elaborate mesh of policies that are making the Palestinians' lives progressively more intolerable, and therefore creating an environment conducive to gradual ethnic cleansing, while at the same time not making any dramatic—Kosovo-like—scene that would alarm the world, inviting condemnation and possible sanctions.[54]

*Israel—The Untenable Essential Contradictions*

Israel's inherent racial exclusivity, as demonstrated above, has convinced many Palestinian citizens of the state that they are not just on the margins, but altogether unwanted. Ameer Makhoul, the general director of Ittijah, the umbrella organization of Palestinian NGOs in Israel, writes:

> The state of Israel has become the most significant source of danger for the million Palestinians who are citizens of the state that was forced upon them in 1948; a state that was erected on the ruins of the Palestinian people... The Palestinian citizens of Israel cannot defend themselves by relying on the legal system and the Knesset. This public has no trust in the state and its institutions, because the Israeli rules of the game enable only discrimination, racism and repression of collective aspirations.[55]

Besides what Palestinians think or want, the question should be posed: Can a state that insists on ethnic purity ever qualify as a democracy, without depriving this concept of its essence? Even Israel's loyal friends have started losing faith in its ability to reconcile the fundamentally irreconcilable: modern liberal democracy and outdated ethnocentricity. Writing in *The New York Review of Books*, New York University professor Tony Judt affirms that

> in a world where nations and peoples increasingly intermingle and intermarry, where cultural and national impediments to communication have all but collapsed, where more and more of us have multiple elective identities and would feel constrained if we had to answer to just one, in such a world, Israel is truly an anachronism. And not just an anachronism, but a dysfunctional one. In today's "clash of cultures" between open, pluralist democracies and belligerently intolerant, faith-driven ethno-states, Israel actually risks falling into the wrong camp.[56]

Avraham Burg, a devoted Zionist leader, reached a similar conclusion. Attacking the Israeli leadership as an "amoral clique," Burg asserts that Israel, which "rests on a scaffolding of corruption, and on foundations of oppression and injustice" must "shed its illusions and choose between racist oppression and democracy."[57]

### *Launch New Visionary and Practical Processes*

*Secular Democratic State: New Horizons*

No matter what our hypocrites, Uncle Toms, or "false prophets" may say, Israel, as an exclusivist and settler-colonial state,[58] has no hope of ever being accepted or forgiven by its victims—and as it should know, those are the only ones whose forgiveness really matters. Despite the pain, the loss, and the anger that relative humanization undoubtedly engenders in them, Palestinians have an obligation to differentiate between justice and revenge, for one entails an essentially moral decolonization, whereas the other descends into a vicious cycle of immorality and hopelessness. As the late Brazilian educator Paulo Freire writes:

> Dehumanization, which marks not only those whose humanity has been stolen, but also (though in a different way) those who have stolen it, is a distortion of the vocation of becoming more fully human... [The] struggle [for humanization] is possible only because dehumanization, although a concrete historical fact, is not a given destiny but the result of an unjust order that engenders violence in the oppressors, which in turn dehumanize the oppressed... In order for this struggle to have meaning, the oppressed must not, in seeking to regain their humanity (which is a way to create it), become in turn oppressors of the oppressors, but rather restorers of the humanity of both.[59]

Rejecting relative humanity from any side, and insisting on ethical consistency, I believe that the most moral means of achieving a just and enduring peace in the ancient land of Palestine is to establish a secular democratic state between the Jordan and the Mediterranean, anchored in equal humanity and, accordingly, equal rights. The one-state solution, whether binational—a notion that is largely based on a false premise that the second nation in question is defined[60]—or secular-democratic, offers a true chance for the decolonization of Palestine without turning the Palestinians into oppressors of their former oppressors. The vicious cycle launched by the Holocaust must come to an end altogether.

This new Palestine should:

1. First and foremost allow and facilitate the return of and compensation for all the Palestinian refugees, as the only ethical restitution acceptable for the injustice they've endured for decades. Such a process, however, must uphold at all times the moral imperative of avoiding the infliction of any unnecessary or unjust suffering on the Jewish community in Palestine;
2. Grant full, equal, and unequivocal citizenship rights to all the citizens, Jews or Arabs;
3. Recognize, legitimize, and even nourish the cultural, religious, and ethnic particularities and traditions of each respective community.

As a general rule, I subscribe to what Professor Marcelo Dascal of Tel Aviv University insightfully proposes:

> [T]he majority has an obligation to avoid as much as possible the identification of the state's framework with traits that preclude the possibility of the minority's commitment to it.[61]

Israelis should recognize this moral Palestinian challenge to their colonial existence not as an existential threat to them but rather as a magnanimous invitation to dismantle the colonial character of the state and to allow the Jews in Palestine finally to enjoy normalcy, as equal humans and equal citizens of a secular democratic state—a truly promising land, rather than a false Promised Land.

That would certainly confirm that Roosevelt is not only dead but is also DEAD WRONG!

## Notes

1. Theodore Roosevelt, *The Winning of the West,* reproduced in Norman Finkelstein, "History's Verdict: The Cherokee Case," *Journal of Palestine Studies* 24, no. 4 (1995): 32–45.
2. For more details about Barak's myth of the "generous offer," refer to David Clark, "The Brilliant Offer Israel Never Made," *Guardian,* April 10, 2002; or Faisal Husseini, "The Compromise That Wasn't: Why Camp David II Failed to Satisfy Minimal Palestinian Conditions," www.AMIN.org, December 12, 2000; or Tanya Reinhart, "The Camp David Fraud," *Yedioth Ahronoth,* July 13, 2000.
3. Barbara Derrick, *Philadelphia Inquirer,* January 16, 2001.
4. Jean-Jacques Rousseau, *The Social Contract* (New York: Penguin, 1968), 52.
5. Several archaeological studies have shown that most of the stories in the Bible used by Zionists to buttress their claim to Palestine were indeed not supported by the region's history, which is "based on direct evidence from archaeology and historical geography and is supported by analogies that are primarily drawn from anthropology, sociology and linguistics," as the archaeologist Thomas L. Thompson has written. (http://www.bibleinterp.com/articles/copenhagen.htm). His findings are supported by the extensive, painstaking, and authoritative research of distinguished Israeli archaeologists, including Ze'ev Herzog (see http://www.prometheus.demon.co.uk/04/04herzog.htm) and Israel Finkelstein (see Aviva Lori, "Grounds for Disbelief," *Ha'aretz,* May 10, 2003).
6. Joseph Weitz, "A Solution to the Refugee Problem," *Davar,* September 29, 1940, cited in Uri Davis and Norton Mevinsky, eds., *Documents from Israel, 1967–1973* (London: Ithaca Press, 1975), 21.
7. "The Origins and Evolution of the Palestine Problem," UN Committee on the Exercise of the Inalienable Rights of the Palestinian People, http://domino.un.org/UNISPAL.NSF/0/aeac80e740c782485266l150 Open Document. June 30, 1990.
8. Henry Kissinger defined as Israel's ultimate objective "a normality that ends claims [from Palestinians] and determines a permanent legal status." Consequently, he has consistently counseled Israel, in return for recognizing a Palestinian state, to insist on a quid pro quo

that included "a formal renunciation of all future [Palestinian] claims." That, he maintained, was "the essence of reasonableness to Americans and Israelis." Henry Kissinger, "The Peace Paradox," *Washington Post*, December 4, 2000, A27.

9. Reuters, "Growing Number of Israelis Seeking Citizenship," *Ha'aretz*, June 17, 2002.

10. Yair Sheleg, "Belgian Prime Minister Apologizes for His Country's Actions during Holocaust," *Ha'aretz*, October 7, 2002.

11. DPA, "Sephardi Jews Demand Recognition from Spanish Government," *Ha'aretz*, October 15, 2002, 18.

12. Celebrated Israeli writers A.B. Yehoshua and Amos Oz wrote: "We shall never be able to agree to the return of the refugees to within the borders of Israel, for the meaning of such a return would be the elimination of the State of Israel." A.B. Yeshoshua and Amos Oz, "Support Barak Conditionally," *Ha'aretz*, December 19, 2000.

13. Amnesty International's examination of Israel's conduct during the current intifada led it to conclude that "there is a pattern of gross human rights violations that may well amount to war crimes." http://www.cnn.com/2000/WORLD/meast/I 11/01/mideast. amnesty.rei.

14. Oona King, "Israel Can Halt This Now," *Guardian*, June 12, 2003. http:/twww.guardian. co.uk/commenVstory/0,3604,975423,00.html.

15. The "separation barrier" has been shown by many researchers to be in effect separating Palestinians from their lands, and isolating them in restrictive Bantustans, fully under the control of the Israeli military. As such, the only proper and accurate name that can be applied to this mammoth barrier is "Apartheid Wall," as many have begun to call it. For details on the wall, refer to the Amnesty International report at http://web.amnesty.org/ pages/isr-index_2-eng, 2-eng, which considers the wall a form of collective punishment, and therefore illegal. See also the Human Rights Watch report at http://www.un.org/ News/Press/docs/2003/galOI79.doc.htm and B'Tselem's detailed position paper at http:// www.btselem.org, or the UNGA resolution condemning the wall at hftp://www.un.org/ News/Press/docs/2003/galOI79.doc.htm.

16. Meron Rappaport, "A Wall in Their Heart," *Yedioth Ahronot*, May 23, 2003. Reproduced at http://1www.gushshalom.org/archives/Wall_yediot-eng.html.

17. Editorial, "A Fence along the Settlers' Lines," *Ha'aretz*, October 3, 2003.

18. Mazal Mualem, "Old Habitats Die Hard," *Ha'aretz*, June 20, 2003.

19. Ibid.

20. Thomas Friedman, "One Wall, One Man, One Vote," *New York Times*, September 14, 2003. http://www.nytimes.com/2003/09/14/opinion/14FRIE.html.

21. Gideon Levy, "Birth and Death at the Checkpoint," *Ha'aretz*, September 12, 2003.

22. John Pilger, "Israel's Routine Terrorism," *The Mirror*, September 16, 2002. http://www. mirror.co.uk/news/alinews/page.cfm? objectid=12202728&method=full&siteid=50143.

23. Chris Hedges, "A Gaza Diary," *Harper's Magazine*, October 2001.

24. Gideon Levy, "Wanted Men," *Ha'aretz*, Friday Magazine, November 8, 2002.

25. B'Tselem, "Sexual Assault in Zeita," June 2003. http:/1www.btselem.org.

26. Ami Eden, "Top Lawyer Urges Death for Families of Bombers," *The Forward*, June 7, 2002.

27. Alan Dershowtiz, "A New Response to Palestinian Terrorism," *Jerusalem Post*, March 11, 2002; cited in Rod Dreher, "Muslims vs. Dersh," *National Review*, November 22, 2002. http://www.nationalreview.com/dreher/dreherl 12202.asp.

28. Shulamit Aloni, "Murder of a Population under Cover of Righteousness," *Ha'aretz*, March 6, 2003. [Translated from Hebrew by Zvi Havkin].

29. Jonathan Cook, "Eyes Wide Open," *Al-Ahram Weekly Online*, August 21–27, 2003. hftp:/ Iweekly.ahram.org.eg/2003/652/op42.htm.

30. Sami Hadawi, *Bitter Harvest* (New York: Olive Branch Press, 1991).

31. Aloni, "Murder of a Population."

32. David Hirst, "The War Game," *The Observer*, September 21, 2003.

33. Israel Shahak, http://www.cactus48.com/jewishlaw.html.

34. Ibid.

35. Edward S. Herman, "Israeli Apartheid and Terrorism," *Z-Magazine*, April 29, 2002. http:// zena.secureforum.com/Znet/ZMag/articies/may94herman.htm.

36. Ibid.

37. *Ha'aretz*, May 22, 2003.

38. *Ha'aretz* January 17, 1986.

39. Lily Galili, "A Jewish Demographic State," *Ha'aretz*, July 1, 2002.

40. Gideon Levy, "Wombs in the Service of the State," *Ha'aretz*, September 9, 2002.

41. "Israeli assimilation" of non-Jewish foreigners is eating away at the Jewish majority, according to recent demographic studies. According to the most conservative—and, in my opinion, misleading—statistics, about 10 percent of the supposed Jewish population of Israel is really non-Jewish. For further details, refer to Yair Sheleg, "Demographic Balancing Acts," *Ha'aretz*, June 13, 2002.

42. Boaz Evron, "Demography as the Enemy of Democracy," *Ha'aretz*, September 11, 2002.

43. Ruth Sinai, "Israelis Can Now Adopt Children from India," *Ha'aretz*, November 11, 2003.

44. Chris McGreal, "Sharon Takes on Rabbis over Jewish Identity," *Guardian*, December 31, 2002.

45. Ibid.

46. Yuli Tamir, "Divide the Land or Divide Democracy," *Ha'aretz*, April 14, 2002.

47. Galili, "Jewish Demographic State."

48. Evron, "Demography."

49. Benny Morris, "A New Exodus for the Middle East,"*Guardian*, October 3, 2002. http:// www.guardian.co.uklisrael/comment/0,10551,803417,00.html.

50. Baruch Kimmerling, "False Logic," *Guardian*, October 5, 2002. http://www.guardian. co.uk/lefters/story/0,3604,805123,00.html.

51. Geraldine Bedell, "Set in Stone," *Observer*, June 15, 2003.

52. Ferry Biedermann, "Interview with the Israeli Military Historian Dr Martin van Creveld," January, 13, 2003. www.rense.com/general34/dutchisraelmilitary.htm. hftp://www.de.indy media.org/2003/01/39170.shtml.

53. Thomas Fuller, "European Poll Calls Israel a Big Threat to World Peace," *International Herald Tribune*, October 31, 2003. http://www.iht.com/ihtsearch.php?id=115858&owner= (IHT)&date=20031031121947.

54. Peace activists Gadi Algazi and Azmi Bdeir explain: "Transfer isn't necessarily a dramatic moment, a moment when people are expelled and flee their towns or villages. It is not necessarily a planned and well-organized move with buses and trucks loaded with people…Transfer is a deeper process, a creeping process that is hidden from view…The main component of the process is the gradual undermining of the infrastructure of the civilian Palestinian population's lives in the territories: its continuing strangulation under closures and sieges that prevent people from getting to work or school, from receiving medical services, and from allowing the passage of water trucks and ambulances, which sends the Palestinians back to the age of donkey and cart. Taken together, these measures

undermine the hold of the Palestinian population on its land." See Ran HaCohen, "Ethnic Cleansing: Past, Present, and Future," www.Antiwar.com, December 30, 2002.

55. Ameer Makhoul, "Looking for a Different Framework of Legitimation, Between the Lines," March 2002. www.between-lines.org.

56. Tony Judt, "Israel: The Alternative," *New York Review of Books*, vol. 50, no. 16, October, 23, 2003. http://www.nybooks.com/articles/16671.

57. Avraham Burg, "The End of Zionism," *Guardian*, September 15, 2003. Reprinted with permission of *The Forward*, which translated and adapted this essay from an article that originally appeared in *Yediot Aharonot*.

58. Even the former deputy mayor of Jerusalem, Meron Benvenisti, says: "In the past two years I reached the conclusion that we are dealing with a conflict between a society of immigrants and a society of natives. If so, we are talking about an entirely different type of conflict...Because the basic story here is not one of two national movements that are confronting each other; the basic story is that of natives and settlers. It's the story of natives who feel that people who came from across the sea infiltrated their natural habitat and dispossessed them." Quoted in Ari Shavit, "Cry, the Beloved Two-State Solution," *Ha'aretz*, August 10, 2003.

59. Paulo Freire, *Pedagogy of the Oppressed* (New York: Herder and Herder, 1972). 28.

60. Binationalism makes two problematic assumptions: that Jews are a nation, and that such a nation has a right to exist as such in Palestine. Clearly binationalism cannot work between Palestinians on the one hand and the world Jewry on the other. But will Israeli Jews define themselves as a nation? Most probably not, since that would contradict the fundamental premise of Zionism. Then do Israelis regard themselves as a nation? Certainly not, since aside from parting with Zionism, that would include the 20 percent Palestinian minority within it.

61. Marcelo Dascal proposes this as a current principle that Israel and its Palestinian citizens ought to uphold as a means of alleviating the conflict between the two identities in opposition. This same principle, however, can be quite useful if applied to the future of a unitary state. Marcelo Dascal, "Identities in Flux: Arabs and Jews in Israel," in G. Weiss and R. Wodak, eds., *Critical Discourse Analysis: Theory and Interdisciplinarity* (Basingstoke, Hampshire: Palgrave Macmillan, 2003), 150–166.

# CHAPTER THIRTY-ONE

## Slow-Motion Ethnic Cleansing

### URI AVNERY

### (10-9-2003)

In his final speech in court, Marwan Barghouti, the Fatah leader on trial, issued a resounding warning: "If Israelis do not adopt the Two-States Solution soon, Israel will disappear. The whole country will become one state, and in this state the Palestinians will soon constitute the majority." I don't know whom Barghouti talked with before using this argument. Probably it was Israeli left-wingers, who are convinced of the brilliance of this strategy.

And indeed, it could be very convincing. Shimon Peres and people like him have been using it for a long time. It is based on the following reasonable assumptions:

- If there is one thing on which 99 percent of Israelis are united, it is the will to live in a state with a solid Jewish majority, whose language and culture are Hebrew.
- This is deeply embedded in the collective Israeli consciousness, partly as a reaction to the persecution of the Jews, the Holocaust, and anti-Semitism in countries where Jews were a minority. Of course, all other peoples want the same, too.
- To the vast majority of Israelis, the idea of a binational state, which means the elimination of the State of Israel, represents the loss of all they have achieved in the country since the first settlers came in 1882.

Therefore, the advocates of this tactic say: don't come to the public with slogans of peace, reconciliation, and hope. That will not work. The Jewish public hates the Arabs and does not trust them. Instead, let's take the feelings of hatred and racial prejudice and use them for a good end. Tell the public that the idea of "two states for two peoples" is the only way to save our state. If it is not realized, the State of Israel will fall apart, a binational state will emerge, and the Jews will become here, too, a fast-shrinking minority. Like the whites in South Africa, they will gradually leave the country. After all, if we have to be a minority, then why in a poor Arab country, as Palestine is liable to become, and not in Canada or Australia?

Marwan Barghouti is not the only one who uses binationalism as a scarecrow. Lately, several Palestinian spokespersons have been waving this flag—not because they believe in it—but in order to frighten Israelis into accepting the two-states plan, which is the only realistic peace plan on the agenda. I warn against this tactic. It is very dangerous. It may seem that there are only two possibilities: one state in the whole country, which will necessarily be binational, or an Israeli state in a part of the country, inside the Green Line, next to a Palestinian state. But there is a third possibility: An Israeli state in all of the country, from which the Palestinian population will be expelled. Few Israelis speak of this openly, but a great many think about it. Good people ignore this alternative because they do not find it thinkable. They imagine Kosovo-style ethnic cleansing: driving millions out in one big dramatic sweep. They console themselves: "The world won't stand for it! Sharon wouldn't dare!"

But there are other ways to implement ethnic cleansing: not dramatically, but slowly, daily, even routinely. Like, for example, what's happening now in Bethlehem. It works like this: Pressure is put on property owners; they are told, "It's better for you to sell us your properties now, before the authorities come and expropriate them for security reasons." (In this case: the security of the nearby Rachel's Tomb). Very high prices are offered. They are promised that a new life will be arranged for them in Canada or Australia, far from the Palestinian organizations that might kill them as traitors. After some time, and after the sellers are safely out of sight, the sale is disclosed to the public. Palestinian tenants are driven out and a new Jewish neighborhood arises.

These methods have served the "redeemers of the soil" (in Zionist terminology) for the last 120 years. The tempo can be increased rapidly. The more hellish the life of the Palestinians becomes—for security reasons, of course—the more the Israeli leadership hopes that the Arabs will go away "voluntarily." Therefore, the idea of "one state from the Mediterranean to the Jordan" cannot be used to frighten Arab-hating Israelis. They see it only as another reason to put up more settlements all over the West Bank, to make sure that Israel will dominate the area. As for the Palestinian population—well, Ariel Sharon and his ilk have a lot of experience in dealing with them. As a matter of fact, there is no need for such tricks to support the idea of two states. It speaks for itself. Slowly and surely it is convincing the Israelis, as it has convinced the "Quartet" and the world community. Those who doubt this should see the statement of the twenty-seven combat pilots (who are now thirty, after two left under pressure and five new ones joined). The "pilots of conscience," who come from the mainstream of Israeli society, are the swallows that announce the spring (as the Hebrew saying goes). People are fed up with the occupation, fed up with the oppression, fed up with the war. There is no need to convince the Israeli public that peace is worthwhile. But they must be convinced that peace is possible. In this respect, people like Barghouti can do a lot; and people in Israel must learn to listen to what they have to say.

# CHAPTER THIRTY-TWO

# Israel's Crimes against Palestinians: War Crimes, Crimes against Humanity, Genocide

## Francis A. Boyle

## (8-28-2001)

### The International Laws of Belligerent Occupation

Belligerent occupation is governed by The Hague Regulations of 1907, as well as by the Fourth Geneva Convention of 1949 and the customary laws of belligerent occupation. Security Council Resolution 1322 (2000), paragraph 3, "calls upon Israel, the occupying Power, to abide scrupulously by its legal obligations and its responsibilities under the Fourth Geneva Convention relative to the Protection of Civilian Persons in a Time of War of 12 August 1949..." The Security Council vote was fourteen to zero, becoming obligatory international law.

The Fourth Geneva Convention applies to the West Bank, to the Gaza Strip, and to the entire city of Jerusalem, in order to protect the Palestinians living there. The Palestinian people living in this Palestinian land are "protected persons" within the meaning of the Fourth Geneva Convention. All of their rights are sacred under international law.

There are 149 substantive articles of the Fourth Geneva Convention that protect the rights of every one of these Palestinians living in occupied Palestine. The Israeli government is currently violating, and has since 1967 been violating, almost each and every one of these sacred rights of the Palestinian people recognized by the Fourth Geneva Convention. Indeed, such violations of the Fourth Geneva Convention are war crimes.

So this is not a symmetrical situation. As matters of fact and of law, the gross and repeated violations of Palestinian rights by the Israeli army and Israeli settlers living illegally in occupied Palestine constitute war crimes. Conversely, the Palestinian people are defending themselves and their land and their homes against Israeli war crimes and Israeli war criminals, both military and civilian.

## The UN Commission on Human Rights

Indeed, it is far more serious than that. On October 19, 2000, a Special Session of the UN Commission on Human Rights (UNHCR) adopted a resolution set forth in UN Document E/CN.4/S-5(L.2/Rev. 1, "Condemning the provocative visit to Al-Haram Al-Sharif on 28 September 2000 by Ariel Sharon, the Likud party leader, which triggered the tragic events that followed in occupied East Jerusalem and the other occupied Palestinian territories, resulting in a high number of deaths and injuries among Palestinian civilians." The UNHCR then said it was "[g]ravely concerned" about several different types of atrocities inflicted by Israel upon the Palestinian people, which it denominated "war crimes, flagrant violations of international humanitarian law and crimes against humanity."

In operative paragraph 1 of its October 19, 2000, resolution, the UNHCR stated that it "strongly condemns the disproportionate and indiscriminate use of force in violation of international humanitarian law by the Israeli occupying Power against innocent and unarmed Palestinian civilians...including many children, in the occupied territories, which constitutes a war crime and a crime against humanity." And in paragraph 5 of its October 19, 2000, resolution, the UNHCR "also affirms that the deliberate and systematic killing of civilians and children by the Israeli occupying authorities constitutes a flagrant and grave violation of the right to life and also constitutes a crime against humanity." Article 68 of the United Nations Charter had expressly required the UN's Economic and Social Council to "set up" the UNHCR "for the promotion of human rights."

## Israel's War Crimes against Palestinians

We all have a general idea of what a war crime is, so I am not going to elaborate upon that term here. But there are different degrees of heinousness for war crimes. In particular are the more serious war crimes denominated "grave breaches" of the Fourth Geneva Convention. Since the start of the Al-Aqsa intifada, the world has seen those inflicted every day by Israel against the Palestinian people living in occupied Palestine: for example, willful killing of Palestinian civilians by the Israeli army and Israel's illegal paramilitary settlers. These Israeli "grave breaches" of the Fourth Geneva Convention mandate universal prosecution for their perpetrators, whether military or civilian, as well as prosecution for their commanders, whether military or civilian, including Israel's political leaders.

## Israel's Crimes against Humanity against Palestinians

But I want to focus for a moment on Israel's "crime against humanity" against the Palestinian people—as determined by the UNHCR itself, set up pursuant to the requirements of the United Nations Charter. What is a "crime against humanity"? This concept goes all the way back to the Nuremberg Charter of 1945 for the trial of the major Nazi war criminals. And in the Nuremberg Charter of 1945, drafted by the United States government, there was created and inserted a new type of international crime specifically intended to deal with the Nazi persecution of the Jewish people.

The paradigmatic example of a "crime against humanity" is what Hitler and the Nazis did to the Jewish people. This is where the concept of "crime against humanity" came from. And this is what the UNHCR determined that Israel is currently doing to the Palestinian people: crimes against humanity. Legally, just like what Hitler and the Nazis did to the Jews.

## The Precursor to Genocide

Moreover, the concept of a "crime against humanity" is the direct historical and legal precursor to the international crime of genocide as defined by the 1948 Convention on the Prevention and Punishment of the Crime of Genocide. The theory here was that to prevent what Hitler and the Nazis did to the Jewish people from ever happening again required a special international treaty that would codify and universalize the Nuremberg concept of "crime against humanity." And that treaty ultimately became the 1948 Genocide Convention.

In fairness, you will note that the UNHCR did not go so far as to condemn Israel for committing genocide against the Palestinian people. But it has condemned Israel for committing crimes against humanity, which is the direct precursor to genocide. And I submit that if something is not done quite soon by the American people and the international community to stop Israeli war crimes and crimes against humanity against the Palestinian people, it could very well degenerate into genocide, if Israel is not there already. And in this regard, the former Israeli prime minister Ariel Sharon is what international lawyers call a genocidaire—one who has already committed genocide in the past.

# BIBLIOGRAPHY

Albano, Terrie. "World Labor Organization Condemns Israeli Genocide." Editorial, *People's World*, March 8, 2002.

Ali, Tariq. "Notes on Anti-Semitism: Zionism and Palestine." *Il Manifesto*, February 26, 2004.

Atzmon, Gilad. "The Old Testament and the Genocide in Gaza." January 8, 2009. www.palestinethinktank.com/2009/01/08/gilad-atzmon-the-old-testament-and-the-genocide-in-gaza.

Boldt, Bob. "No More Silence." July 21, 2006. www.mwcnews.net/index2.php?option+com_content&task+view&id+8199&pop+1&page.

Boyle, Francis. "Palestine Should Sue Israel for Genocide," [Copyright December 13, 1997], *First publication in MSA News*, March 20, 1998.

Brandabur, Clare. "Roadmap to Genocide." September 3, 2008. www.nobleworld.biz/images/Brandabur.pdf.

Cattori, Sylvia. "An Interview with Aharon Shabtai." February 25, 2008. www.silviacattori.net/article384.html.

Christison, Kathleen. "Can Palestine Be Put Back into the Equation?" August 26, 2005. www.counterpunch.org/christison08262005.html.

Cook, William A. "The Myth of Middle East Peace: Deception as Truth." November 23, 2007. www.counterpunch.org/cook11232007.html.

———. "An Open Letter to the New Congress—Investing in Hate: America's Support of Israel." December 6, 2006. www.atlanticfreepress.com/index2.php?option=com_content&task=view&id=389&.

———. "The Real Axis of Evil—A State without Mercy." October 22, 2006. www.atlanticfreepress.com/content/view/83/32/.

De Rooij, Paul. "Ambient Death in Palestine." June 21, 2003. www.dissidentvoice.org/Articles6/DeRooij_Ambient-Death.html.

Habeeb, Sameh. "Lawyers: Israel Used Uranium in Gaza Genocide." June 11, 2009. www.paltelegraph.com/palestine/gaza-strip/1091.

HaCohen, Ran. "A Midwinter Night's Dream." January 29, 2007. www.antiwar.com/hacohen/?articleid=10417.

Ignatiev, Noel. "Zionism, Anti-Semitism, and the People of Palestine." June 17, 2004. www.counterpunch/ignatiev06172004.html.

Levy, Gideon. "Israel Does Not Want Peace." May 9, 2007. www.counterpunch.org/levy04092007.html.

Martin, Andy. "The Palestinian Genocide." June 28, 2006. http://.world.mediamonitors.net/content/view/full/31916.

McMahon, Sean. "Israel's Strikes on Sudan: Globalizing Politicide." May 13, 2009. www.counterpunch.org/mcmahon04132009.html.

Pilger, John. "Imprisoning a Whole Nation." May 22, 2007. www.johnpilger.com/page.asp?partid=438.

Polya, Gideon. "Apartheid Israel's Gaza Concentration Camp and Palestinian Genocide." February 1, 2008. www.mwcnews.net/index2.php?option=com_content&task=view&id.

———. "Palestinian Genocide: Apartheid Israel Killing Arab Infants." March 23, 2007. www.mwcnews.net/index2.php?option=com_content&task=view&id=1341.

Raimondo, Justin. "Ein Volk, Ein Fuehrer, Ein Israel." *Antiwar.com*, July 12, 2002. www.antiwar.com/justin/j110703.html.

Salam, Kawther. "Letter to EU Ministries of Foreign Affairs." December 31, 2008. http://www.kawther.info/wpr.

Scheer, Robert. "A Form of Ethnic Cleansing." *Los Angeles Times*, April 16, 2002.

Shamir, Israel. "Battle for Palestine." March 11, 2002. www.serendipity.li/hr/shamir.html.

# SUBJECT INDEX

genocide, 2, 4, 5, 6, 22–5, 29, 30,
37–40, 42, 56, 61, 70, 79, 80, 81,
88–91, 93, 100, 103, 105, 109, 110,
111, 122, 123, 124, 132, 133, 159,
163, 165, 168, 169, 172, 174, 181–4,
187, 188, 195, 198, 199, 201,
207–19, 222–4, 226, 229–31, 237,
243, 259, 261–4
  etymology of, 214, 217
  Lemkin's definition, 4, 222, 223
  UN Convention on, 90
Golan Heights, 136, 140, 141, 142
Green Line, 129, 135, 140, 256
Grenada, 145

Ha'aretz, 1, 26, 30, 33–8, 63, 76, 80,
93, 116, 127, 135, 144, 156, 157,
158, 160, 161, 162, 196, 199, 200,
220, 238, 240, 241, 242, 246,
251–4
Haganah, 1, 6, 7, 9, 10, 11, 15, 19, 20, 21
  Oath, 20
Hague Regulations (1907), 259
Halacha, 244
Hamas, 31, 34–7, 43–7, 51, 57–61, 65,
68, 76, 93, 97, 106, 109, 110, 111,
114–17, 125–8, 131, 135, 137, 140,
154, 156, 187, 188, 192, 195, 196,
202, 203, 208, 219, 220, 225
  democratic election of, 131
Har Homa, 130
Hassidic, 244
Hebron, 76, 104, 126, 165, 226,
227, 244
Herzliya Conference, 137
Hezbollah, 59, 65, 67–9, 111, 116, 135,
137, 143, 148, 153, 156, 185, 196
Holocaust, 7, 23, 27, 39, 40, 42, 55, 56,
61, 94, 103–8, 110, 113, 114, 133,
147, 163–9, 177, 178, 183, 207, 209,
218, 238, 239, 250, 252, 255
  definition of, 40
human rights, 15, 22, 25, 29, 30, 35–8,
44, 48, 53, 71, 78, 80, 81, 84, 88,

90, 100, 104, 113, 125,
126, 147, 149, 152, 154, 156,-7,
173–5, 183, 187, 201–2, 211, 212,
217, 224, 226–8, 231, 240, 244,
252, 260
Human Rights Watch, 226, 227,
231, 252

Indonesia, 147
International Atomic Energy Agency
(IAEA), 193
International Court of Justice (ICJ), 30,
89, 90, 100, 154, 173, 189, 212,
214, 230
International Covenant on Civil and
Political Rights, 30, 78, 230
International Criminal Court, 154, 209
International Criminal Tribunal for the
former Yugoslavia, 233
International Institute for Strategic
Studies, 186, 199
international law, 15, 19, 24, 29, 30, 32,
33, 35, 36, 38, 53, 80, 88, 99, 100,
107, 114, 136, 149, 154, 172–6, 187,
188, 189, 208, 217, 225, 231,
259, 262
International Solidarity Movement,
94, 126
Intifadas, 143
  see also Second Intifada, 30, 82, 83,
88, 142, 156
Iran, 69, 70, 99, 100, 110, 111, 119, 120,
135, 143, 148, 152, 156, 157, 165,
186, 187, 189, 190–5, 197, 198, 199,
208
Iraq, 32, 38, 42, 44, 57, 63, 67, 69, 70,
81, 91, 100, 111, 120, 121, 147, 148,
152, 165, 173, 174, 186, 189, 192,
194, 195, 197, 198, 208, 214, 215,
216, 218
  invasion of, 100, 218
Irgun Hagana, 1, 6, 13, 19
Iron Dome, 116
Iron Wall, The, 158

# NAME INDEX